PRAISE FO
CHALLENG

MW00639401

'A thoroughly comprehensive tour through the latest and best thinking in marketing and branding by our industry's thought leaders. Sharp, succinct and refreshing. A no-nonsense journey through what it takes to make the best brands.' **Charles Cadell, President – Asia Pacific, McCann Worldgroup**

'What this book understands so well is that marketing is a little like chess: there are few hard and fast rules, but there are recurring patterns. To be able to spot a pattern in one place and then to apply it somewhere completely different is often the talent which separates the grand-masters from the rest.' **R H Sutherland, Vice Chairman, Ogilvy & Mather UK**

'*The Brand Challenge* is the most complete and up-to-date account of brands and branding that I have read. I am tempted to paraphrase Malvolio: "Some are born brands, some become brands, and some have branding thrust upon them." This is not meant to sound cynical: it just reflects the hegemony of branding practice, based on its proven utility and high value to so many industries. The editor, through his passion for the subject, his persuasiveness and charm, has assembled an outstanding cast of authors – some old friends to followers of branding, but several rising stars too – to discuss the contribution of branding "discipline" to relatively new areas, like football, not-for-profit, and fashion. Peter Fisk has written an outstanding piece on innovation: read this. Read it all.' **Tom Blackett, Brand Advisor**

'Kartik Kompella's *The Brand Challenge* provides a valuable and unique view into branding. The book offers a solid foundation into branding principles as well as insightful expert advice into how branding works across a broad set of categories and markets. Essential reading, it is both stimulating and instructive.' **Kevin Lane Keller, E B Osborn Professor of Marketing, Tuck School of Business**

'Branding is brought to life by seasoned experts in a dozen fascinating settings including luxury goods and much more.

If you have a branding problem, then an innovative solution may lie in what someone else did in another category. This book provides dozens of impressive and varied examples.' **David Aaker, author of** *Brand Relevance: Making competitors irrelevant*

'Although there are many branding books available, this new book of readings edited by Kartikeya Kompella presents content that is different from all of the others. Expressing diverse (and sometimes extreme) points of view, the industry experts and academics in this text investigate the myriad ways branding can be used across many sectors. The collection provides a comprehensive over view of the magic of branding. Anyone interested in the nuances of how branding can be used effectively will find something new and useful in this collection.' **Barbara E Kahn, Patty and Jay H Baker Professor, Director, Jay H Baker Retailing Centre, Professor of Marketing, The Wharton School**

'I've read dozens of brand strategy and advertising books along my career, but Kartik's is a truly unique one. His approach in examining branding across multiple different industries and categories unravels insights that cannot be found in traditional marketing textbooks.

The book combines vital branding concepts with the application of branding forming a powerful combination for readers. The experts who write the chapters display a wealth of knowledge in each reader-friendly chapter.

Filled with easily applicable ideas and hundreds of real-life examples, this book feels like a complete "MBA in Branding", which I strongly recommend both for those just starting a career in marketing, as well as the experts on the topic. I hope you enjoy the reading and learning as much as I did!' **Andre Felippa, Marketing, Product and Communications VP, Latin America, Alcatel Onetouch**

'*The Brand Challenge* offers a kaleidoscopic view of the world of branding, inviting readers along on an exciting journey through brand management theory and practice in diverse industries. In doing so, it crystallizes the essential truths of branding at the same time that it uncovers the idiosyncrasies that defy them in particular product categories. A true celebration of the scope and complexity of branding, this edited book includes the experiences of seasoned veterans, as well as intriguing, new voices in the field.' **Dr Jill Avery, Senior Lecturer, Harvard Business School**

'Every brand challenge need not be won on deep category knowledge and heritage. It can also be inspired by learning from deliberately diverse categories, and purposefully focusing the right lessons on to your own brand story in a new way, so long as the story is told and delivered in a distinctive way, a way that resonates and indelibly occupies the mind space of your target consumers and customers.' **Phil Chapman, VP Marketing Communication and Brand Equity, Mondeléz**

'*The Brand Challenge* is a comprehensive look at creating and nurturing successful brands by explaining how brand building is done in multiple categories. A must-read for any professional who wants to grow their business in a crowded marketplace.' **BJ Bueno, co-author, *The Power of Cult Branding***

The Brand Challenge
Adapting branding to sectorial imperatives

Edited by Kartikeya Kompella

KoganPage

LONDON PHILADELPHIA NEW DELHI

First published in Great Britain and the United States in 2015 by Kogan Page Limited

2nd Floor, 45 Gee Street	1518 Walnut Street, Suite 1100	4737/23 Ansari Road
London EC1V 3RS	Philadelphia PA 19102	Daryaganj
United Kingdom	USA	New Delhi 110002
		India

www.koganpage.com

© Kartikeya Kompella and the individual contributors, 2015

The right of Kartikeya Kompella to be identified as the editor of this work, and of the individual contributors to be identified as the authors of this work, has been asserted by them in accordance with the Copyright, Designs and Patents Act 1988.

ISBN   978 0 7494 7015 9
E-ISBN   978 0 7494 7016 6

British Library Cataloguing-in-Publication Data

A CIP record for this book is available from the British Library.

Library of Congress Cataloging-in-Publication Data

The brand challenge : adapting branding to sectorial imperatives / [edited by] Kartikeya Kompella.
    pages cm
  ISBN 978-0-7494-7015-9 (paperback) – ISBN 978-0-7494-7016-6 (ebook) 1. Branding (Marketing)
I. Kompella, Kartikeya.
  HF5415.1255.B717 2014
  658.8'27–dc23
                                                                                                    2014028451

Typeset by Amnet
Print production managed by Jellyfish
Printed and bound by CPI Group (UK) Ltd, Croydon, CR0 4YY

CONTENTS

04   Bridging the gap between brand idea and delivery in a move-faster-but-be-certain market: Why the traditional process of building a brand needs a reboot 83
Allen Adamson

05   Luxury branding 97
Jean-Noël Kapferer

12   Research advances in the building of hotel brands 253
Professor John O'Neill

13   The city as a brand 271
Jeremy Hildreth and JT Singh

FOREWORD

Good lord, another book on brands! The brand-lover I've always been couldn't help but be curious about such topics: trademarks, brands, lovemarks – the debate remains fierce and vivid whether traditional branding practices have become stultified. Unsurprisingly, I will tackle upfront the digital landslide: following the example of advertising or communication, brands have to be up to this formidable task. And the clock is ticking, given the unprecedented pace of this revolution.

Brands are facing three challenges.

The first is to actually take into account what is radically, deeply and irreversibly changing in the very workings of society. Forget product-centric branding, brand funnel or branding matrices. The time of client empowerment has come, and it's here to stay. Courtesy of sharing and instantaneousness, the consumers' behaviour is changing much faster than the marketers' reflexes. Hence the pressing need for brands to stay attuned to consumers. (Having set aside the client, Gap learnt the lesson the hard way when online voters vetoed its proposed new logo.) This precious bond is obviously essential for retail, given the rise of e-commerce, but also for B2B in terms of customer relationship. Although a strong brand means a strong identity, this can't hamper flexibility: you have to be able to adapt; if not, a Kodak-like fate is looming.

The second challenge is the one confronting brands themselves. What does a brand become when the boundaries between IT, marketing and sales are blurring? A unique motto, an identified logo, awareness and recall, or online rankings? I reckon that it is still about respect and love, since emotions are more than ever the key elements, but digital is resetting the base. First in terms of intimacy, as the sky is almost the limit for brands 2.0 with instant feedback and personalized messages. Second in terms of rationality, when aggregators and comparison tools tend to focus on data, as opposed to the mystery or mythology of brands. Big Data and Smart Data will never be enemies of brands – the 80 per cent emotional/20 per cent rational ratio will stick – but brands must early on rethink themselves in a datafied world. Third, in terms of materiality, when the 'always-on' mindset is all about usage rather than ownership. Brands used to be about the products, then about the customers; now they're mainly about a user experience – both online and offline.

Third, brands are people, their values, a psyche. Soaring blogs and social networks, spurred by the skyrocketing popularity of smartphones, call for a previously unseen transparency. Brands will have to be able to justify what they do, at any time and in public. Hackneyed positions on SRI will not suffice: customers duly ask questions and they expect answers. A company like McDonald's successfully pre-empted it by engaging in online discussions on meat certification. Customer relationship becomes a horizontal network ecosystem. Should a situation materialize – let's think about over-bleached clothes – brands must trust customers, like the detergent brand that let online comments prove the powder was not the issue, improper use was.

I trust brands are already reinventing themselves in this digital age, and cross-sectorial insights are more than ever valuable assets. At Publicis, we are able to steward brands on this journey daily, since we early on invested in this digitized world – e-commerce, customer relationship management, real-time bidding, audience-on-demand – and we continue to passionately believe in magnificent, creative and overwhelming brands. Kevin Roberts, Saatchi & Saatchi CEO, prefers to call them lovemarks – I do agree.

Maurice Lévy,
Chairman & CEO – Publicis Groupe

PREFACE

One of the charms of the communication and brand consulting businesses is the infinite variety of branding challenges that one faces. It's not just that each brand is unique and that one has to understand the brand and its competition; it is also that brands operate in sectors and each sector is a different playing field.

The consulting business presumes that given enough exposure you will be a Federer who can prevail on any surface, and in reality one does learn enough to manage reasonably well. Often enough this is achieved by quickly learning sectorial conventions and applying them.

The entire notion of understanding sectors is important yet restrictive. Many companies are obsessed with working with sectorial experts. This is a wonderful recipe for creating dullness and sameness.

While on the one hand, it is silly to assume that if you are a bank you need not be responsible for your customers' funds and build and retain their trust; on the other hand, this does not automatically mean that you should conduct yourself with insufferable dullness.

One has to be mindful of, yet not restricted by, sectorial conventions. Importantly one should understand what customers really want from a brand and not be obsessed with how others in the sector are conducting themselves.

Today there are a happy set of brands that are defying the conventions of their sectors and succeeding. The secret of these brands seem to be that:

- they obviously understand branding very well;
- they understand their customers' real requirements very well; and
- they know when to follow the rules of a sector and when to flout them.

This seems to be a good understanding to have, and one way that it can come about is through an understanding of multiple sectors and how they work.

There are sector-specific books such as those on pharma branding, place branding, technology branding and so on, that presumably are devoured by professionals in these fields. There are other books on branding that provide perspectives to branding or explain principles that can be applied across brands and sectors.

There does not seem to be any book that helps put sectors in perspective by showing what are the real drivers of different sectors and how brands in different sectors have succeeded.

I thought a book of this nature was important because it would help readers understand how certain sectors operate, how to look at a sector deeply to understand what its real rules are, and to realize what is similar across sectors and what is different. Importantly, it would help readers understand how to take certain aspects of one sector and implement them in another sector, thereby creating innovation in these sectors. And innovation is an important creator of differentiation, growth and wealth for brands.

The lack of awareness of what consumers want and the adherence to meaningless sectorial conventions are making some brands deliver far less than they should.

The tech brands that confuse customers with technobabble and the detergent brands so wrapped up in their attributes and benefits monologue that they can't show a bigger picture and greater purpose to consumers are examples of the types of brands that need to change. In today's more connected world, brands need to find ways of building emotional bonds with consumers, not hide behind conventions and distance themselves.

I've always been a huge believer that good literature is the first step to take for a practice to improve. I'm a big fan of edited collections that bring a variety of expert perspectives together in one book.

I decided to build a collection that provided readers with a perspective of branding from a sectorial standpoint. I felt this could help them build innovative brands or build brands innovatively.

The way to do this seemed to be to get experts from different sectors to explain how these sectors work. By learning about different sectors, some of which are in stark contrast to others, one sees what is common across sectors and what is different.

I solicited the help of people who were best-in-class experts in their respective topics, many of whom had written entire books devoted to the topic of their chapter. The advantage of this was that they knew the subject so well that they could provide a very tight, accurate and powerful understanding of their subject. This book is indeed the product of some very fine experts.

The book has two sections – the first is a set of four foundation topics that apply across sectors and put branding as a subject into context. The second section is a detailed look at specific sectors.

Over the next couple of pages, I will try to explain why I chose the authors and their respective topics.

Al Ries' contribution to marketing and branding cannot be overemphasized. I've always believed that his book on focus highlighted one of the most important aspects of branding. I requested him to write on this subject so that its value is reinforced with contemporary examples.

Identity is a much-used term in branding that's probably not as well understood as it should be. For too many, all it means is following a typeface in a certain size and ensuring that a logo matches a particular pantone colour. Tony Allen has an excellent appreciation of the big picture of 'identity' and I was very glad when he agreed to join this project.

Innovation is a buzz word now applied more to products than to brands. I felt most people don't appreciate the several perspectives on innovation that exist for brands. Peter Fisk has a masterly understanding of the topic and I felt a chapter from him would provide great clarity on the topic.

I had contacted Allen Adamson for a chapter on 'Differentiation', something I believe is a cornerstone of branding, when he suggested he'd prefer writing on something to do with 'prototyping the brand experience'. I didn't quite get what he meant at first, but as he explained the topic, I realized that this was a new and exciting perspective that I couldn't afford to miss out on.

It was more of a challenge to find authors for the sectorial section, but I always believed that if I searched hard enough I could find excellent authors, and I wasn't wrong.

The branding of luxury goods is something that always intrigued me. Professor Jean-Noël Kapferer is someone I admire enormously and his wonderful book on luxury branding made him the ideal person to write a chapter on this subject.

Retail branding is a complex area with elements of real estate and service. There are also a variety of retail brands, from discount stores to luxury retailers, thereby making the subject even more complicated. I came across Jesko Perrey and Thomas Meyer's book on retail branding, and realized that these were two people who understood this complex subject very well.

Much of branding discussions focus on consumer brands, but B2B is a large and important aspect of the business world. My experience with B2B brands had shown me that there was a large role that branding could play and I wanted someone who understood this area really well. Lippincott is a brand consultancy that is very strong in this sector and Michael D'Esopo and Simon Glynn of Lippincott have demonstrated great expertise in the topic.

I've never handled a television channel but I've always been fascinated at how they create new products for viewers to consume every day, living and dying by TRPs, constantly rejigging themselves to create and sustain interest in viewers. Professor Walter McDowell is someone who has the rare experience of not just working in the field of media but also teaching about it. He was kind enough to agree to share his experience through his chapter.

Finance is a truly specialized subject today and many brands operate in this field. They range from the mundane to the very specialized. They mostly come across as boring and humourless. Mike Symes wrote an excellent book demystifying and challenging finance brands and his thoughts and approach to branding resonated so powerfully with mine that it was impossible not to invite him aboard this project.

Non-profits are another sector that I've found fascinating. Most of them are built on ideologies, values and principles and driven by hope and not commerce. In Jocelyne Daw, I found an expert who understood how to make branding work for non-profits.

Fashion is a rather tough sector to understand. My discussions with people in the fashion business led me to believe that it was about great designers creating fantastic or bizarre clothes that are put up at fashion shows and celebrated through awesome photography. Professor Joseph Hancock's book on fashion branding and his belief that fashion branding is about storytelling was compelling and rang true for me.

The hospitality industry is a service industry that has great scope for varied product offerings that are conceptually easy to match. Branding is at the soul of this industry and Professor John O'Neill was in a great position to explain how it operates.

I've been involved in many discussions on place branding and I've always been struck by the 'givenness' of such brands. You can't change a place, you can't lie about it, you can't say what you want and expect others to see it the way you do. You're stuck and have to make the most of what you have. As I researched experts on place branding I found Jeremy Hildreth and JT Singh and thought that their perspectives on the topic were brilliant.

Technology brands can spew deathly serious technobabble or exhibit a very quirky sense of humour. Most tech brands are placed somewhere between the two extremes of either taking themselves too seriously or not seriously at all. DeSantis Breindel is a very sound consultancy that understands this space very well and Howard Breindel, Jonathan Paisner and Seth Margolis have an exceptionally fine grasp of the nuances of tech branding.

The branding of sports is a fascinating subject. An arena where legends are created in seconds and extreme passions rage constantly is always going to be an area worth studying. Football reflects sports branding very well and I was delighted to find Sue Bridgewater, the author of *Football Brands* and convince her to share her vast knowledge of the subject.

As you will have noticed from my mixed selection of sectors, I tried to focus on the more interesting challenges (fashion, luxury) as well as the more straightforward (retail, hospitality). There's no way I could have covered all sectors, so I chose the normal and exotic.

I quite liked the idea of place branding and football branding being in the same book as financial branding and tech branding, because I thought it would demonstrate what was the same or different across sectors if at all, and could help plant innovative thoughts in readers' heads. I have learned a lot from this book and hope you will too.

I'd like to express my deep gratitude to all the authors for taking the time and effort to produce wonderful chapters at the request of a total stranger. This book would not exist but for the generosity of these fine people.

Specifically I'd like to thank Al Ries and Professor Kapferer whose books I read with great interest as a youngster. I've had the good fortune of working with them in the past too and they were the first people to give me the confidence that I could edit books on branding.

I'd also like to thank the many important and busy people who were kind enough to take the time and effort to read and endorse this book. Special thanks to Monsieur Maurice Lévy for writing the foreword.

As would be expected, there are many people involved in converting a book from an idea to reality. I'd like to thank Matthew Smith, my publisher at Kogan Page for seeing merit in the proposal and then supporting me in every way possible to help me make this book as good as I can.

I must put on record my appreciation for the cheerful and enthusiastic Geraldine for helping me with every query I had on matters to do with the legal and production aspects of the book. Melody Dawes came in and helped this book reach a happy ending.

Many thanks to Subbu, Ashish and Bhavneet for their many discussions with me as I was formulating the book concept.

Thanks to Ramanan and Sudeep who rendered invaluable help and advice as I sought to market this book.

My thanks to my parents and brothers who helped me develop into the kind of person I am.

Last but not the least I need to thank my wife Vinitha and daughter Mithya. Vinitha, for being a constant source of encouragement and a calming influence. My daughter Mithya's evident pride in my creation of a book made me want to make it as good as I can.

It's been a long journey and a fulfilling one.

I really hope you like the book and I look forward to your comments. Send them in to **kartik@purposefulbrands.in**

*To my wonderful wife Vinitha who's stood
by me in every challenge.*

Focus
The future of your company depends on it

AL RIES

In 1981, Jack Trout and I wrote a book entitled *Positioning: The battle for your mind*. In the years that followed, 'positioning' became one of the most talked-about concepts in the marketing community.

To date, more than 1.5 million copies of *Positioning* have been sold, including 400,000 in China alone.

As recently as 2009, readers of *Advertising Age*, the leading American marketing publication, selected *Positioning* as the best book they've ever read on marketing. (That same year, the Harvard Business School Press published a book entitled *The 100 Best Business Books of All Time. Positioning* was one of them.)

Before positioning, the emphasis was on the product and its competition. The leading marketing theory was Rosser Reeve's 'unique selling proposition'. You looked for ways your product differed from its competitors and then advertised one of those unique differences.

We reversed that idea. Instead of looking at your product and its competitors, you looked in the mind of your prospect in order to find an 'open hole' you could fill. Lexus, for example, filled a hole called 'Japanese luxury vehicle' and became a very successful brand.

Focus versus positioning

Today, positioning is an accepted marketing concept. Focus is not.

Today, virtually every marketing plan contains a statement about the 'position' the brand is hoping to obtain.

Focus is a much newer concept. It wasn't until 1996 that I wrote the book, *Focus: The future of your company depends on it*. Since then 'focus' is slowly making some progress in the marketing community.

But even now, very few marketing plans are built around the idea of 'narrowing the focus'. Actually, it's the reverse. Most marketing plans are built around ideas for 'expanding the brand'.

As compared to 'positioning', I believe that 'focus' is a more helpful conceptual idea because it tells companies how to establish a position. You literally get into minds by 'narrowing the focus' much like a sharper knife cuts better than a dull knife.

BMW, for example, narrowed its focus to 'driving' and became the world's largest-selling luxury car brand. Volvo narrowed its focus to 'safety' and became the No 1 luxury brand in the United States for 15 straight years until they branched out in other directions.

'Focus' is a particularly helpful concept because it goes against conventional wisdom (much like 'positioning' did when it was first introduced). Most companies don't want to focus their brands. They want to expand their brands into more products, more services, more price levels, more distribution outlets.

Am I opposed to expanding a company's sales? No. But not by expanding brands. The best way to expand a company's sales is by launching a second brand. (Or a third or a fourth brand.) But companies don't want to do that because they think it's too expensive to launch a new brand, especially because of the high cost of advertising.

There is an answer for that problem, too, and it's contained in the book, *The Fall of Advertising and the Rise of PR*, which I wrote with my daughter Laura Ries.

Companies should launch new brands with PR, not advertising. Advertising today doesn't have the credibility to put a new idea into human minds.

Focus on the brand

Not the product.

JK Rowling is the first author to become a billionaire by writing books. Her 'Harry Potter' books were translated into 55 different languages and sold more than 325 million copies. The eight motion pictures made from her books took in $7.2 billion in revenues. In total, the Harry Potter franchise (books, movies, DVDs and toys) recorded $24.8 billion in revenues.

So what happened when JK Rowling wrote a novel (*The Cuckoo's Calling*) and had it published under a different name (Robert Galbraith)?

Nothing. In spite of very favourable reviews, *The Cuckoo's Calling* sold less than 1,000 copies. Then the word got out that the book was actually written by JK Rowling and it almost immediately jumped to the top of the best-seller lists. In just a few months, the book had sold 1.1 million copies.

What's more important, the book or the author? What's more important, the product or the brand?

It has become increasingly obvious that the brand is more important. That the brand is the key to success, not the product.

Yet many companies today are spending most of their efforts on designing, building and distributing 'better products'. Only after the product is ready for the market do companies turn to their marketing people and say, 'It's time for you to do your job'.

By then, it's probably too late. Seldom can you win in the marketplace by building a better product. So how can you win in the marketplace?

By narrowing the focus.

A real estate example. In 2008, Duncan Logan came to San Francisco from England to set up an online real estate service. It failed in less than two years.

In 2010, he found a building scheduled to be knocked down in two years which meant its owner couldn't write long-term leases. The owner agreed to give Duncan Logan some space in exchange for a share of the profits.

To test the market for temporary office space, he put an ad on an internet site. It drew eight responses. Then he repeated the ad, but added the phrase 'tech companies only'. It drew 15 responses, almost double.

That was the key insight that led to a successful brand called 'RocketSpace', focused on high-tech start-ups. Today, the company leases 580 desks, charging $700 to $800 a month, which real estate experts say is a 20 per cent premium to current rental prices. By the end of 2013, RocketSpace hopes to fill a thousand desks.

It's hard to know for certain, but I believe the simple step of adding 'for tech companies only' was the key decision that built the Rocket-Space brand.

A restaurant example. In 1940, two brothers started a barbecue restaurant in California. Eight years later, the two brothers weren't happy with sales so they analysed their business.

After discovering that most of their profits came from hamburgers, the brothers closed their restaurant for three months and reopened it in 1948 as a walk-up stand offering a menu with just nine items.

Four items to eat (hamburger, cheeseburger, malt shakes and French fries) and five items to drink (Coca-Cola, orange, root beer, coffee and milk).

The brothers, of course, were Dick and Mac McDonald and the chain they started is now the world's largest restaurant chain with sales in a recent year of $27.6 billion and net profits after taxes of $5.5 billion, a net profit margin of 20 per cent.

Today, a typical McDonald's restaurant has 145 items on its menu. Suppose Dick and Mac McDonald had opened a restaurant with those same 145 items in 1948. Would it have had a chance of becoming successful? Of course not.

There's a second question where the answer is not quite so obvious. Suppose McDonald's today had kept much of its original menu (with minor changes and additions). How successful might it be?

Virtually every company in the world follows the McDonald's formula. Narrow the focus, build a brand and then expand the brand as rapidly as possible.

But this expansion has actually weakened the McDonald's brand. In its latest 'Consumer Picks' survey by *Nation's Restaurant News* magazine, McDonald's ranked 149 out of 152 restaurant chains with a score of 38 per cent. The No 1 brand (In-N-Out Burger) had a score of 72 per cent.

In-N-Out Burger is much like the original McDonald's. Just 15 items on the menu. Four items to eat (hamburger, cheeseburger, double hamburger and French fries.) Eight beverages and three flavours of shakes.

Furthermore, the average In-N-Out Burger does $2.2 million in annual sales versus $2.3 million for the average McDonald's. That's particularly surprising because In-N-Out Burger is a weak 'generic' name and has regional coverage, the West Coast of America only. (See the section 'Focus on the global market' for why this is a weakness.)

Focus on the mind

Not the marketplace.

The word 'marketing' can lead marketing people astray. It implies that the objective of a marketing campaign is to capture a piece of a market. So marketing people study markets, their size, their composition, their competitors.

Not true. The objective of a marketing programme is to dominate 'something' in consumers' minds. (Instead of 'marketing', it might have been better to call the discipline 'minding'.)

Take Starbucks, now a global coffee chain with more than $13 billion in annual sales. (Net profit margins are 10.4 per cent.)

One can visualize how Starbucks got started. The United States is filled with 'coffee shops' that sell a variety of foods and beverages. So the initial decision was to narrow the focus. In Starbucks' case to 'coffee only'.

Would that have worked? No. Why would anyone have gone to Starbucks when they can get coffee at McDonald's and every other fast-food chain in addition to the traditional coffee shops?

The next decision was to 'narrow the focus' to high-end coffee only. But that would not have worked either. How would consumers know the coffee at Starbucks was significantly better than the coffee at thousands of other 'coffee shops'?

Too often, however, marketing people stop at this point. We'll introduce a 'better' coffee at similar prices and capture a large share of the existing market. (This is the traditional 'better product' approach.)

Starbucks' next decision was to charge higher prices. Much higher prices. Two or three times as much as the traditional coffee shop.

Why did that work? Because consumers instantly assumed that Starbucks must have better coffee.

Is the coffee at Starbucks better than the coffee you get at a traditional coffee shop? Probably. But without the higher prices, it would have been much more difficult to get consumers to accept that idea.

In every step of the development of Starbucks coffee, decisions were made to create the desired effect in consumers' minds, regardless of whether or not they made sense in the marketplace.

Every business is different, but conceptually they are all the same. Before you can win in the marketplace, you have to win in the mind.

Take the automobile business. Subaru is one of the smaller Japanese imported vehicles in the US market. In the early 1990s, Subaru was in serious trouble. In 1993, for example, Subaru lost $250 million in the American market on sales of $1.4 billion.

Subaru had one advantage over other automobile brands. It had pioneered four-wheel-drive vehicles. In 1993, for example, 48 per cent of its sales were four-wheel drive and 52 per cent were conventional two-wheel drive. (Few other brands sold any four-wheel-drive vehicles.)

That made sense. Up north where snow and ice are common, four-wheel-drive vehicles have a place in the market. Down south, however, few car buyers want to pay extra for four-wheel drive.

In 1994, the company hired George Muller as the new president of Subaru of America. His first decision: Focus on four-wheel drive, even though four-wheel-drive vehicles accounted for less than half of Subaru's sales.

The new advertising theme: 'The beauty of all-wheel drive.' (What the automobile industry calls 'all-wheel drive', consumers call 'four-wheel drive'.)

It didn't take long to turn the brand around. Three years later, Subaru was essentially a four-wheel-drive brand and sales were up from 104,179 to 120,748 units, a gain of 16 per cent.

In the 16 years since then, Subaru has registered sales increase in 14 of those years. In 2012, Subaru sold 336,441 vehicles in the United States, ahead of brands such as Chrysler, Mercedes, BMW, Mazda, Lexus, Buick, Acura, Cadillac and Audi.

In the 19 years since making the decision to focus on four-wheel drive, Subaru sales are up 223 per cent, while the total automobile market was up just 4 per cent.

But here's the most important point. Subaru did not decide to focus on the four-wheel-drive 'market'. Since very few brands sold four-wheel-drive vehicles, the market itself was rather small. Nowhere near the number of vehicles Subaru eventually wound up selling.

Subaru decided to focus on four-wheel-drive vehicles and discontinue making two-wheel-drive vehicles. Now the brand had a unique idea even though the initial four-wheel-drive market was rather small.

By promoting its unique advantage, Subaru was able to dramatically increase the market for four-wheel drive. And naturally capture the lion's share of this market.

Focus on the market leader

If you're not the market leader.

While the objective of almost every marketing programme is to become the dominant brand in the category, that's not always possible. Brands like Coca-Cola, Red Bull, McDonald's, IBM and many others are so strongly entrenched in first place that they can never be overtaken. So what do you do if your brand is in one of these categories?

Be the opposite of the market leader.

There are two profitable positions in every category. The No 1 brand and the No 2 brand. It's the third-place brand that is generally unprofitable.

In the United States, Coca-Cola has about 55 per cent of the cola market. Pepsi-Cola has about 35 per cent. And the No 3 brand, RC Cola, has just 2 per cent.

An energy drink example. Red Bull was the first energy drink and today is a $6.3 billion global brand. One of the secrets of Red Bull's success is its 8.3-oz can. Like a stick of dynamite, the small-size can symbolizes 'energy'. So it was logical for hundreds of competitors to also launch energy drink brands in 8.3-oz cans.

Except Monster. It was the first energy drink brand to be introduced in 16-oz cans. Was the larger size a better choice for an energy drink? No, but it was different and that fact alone caught the attention of energy drink drinkers.

Furthermore, the choice of the name 'Monster' also helped hammer in the idea of a larger-size energy drink.

Today, Monster is a strong No 2 brand with a 36 per cent share of the US market. (Red Bull has 43 per cent.)

The No 3 brand, Rockstar, has just 11 per cent, again illustrating the idea that in the long run most categories end up being dominated by two major brands.

That seems illogical when you realize that there were more than 1,000 energy drink brands introduced in the United States. But there's no room in the mind for a thousand energy drink brands. For most consumers, two brands are enough.

It's also worth noting that the Pepsi-Cola brand got established the same way the Monster brand did. Back in the 1930s, Coca-Cola was only available in its iconic 6-oz contour bottle. Pepsi-Cola, however, came in 12-oz bottles. At the time, a famous radio commercial made a deep impression on cola drinkers and rapidly established the Pepsi brand:

Pepsi-Cola hits the spot.
Twelve full ounces, that's a lot.
Twice as much for a nickel, too.
Pepsi-Cola is the drink for you.

A condom example. For more than 80 years, Trojan has been the United States' No 1 condom. Then Trojan did what many leading brands ought to do. Compete with themselves, using the classic strategy for building a No 2 brand: be the opposite.

How do you become the opposite of a condom? The same way Pepsi-Cola became the opposite of Coca-Cola and Monster the opposite of Red Bull. Trojan introduced a large-size condom with the 'Magnum' brand name. Currently, Magnum condoms have a 19 per cent market share.

A perfume example. A number of years ago, all perfume brands were feminine. So Revlon introduced a perfume brand with a masculine name, 'Charlie'. For three straight years in a row, Charlie was the world's best-selling perfume. (Why isn't Charlie a big brand today? That's because fashion brands like perfume have a limited life. In fashion, consumers look for what's new and different.)

A cosmetics example. Most cosmetics companies add fragrances to their brands. It's logical. You'd expect a cosmetics brand to smell nice.

But not Clinique, one of the first cosmetics brands to be 'fragrance free' (some consumers are allergic to fragrances).

Clinique has become one of the leading global cosmetics brands using the slogan, 'Allergy tested. 100% fragrance free'.

A rum example. Bacardi is the world's leading rum brand. But what's the No 2 rum brand?

It's Captain Morgan, one of the first 'spiced rums'. In other words, not necessarily a 'better' rum, but certainly a totally 'different' rum.

A pickle example. Vlasic is the largest-selling pickle brand in the United States and Claussen is No 2. Like almost every pickle brand, Vlasic is sold on supermarket shelves. But Claussen can be found only in refrigerated sections of supermarkets.

Do Claussen pickles need refrigeration? I don't know, but it certainly creates the perception that the Claussen brand is somehow superior to other pickle brands. 'The crisp pickle' is what Claussen calls itself.

Claussen is using an effective marketing technique that might be called the 'one-two approach': (1) create a tangible difference between your brand and the leading brand; and (2) connect that difference to an intangible benefit. In other words: (1) sell the brand in refrigerated sections; and (2) promote the brand as 'the crisp pickle'.

It's difficult to establish intangible benefits such as high quality, low maintenance, superior performance and even 'crispness'. Hooking an intangible benefit to a tangible difference is a technique that greatly increases believability.

A candy example. Candy bars in the United States are usually advertised to children. The Snickers brand, however, did the opposite. The brand was advertised to adults with the theme, 'The adult candy bar'.

Today, Snickers is the No 1 candy bar brand in the United States with 2012 sales of $2.0 billion, far ahead of the No 2 brand, KitKat, with sales of $948 million.

A mouthwash example. The first mouthwash in America and still the leading brand is Listerine, a bad-tasting mouthwash. (Typical headline of a Listerine advertisement: 'I hate it, but I love it.)

The assumption was a mouthwash has to taste bad if it is going to kill germs. So many competitive brands (Colgate 100, Cēpaco, Micrin and others) were also introduced as 'bad tasting' mouthwashes.

Except Scope, the first good-tasting mouthwash which eventually became the No 2 brand.

A pen example. Cross was the leading high-end pen brand, with a thin, elegant design. Then Montblanc was introduced as a 'thick' pen and eventually became the global leader with a 28 per cent market share.

A furniture example. Almost every furniture store is focused on selling individual items of furniture. But the largest furniture chain in the United States uses the opposite approach. The chain is 'Rooms To Go' and as its name implies, it is focused on selling 'rooms'.

Its slogan: 'Buy the piece, save a little. Buy the room, save a lot.'

Another cola example. Like many other brands, Pepsi-Cola has tried many different advertising campaigns. One campaign that was particularly effective was 'The Pepsi Generation'.

Consumers perceive its competitor, Coca-Cola, to be the old, established cola. 'The brand your parents drank.' So Pepsi-Cola became the opposite by focusing on younger people.

I have written frequently about the success of this campaign and wondered why Pepsi decided to drop it. (Nothing works better in marketing than consistency.)

A jewellery example. A number of years ago, Scott Kay arrived at our offices and said, 'I came here to thank you for writing about the Pepsi generation campaign. I've done the same thing.'

'But Scott,' I said, 'you sell expensive jewellery. How could you use the same idea as a cola campaign?'

'Well,' he said, 'I sell wedding and engagement rings to young women. So my advertising implies that my prospects don't want to wear what their mothers wore. They're the Platinum Generation.'

'Scott Kay,' the brand, has become the leading brand of platinum jewellery. Scott Kay, the entrepreneur, is credited with creating the trend from gold to platinum. A recent survey of brides showed that 24 per cent prefer gold, 37 per cent prefer white gold and 38 per cent prefer platinum.

Many marketing people spend most of their time studying ideas and trends in their own industries. Yet most breakthrough ideas come the Scott Kay way. Taking concepts that may initially have nothing to do with your own industry and transforming them to fit your situation.

Focus on the short term

Not on the long term.

One popular corporate activity is developing a 'vision' statement for each brand. Where does the company hope the brand will be in five years, or in 10 years?

If you don't have a goal for your brand, goes the thinking, you won't be moving in the right direction in order to achieve that goal.

Nonsense. No one can know what the competition might or might not do in the years to come. No one can predict what consumers are going to want.

Deal with what's on the table today. If you can build a strong position for your brand today, then it has a much better chance to be successful tomorrow.

Take Amazon.com, for example. Today, Amazon.com is by far the most successful site on the internet selling merchandise. In 2012, Amazon.com sold $61 billion worth of goods and services and the company has been growing over the past decade at an average rate of 31 per cent a year.

Today, Amazon.com sells, among other things, apparel, books, computers, consumer electronics, groceries, health and beauty, home and garden, shoes, sports and outdoor, tools and industrial and toys.

But Amazon didn't start that way. Amazon started with books. 'Earth's biggest bookstore' was the advertising slogan, making the implied comparison with the Amazon in South America, earth's biggest river.

For a new internet site, books were a good choice. The average bookstore carries perhaps 120,000 titles. But Amazon.com carried millions of titles and sold them profitably at prices that were 30 to 40 per cent less than at physical bookstores.

Suppose Amazon.com started out selling a full line of merchandise similar to what the site is selling now. Would that have been successful? I think not.

Selling something specific (books) put the Amazon name into consumers' minds. (The power of a focus.) Even today, Amazon is perceived as a 'book site' that sells a lot of other merchandise.

No one can predict the future. What allowed Amazon to profitably sell other merchandise was the failure of potential competitors to launch similar 'narrowly-focused' sites. The one competitor that did so (Zappos.com focused on shoes) was extraordinarily successful and subsequently purchased by Amazon.com for $1.2 billion.

What if a dozen or more Zappos-type sites were launched after the initial success of Amazon.com? They would have seriously undermined the ability of Amazon to branch out into other merchandise.

From a long-term point of view, the best strategy is to start with narrow focus and build a strong position. Then see what happens in the marketplace. Sometimes you can expand your position and sometimes not. It all depends on the competition.

Oftentimes, a successful line extension (like Amazon's) is not a sign of a successful strategy. It's a sign of unsuccessful competitive reactions to your initial strategy.

The success of Amazon drew many physical retailers to the internet. Wal-Mart, Target and virtually every department store chain of any size. But virtually all of these companies made the classic line extension mistake. They used their physical brand names on their internet sites.

None of these chains have done particularly well on the internet. Take Home Depot, the giant home improvement chain with $74.8 billion in annual revenues. Only 2 per cent of that $74.8 billion comes from online purchases.

Focus on the global market

Not just your domestic market.

The world's most successful companies are those building global brands. Here is a list of the 10 most valuable global brands, according to Interbrand, a brand consultancy.

1 Apple.

2 Google.

3 Coca-Cola.

4 IBM.

5 Microsoft.

6 General Electric.

7 McDonald's.

8 Samsung.

9 Intel.

10 Toyota.

Eight of the ten most valuable global brands are from the United States. What makes the country economically successful is not its people, its location, its resources or its government. What makes the United States economically successful is the creation of these and many other global brands. (55 of the 100 most valuable global brands are from the United States.)

Look at Samsung with 2012 sales of $188.4 billion (ahead of Apple with sales of $156.5 billion) and a net profit margin of 11.5 per cent. If the company had stayed in Korea, a relatively small country with a population of 50 million, would it have become nearly as successful?

Even worse. Would Samsung have even existed today? Would most Koreans have bought Apple and Sony products instead of Samsung products because they were better 'brands'?

I think so. 'Imported' products are often considered superior to 'domestic' products, especially if those imported products are also well-known global brands.

One of the rationales for building a global brand is to protect a company's domestic business from competitive global brands.

Look at Toyota, the world's largest automobile manufacturer and the world's most valuable automobile brand. Obviously Toyota is the best-selling vehicle brand in Japan, but would that be so if Toyota was just a domestic automobile producer? I think not.

Where would Red Bull be if it had stayed in Austria, a country of 8.5 million?

In many categories, domestic-only brands are being overtaken by global brands that have the twin advantages of (1) scale and (2) a worldwide reputation.

One of the reasons brands stay home instead of going global is the perceived difficulties of expanding into other countries. Here is a strategy, however, that can be helpful.

First, and most important of all, a brand needs to dominate its category at home before going global. Domestic 'leadership' gives the brand the 'credentials' needed for expansion into another country.

(There are examples, of course, where No 2 and No 3 brands have successfully gone global. BMW and Audi in Germany, for example. But these are untypical and there is usually a reason why this happens. Germany, the country that invented the automobile, has a powerful automotive perception that can support multiple brands.)

Italy is known for pasta. When Barilla, the leading pasta brand in Italy, moved into the US market, it used the slogan 'Italy's #1 pasta'. Within three years, Barilla was the No 1 pasta in the United States.

Second, a brand needs to move into one country at a time. Don't spread your resources over several countries at once. It's better to take them on one at a time.

Third, franchising can be very helpful in building a global brand. Starbucks has more than 18,000 retail stores, 11,000 in the United States and the rest in the global market. Most of the US stores are owned by Starbucks, but most of the foreign stores are franchised by local entrepreneurs. Without franchising it would have been much more difficult to build a global Starbucks brand.

Franchising makes sense on the global market, not only because it reduces the need for capital, but also because it attracts entrepreneurs with knowledge of local markets. What works in one country doesn't necessarily work in another country.

Focus on a single word

Not a list of attributes.

What do consumers look for when they buy an automobile? Everything.

They walk around the vehicle to check its looks. They make sure the interior is nice. They note the expected fuel consumption. They put the kids in the back seat to see if there's enough room. They take it out for a test drive. They read magazine reviews to check its reliability. And, of course, they check the price.

That's why many automobile manufacturers run advertising that tells the whole story about their new vehicles.

Some 50 years ago, when BMW arrived in the United States, the company followed a similar path. Early BMW advertisements claimed just about everything. Typical headline: 'Our new BMW is a unique combination of luxury, performance and handling. And it's amazingly easy on fuel.'

A decade later, in 1974, BMW sold 15,000 automobiles in the US market, which made the brand the 11th largest-selling European imported vehicle.

The following year, BMW's new agency (Ammirati Puris AvRutick) launched an advertising campaign that would make both the brand and the agency world famous: 'The ultimate driving machine.'

In other words, they focused the brand on one attribute, 'Driving'.

In the decades that followed, BMW became the largest-selling luxury vehicle in the world. 'The ultimate driving machine' may well be the most effective marketing slogan ever created. It took a brand that was going nowhere and made it the No 1 selling luxury car brand in the United States and also No 1 in many other countries of the world.

The most effective marketing programmes are built around owning a single word:

- Google – Search.
- Prius – Hybrid.
- Volvo – Safety.
- Mercedes – Prestige.
- Ikea – Unassembled (furniture).
- The Body Shop – Natural (cosmetics).

Focus on a single visual

Then use it to hammer your word into consumers' minds.

Everyone has two brains, a left brain that handles words and a right brain that handles visuals. The right brain is also the site of a person's emotions. That's why visuals are emotional in a way that words are not.

Watch people in a motion picture theatre. They will often laugh out loud or cry out loud. Now watch a person reading a novel on which the same motion picture was based. Same heroes, same villains, same story, but you seldom see any outward signs of emotion. Words don't have the ability to create emotions that visuals do.

When you combine the emotional impact of a visual with a word that communicates the essence of the brand, you have a powerful combination.

BMW didn't just say, 'The ultimate driving machine'. They ran television commercials showing happy owners driving their BMWs over winding roads. The visual hammered the verbal into consumers' minds. (We call the visual the 'hammer' and the verbal the 'nail'.)

When Corona, a Mexican beer, was brought into the US market, the importers had the brilliant idea of serving the beer with a slice of lime on top of the bottle. That was the brand's visual hammer that communicated the idea that Corona was the authentic Mexican beer. (The United States is associated with lemons, one of our most popular citrus fruits. Mexico is associated with limes.)

Today, Corona outsells Heineken, the No 2 imported beer, by more than 50 per cent. It has also become the 93rd most valuable brand in the world, worth $4.3 billion, according to Interbrand, a branding consultancy.

All because of a lime.

In the world of professional golf, there are four major championships: (1) the US Open; (2) the British Open; (3) the PGA Championship; and (4) the Masters. The first three are hosted by major golf organizations, but the Masters is hosted by a private club, the Augusta National Golf Club.

Yet, the Masters gets more attention than any of the others. Why is that? Because the winner of the Masters gets a Green Jacket. The Green Jacket is the visual hammer that has made the Masters the world's best known golf tournament.

Another effective visual hammer is Coca-Cola's contour bottle, famous around the world. It communicates the idea that Coca-Cola is the original, the authentic cola, the real thing.

Before Marlboro, all cigarette brands were unisex, appealing to both men and women. Marlboro was the first 'masculine' cigarette. Without the cowboy, however, this verbal idea would have never gotten into smokers' mind. Today, Marlboro is the world's largest-selling cigarette brand, out-selling the No 2 brand (Winston) by 130 per cent.

In today's overcommunicated society, words are no longer enough. To put a brand into consumers' minds also takes a visual.

Focus on multiple brands

And keep your core brand focused.

The most common marketing strategy used by most companies is 'line extension'. What other products and services can we market under our brand name?

A significant percentage of all advertisements are dedicated to launching extensions of existing brands. Many companies don't consider any alternate possibility. Yet there is one that can be remarkably productive. Instead of introducing a line extension, why not introduce a second brand?

There are two advantages of the 'second brand' approach: (1) it keeps the core brand focused; and (2) it can result in a substantial increase in sales.

Take Toyota. Instead of introducing an expensive Toyota, the company launched a second brand called 'Lexus'. For a number of years, Lexus was the largest-selling luxury vehicle in the United States, out-selling BMW and Mercedes-Benz. Currently, Lexus is close in sales to the two German brands.

In 2012, Mercedes sold 295,013 vehicles in the United States. BMW sold 281,460 vehicles. And Lexus sold 277,046 vehicles. These three brands were well ahead of the other luxury vehicle brands: Cadillac (149,782); Audi (139,310); and Lincoln (82,150).

Would an expensive Toyota sell as well as a Lexus? I think not. Expensive versions of the two inexpensive Korean vehicles (Hyundai and Kia) have not sold well.

Well, you might be thinking, automobiles are one category where brands are particularly important. But that's getting to be true in almost every category.

Take the three US companies selling computers and other high-tech equipment: Apple; Hewlett-Packard; and Dell.

Hewlett-Packard and Dell are single brand companies, selling almost everything under their corporate brand names.

Apple is not a single brand company. Nobody says, I bought an Apple. They say, I bought an iPhone. Or an iPad. Or an iPod. Or a Macintosh. These are the brand names. Apple is the company name.

Hewlett-Packard and Dell are in serious trouble. Michael Dell has just sold his company to a private equity firm and in 2012 Hewlett-Packard lost $12.7 billion.

Apple, on the other hand, has become one of the most valuable companies in the world, worth $435.9 billion on the stock market. (Hewlett-Packard is worth $40.3 billion. Dell is worth $24.2 billion.)

Multiple brand companies tend to be more profitable than single brand companies. Apple's profit margin in 2012 was 26.7 per cent. Coca-Cola (11 brands with revenues of more than $1 billion each) had a profit margin of 18.8 per cent. Procter & Gamble (25 brands with revenues of more than $1 billion each) had a profit margin of 12.9 per cent.

The average profit margin of a large US company is about 5 per cent.

Focus your company

The same way you focus your brands.

Years ago, most consumers didn't care who made the brand. They just cared about the brand itself.

That's not true today. Most consumers are not only aware of who makes what brands, but they also give a lot of weight to the company brand as well as the product brand. (Witness the power of the Apple company brand.)

I use a 'brand tester' to measure the power of a brand. Just drop the brand name in the empty slot, 'What's a _____?' Then answer the question with the typical consumer perception.

What's a Starbucks? It's a high-end coffee shop.

What's a BMW? It's a fun car to drive.

What's an Apple? It's a high-end electronic device.

What's a Dell? It's a personal computer.

While consumers think Dell is a personal computer, that's not true for the company itself. Dell is moving from personal computers to software and services for corporate clients.

One reason for the move is that Dell doesn't have a strong global position in personal computers. (It's now in third place after Hewlett-Packard and Lenovo.)

A better answer to 'What's a Dell?' would have been 'It's the leading brand of personal computers'.

Nor has Dell's shift to 'software and services' panned out. Dell shares fell more than 30 per cent over the five years before the company announced its plan to sell itself in February of 2013.

Since 2009, Dell has spent $12.7 billion on acquisitions. Presumably this was money spent to get into 'software and services' businesses.

Wouldn't it have been better to spend a good portion of this money 'shoring up the base'? That is, spending the money on building the Dell personal computer brand.

The market is there. An estimated $270 billion was spent on personal computers last year, of which Dell received only $28.5 billion, or 10.7 per cent.

Dell is a hardware company moving into software and Microsoft is a software company moving into hardware. Both are making a mistake.

Microsoft's latest acquisition is Nokia's phone operations for which the company paid $7.2 billion.

One might have thought Microsoft would have been leery of hardware since it took a $900 million charge in the second quarter of 2013 on its Surface tablet computer.

Will its Nokia acquisition help Microsoft? Nokia used to be the world's largest cellphone manufacturer, but made the classic mistake of putting the Nokia brand name on its expensive smartphones.

What's a Nokia? It's a cheap cellphone. Not an expensive smartphone.

When Nokia becomes part of Microsoft, will the addition of the Microsoft corporate brand name help turn around its smartphone business? I think not. It will just confuse the issue. What does a software company know about hardware?

Like Microsoft, Google is another software company trying to get into hardware with its $12.5 billion purchase of Motorola Mobility.

What's a Motorola? Just another smartphone without a position.

Will the addition of the Google corporate brand name help Motorola become a winner? Unlikely.

On the other hand, Google's purchase of Android has become a big success. As an independent software company, Android, Inc had little chance of convincing big corporations like Samsung to take a chance on a new smartphone operating system. But when backed by Google, it did make sense.

As the search market becomes increasingly mobile, its Android software will help Google become as dominant in mobile search as it is in personal computer search.

These are only a few of many examples where applying the principles of focus to company brands makes as much sense as applying the same principles to product brands.

Focus is a powerful conceptual tool for both product brands and company brands and it's a shame that more companies don't realize this.

Biography

Al Ries is a graduate of DePauw University in Greencastle, Indiana (United States). He served in both the US Merchant Marines and the US Army before joining the advertising department of General Electric in 1950. Later he worked for two New York City advertising agencies before founding his own agency, Ries Cappiello Colwell. After 28 years, he and Jack Trout formed Trout & Ries, a marketing consulting firm. The two men pioneered the widely accepted 'Positioning' concept, which has gained worldwide acceptance. In 1994, he and his daughter Laura Ries founded Ries & Ries, a marketing consulting firm located in Atlanta, Georgia (United States). Together the two have written five books on marketing, including their latest, *War in the Boardroom*. Over the years, Al Ries has worked with many of the world's largest companies, including Microsoft, Intel, Procter & Gamble, Samsung, Siemens, Apple, Xerox, Disney and many others.

Identity
Don't lose it

TONY ALLEN

> *Low, Rockall, 9 7 3 moving northwards, losing its identity by same time. New low expected Malin by that time.* (BBC RADIO FOUR, THE SHIPPING FORECAST)

Devotees of Atlantic weather systems love a good front that's *losing its identity*. Those pumped up isobars collapsing into drizzle. Does the same happen to us?

Fans of identity might enjoy that Ethel Gumm sensibly changed her name to Judy Garland, whereas John Bongiovi only had to tweak his. And that Michael Caine is better than either Michael Scott or Maurice Joseph Micklewhite, his former names. Is it the hard 'C' or the imaginary Co' in front? Or that 'My name is Michael Caine' scans better in a Cockney drawl?

Eleanor Gow, Alicia Foster, David Williams, Susan Weaver, Margaret Hyra and Florian Cloud De Bounevialle Armstrong all felt a bit like Maurice Mickelwhite. With the possible exception of Florian they'd all been dealt fair hands by their parents but grew up feeling there was room for improvement. They changed, in respective order, to Elle McPherson, Jodie Foster, David Walliams, Sigourney Weaver, Meg Ryan and Dido.

The faces of identity

Identity is who you are, what you do, how you do it and where you are going. Identity enables us quickly to recognize a brand or a person. For example, Federer, Nadal, Djokovik, Sharapova, Murray are easily recognizable by their looks, habits, grunts, groundstrokes and on-court behaviour. Their identities are composed of small but unique signals that express their individuality. Thinking about how easily we recognize giants in sports, music, film and TV as well as those in our own friends and family, it's exactly the same for brands. When we develop a branding strategy we are trying to work out the kinds of messages and signals we need to express to encourage people – and that means behavioural as well as physical signs – to associate our brand with certain feelings. These could be to do with attributes such as safety and reliability – how do you look and behave in a safe and reliable manner? Think of the boxy design history of Volvo. Or attributes such as fun, glamour and risk, or health, purity and hygiene. And one of the big questions for a professionally cre-ated identity is how aspirational it should be, meaning how much of our future vision do we want to reveal in the way we design our identity? Virgin is a great example that sets out a future agenda, start-ing with its name. 'Virgin' looks at the world with innocent eyes and continually challenges the way things have been done with a fresh approach – whether in retailing, travel or communications.

By definition, identity can't be an understatement, but it is some-times understated by companies, brand managers and individuals. Identity is the delectable, experience-enhancing part of branding. A great identity is like a rousing Berlin Philharmonic orchestra of sen-sory signals conducted by a Herbert von Karajan of a brilliant organ-izing idea. A really powerful identity starts with an equally powerful reason for being. Companies with a crystal clear sense of purpose beyond simply making profits for their shareholders are few and far between but when they do come along, they are so strong they not only create completely new competitive benchmarks, they actually persuade us to adapt our behaviour. Take the most prolifically quoted example of the 21st century – it is of course *that* computer company. Superior product design, packaging, operating software, retail expe-rience, record of inventiveness, new store openings, store designs, Genius bar, i-Tunes, phones, i-everything in life, groupies, black polo necks. It has it. It has an identity that many brands love to emulate. *That* computer company has left others standing. The influence of its imagination and design ability has bonded people with technology in ways unimaginable before and has helped transform the way many lead their lives today.

At worst, poor identities are instantly forgettable. They're blends and 'Frankensteins', interchangeable and mute, like imagining being marooned in a motorway service station, aware that the 400 passing HGVs have made your eyes tired with their non-idea, lorry-like iden- tikits. But while there may be less need for the motorway's *Mittelstand* to have identities, it would be boring and non-productive if all of commercial life also adopted a commercial identikit. And sadly this happens too often because original thinking is hard but copying is easy. Readers might agree that high streets get worse the more they are stocked with professional chains, and that business parks selling modern workplace lifestyles are generally soulless. Is it the oxymo- ronic name? When looking for superlative examples of identity we need to study two groups of brands: first, those that have not been interfered with because the chances are they'll be genuinely interest- ing. Examples of this include the resident retailers, amazingly of one of central London's shopping streets, Chiltern Street that is full of only one-of-a-kind, intriguing, individualistic and 'non-branded' shops and which runs parallel to a major high street containing exactly the opposite – all the usual brand names you see every day. Examples of the other kind of brand worth studying are those 'pros' that have succeeded in crafting brilliantly clever solutions year after year. The mid-ground is not interesting. We'll stick to the peaks in this chapter.

Like truly great actors, a great identity has originality in its bones and is able to self-replenish, to become contemporary again while barely changing its fundamental components. Coca-Cola's name and swirly script logo were created in 1886, the same year that Karl Benz patented the first automobile and Johnson & Johnson created its identity. General Electric's current logo was created in 1900, Lilly's in 1933 and IBM's in 1956. Great trademarks, which are the tips of great identity icebergs, remain relevant because they were distinctive when conceived, they make sense today, and expert guardians have carefully managed their use over time.

Don't buy an identity if you're not prepared to value it and invest in it continuously. And don't expect a great identity to be cheap. The famous example quoted at the beginning of this chapter embodies simplicity but only by working tirelessly and obsessively, and only by investing heavily ahead of the curve. It is also reputably and easily believably one of the toughest and most exacting companies on earth to work for.

By the same token, well-managed identities know when it's time to change, when they look like they are dressed in clothes from the '70s – those flares might be back in but not with Mickey Mouse emblazoned on one leg, or, they are communicating the wrong things for the time. UPS changed in 2003 and in the process removed the designer Paul Rand's famous parcel motif. Was that the end of parcels, or the beginning of logistics? Companies that are conscious of their *identity* know when to smarten up, especially when joining a new and superior peer group. This time their whole being needs a *new identity*. And there's that phrase we all recognize, *a new identity*, the Gumm Sisters versus the Garland Sisters. Gumm is distinctive but Garland does a better job at suggesting sweetness and harmony.

We all know what a new identity means. People assume that's what Lord Lucan did after his household's murdered nanny was discovered in 1974. Some think South American countries are teeming with individuals running from their old identities. A new identity is about change on a grand scale, change that's worth going through pain for because we can be successful if people perceive us differently. But if it's so obvious what identity is, why do we need a chapter on identity in this book on branding?

Perhaps it's precisely because *identity* is so obvious, so intuitive to humans that we tend to forget how important it is to business and to the success of a brand. This chapter is titled 'Identity – don't lose it' because there is a chance that with the over use of 'brand' and its deft positioning at the right hand of financial success, that *identity* could be relegated to a lower level need – simply a name, a logo and a collection of smiley photos from a mid-priced stock library. That would be terrible and is far away from an identity of real value. A full and creative identity is as important in business as it is in life. 'Brand' and 'identity' co-exist as equally powerful strategies in applied branding. A brand without an identity is nonsensical but an identity lacking a brand idea is a frequent occurrence (please check out low-branded industrial categories for examples of this). A charismatic identity can make a business and brand famous.

Identity is the creative twin to branding's strategic sage. Identity is a business creator, an interpreter and a lifesaver. Without an identity, great brand ideas wouldn't get off their starting blocks because nobody would know what they are about. Great identities feed on ambition. The people who manage them – passionate CEOs and brand owners – value them and want them to be the winners when they and their competitors are knocking on the same doors for business. The positive effect of a strong identity, and the enervating effect of the opposite enable us to see, filter, accept and discard thousands of ideas that bombard us every day. Identities are all around. Identity exists in big game-changing behaviour like Twitter, e-mail and the internet. The identity of Twitter is not its logo, it's the 140-character rule that dictates how we communicate. The identity of Twitter is also our identity. Social media has created universal shared pools of identity. This is really the first time in history, aside from social movements, that identity is communally shared and managed. Of course identity is also the sensory stimulation that makes us behave and react to our environment in a certain way. It comprises hundreds of signals that we gather individually or collectively into our conscious – wordplay, names and naming, sounds, pictures, symbols, behaviours, materials, textures, tastes, scents, atmospheres, aftershaves and even hairstyles. What would the great smell of Brut say about you in the context of today's myriad designer fragrances – that you are an old timer, or that you are a radical? Talking of hair, Hillary Clinton wisely noted its power to persuade, 'If I want to knock a story off the front page, I just change my hairstyle.' Have you considered the identity value of today's reverse mullet? It takes you by surprise to see such a very long fringe. Does the mullet originate from the Beastie Boys' song *Mullet Head*, or from the habits of Icelandic fisherman who wanted to keep their necks warm, or the French '70s fashion guru Henri Mollet, or Pat Sharp, the UK children's TV presenter? How can the personal identity phenomenon of the mullet colonize the planet without a brand book or guideline? The mullet is alive in the United States as variously, BIFRIB (business in front, rocking in the back), the Tennessee Top Hat, the Kentucky Waterfall, the Missouri Compromise and the Bouncing Cobra. In Germany and Austria the mullet is Vokuhila or Motch Kopf (carpet head); in Sweden it's known as the hockey helmet and perhaps best of all, in Montreal, in French, the look is named after a soulless suburb called Longueil, so, a 'Coupe Longueil' or Longueil Cut. Enough hair. The point is that strong identities have the power to travel, with or without a brand idea.

Identities enable us to see, appreciate and understand a person, a company, a country, a country's fight for independence, a public space, a political party, a brand, a religion, poor and gentrifying neighbourhoods in your city, a protest movement, or something as core to enjoyment as a first pressed olive oil from a favourite supermarket.

We recognize strong identities without needing confirmation of their logos – *the* pink pages of the FT, *that* lemon yellow carrier bag from Selfridges & Co, *those* precious light medium robin egg blue boxes unique to Tiffany & Co, *the* ubiquitous orange low cost carrier easyJet, *those* famous chocolate brown and gold delivery vans of UPS, *that* most fashionable of champagne marques, the orange label of 'Widow Clicquot'. Recognizing a brand through its identity is about more than visual recognition. Sonic identities twitch at us constantly from every PDA, smartphone, laptop, railway station, airport terminal and department store. Apple has patented the 'diagnostic completion' sound its Mac computers make when booting up. The sound, based on a slightly flat G flat/F sharp major chord follows a long history of 'designed' sounds as part of the experience that distinguishes Apple from others. Meanwhile famous sonic trademarks include Nokia's 1993 ringtone that used a guitar solo from Grand Vals by Francisco Terraga, Brian Eno's classical-inspired sonic start up for Microsoft in '95, Intel's 'bong' created by Walter Werzowa, and the MSN/Live Messenger Notification sound that features in DJ David Guetta's re-mix. The motto of the Audio Branding Congress that holds its annual events in different cities of the world is 'sound opportunities'. Those who have disembarked from the *Eurostar* at *Paris Nord* cannot have missed the chanteuse 'da-da-da-ing' of SNCF's sonic identity as they dart their way to the Metro. This is one of the most distinctive public place announcement strategies – a proper identity designed to care for and relax you, not a jingle. It's also so *very* French.

Olfactory identities create sensations of pleasure, comfort and reassurance. London's Connaught Hotel's choice of signature scent is Cire Trudon's Solis Rex, a candle scent homage to the waxed floors in *the Hall of Mirrors* at the Palace of Versailles. The Four Seasons Buenos Aires deploys Bayo scent, created by Fueguia 1833, a fragrance composed of organic and native ingredients that reflect the diversity of Argentinean ecosystems. Singapore Airlines patented its own scent – Stefan Floridian Waters, worn by flight attendants and infused into the hot towels. Crayone patented its smell as a way to ensure its colour pens could not easily be substitutable. 'New car smell' is used to market odour eliminators. The manufacturer Dakota markets a product called the Dakota New Car Scent Odour Bomb that eliminates smells in up to 6,000 cubic feet of space. In a Fast Company article, according to the Sense of Smell Institute, the average human being is able to recognize approximately 10,000 different odours. What's more, people can recall smells with 65 per cent accuracy after a year, while the visual recall of photos sinks to about 50 per cent after only three months. This fact may lie behind Pizza Hut's decision to launch *Eau de Pizza Hut* as part of a Valentine's Day promotion in early 2013. Kurt Hane, CMO of Pizza Hut, commented about this in a press release to HuffPost Food, 'Eau de Pizza Hut is one of the most sought-after and rarest of scents available'. Indeed.

Verbal identities amuse us with their cleverness – Ben & Jerry's ice cream names being a classic example that include 'Cherry Garcia' after the late guitarist, singer and songwriter of the Grateful Dead Jerry Garcia, and 'Scotchy Scotch Scotch' after Ron Burgundy's favourite tipple. Verbal identities can also irritate, certainly when the owner adopts an overly breezy tone about things that are inherently dangerous such as payday loans, or waxes lyrically about uninteresting events such as current accounts. And especially when the desire to connect with people overtakes the knowledge of what is likely to be annoying to them, such as over enthusiastic public announcements, the trend towards letting train conductors loose with the microphone and long-winded nannying on airlines. Those who travel frequently will know an express service somewhere in the world that connects the airport to the city with no intervening stops. Despite such a contained and secure journey the itinerary is still broadcast in four languages.

Tactile identities create ownership among their audiences. The aluminium casings of MacBooks help to dissipate heat that keep the insides cooler in order to make the laptop seem always cooler to the touch. Lamborghini emulated a fighter plane in 2007 and the world has gone mad for matte finishes that evoke the feel of Teflon. And what all of this confirms is that identity is a vital, relevant, creative and progressive pillar of the branding process. With more technologies at our disposal than ever before, including 3D printing, making our mark by imaginatively managing sensory signals should be irresistible. Identity can do this if we properly balance the branding process with this goal in mind.

How identity works

Identity envelops a business idea and makes it accessible, communicate-able, durable, campaign-able, brand-able, target-able and ultimately do-able. 118118 is a great example of a campaign-able identity.

When the United Kingdom deregulated its telephone directory enquiry service, numbers were auctioned to bidders who would provide new, competing services. The bidders included incumbents such as BT and new operators such as The Number, a subsidiary of a US provider. Deregulation sparked an intense media advertising battle to get users of directory services to remember their number. All numbers started with 118 but had different combinations thereafter. Number recognition was the game, operators needed to give an *identity* to their number. The Number paid for the rights to use 118118 and developed a distinctive campaign using runner twins each with 118 on their vests. The running twins aped the appearance of a famous British long distance athlete whose career spanned the 1970s and would be instantly recognizable to people in their forties and above, the users of old style phone books. David Bedford, who the runners were based on, had a characteristic moustache and later sued the Number for improper use of *his identity* – but this distinctive identity *idea* and the campaign that have evolved over 10 years enabled 118118 to clean up over its rival. Today 118118 has taken its brand in the direction of financial services. This is a great example of the power of a daring identity to break new ground and open future opportunities.

Why is identity a big deal? Identity does its work through a driving idea. This is usually inspired from a *brand platform* – the net impression a person, company or product manager wants to create in the market – and elements – which include graphics, words, images, textures, sounds, tastes, style etc, plus big concepts that bring an inert proposition to life by stimulating all the senses. Starbucks' 'place between home and work' explains a driving idea that has led to the familiar look and feel we all know today. Identity is the experience people have of us through our products and services, our online and offline environments, our communications and the way we behave. Creating and managing an identity goes far beyond the logo.

The famous saying about retail, 'no concept, no business' is as accurate when said about an identity. Without an idea then sameness fills the identity void – a recipe for disappointment surely, if not disaster? Companies, brands and people suffer needless anonymity when they fail to address a poor identity. Identity works to communicate, explain, stretch and position a brand. We would be crazy not to stress its importance and ask for more from our identities when we undertake a branding initiative.

A strongly conceived identity can also have the power to grease the wheels of a half-baked strategy. And on many occasions, the exciting visual identity of a brand can temporarily mask short falls in its service. Think of mobile/internet entries over the past 10 years – their identities needed to promise the future even when their present was still being formed (the early days of '3' and Beeline in Russia). But brilliant ideas do demand and thrive in the hands of a great identity – ideas like the reinvention of mobile telephony by Hutchinson Whampoa. Here, in 1993, the promise of per second billing deserved a name and identity different to anything the market had seen. Chris Moss, who was part of the internal team at Hutchinson Whampoa responsible for pushing through 'Orange', already had 'Microtel' as a candidate brand. However, launching against British Telecom's Cellnet and Vodafone, 'Microtel' would have been a 'so-what'. The point of Hutchinson's unique business model would have been undersold.

Moss and his colleagues set out to create difference. Fighting to persuade the bosses at Hutchinson to take 'Orange Personal Communications Services' instead of 'Microtel' was the breakthrough. Supported by a smart phrase, 'The future's bright, the future's Orange', and an archetypal tonal and graphic identity that championed friendliness in an original and captivating way, Orange's brand identity remains an outstanding reference in identity development.

Change-provoking identities like Orange influenced modern business. They capitalized on the early internet age and were designed to be gold dust as markets globalized and the power of universal and differentiated brand ideas to cross borders was seen by all. In the late '80s and '90s companies also started to use identity to make friends with their customers instead of for simply indicating property ownership. They recognized they had to earn the interest of people who had more interesting things to do. This also meant that customers couldn't be herded into the same box. Midland Bank, now branded HSBC, carried out research to understand customers who appeared to hardly ever make a branch transaction. Since the point of a branch is to upsell higher margin products, those who avoid branches will prove limiting to any bank. Midland had to find a way to woo its recalcitrant account holders. Its research helped. Midland concluded that there would always be a percentage of customers that hated queuing and furthermore, that these people might turn out to be affluent. First Direct from Midland Bank was born in 1989, a bank whose identity is its service, it has no branches, only the most superb customer banking staff that operate entirely on the telephone (the bank is now online as well). First Direct is an example of a different idea, a bank where you never need to stand in line, one that's open 24 hours a day, 365 days a year where in a few seconds you can organize everything you need painlessly. And to make this idea an experience, the identity of First Direct exists through the behaviour of its staff as much as, and probably even more so than it does through its graphics, though these are also highly distinctive (they only use black and white). Mark Mullen, First Direct's CEO describes why First Direct is different: 'It's as simple (or not) as do you believe what I am going to say next?' Mark is referring to telephone customer service, a style that is helpful, never pushy; alert, never questioning; and quick. Because First Direct's customers experience a different voice every time they call the bank, this means the culture, training and recruiting policies of First Direct have to be more precise than those who operate traditional branches. And there is something else here that's worth mentioning – the value of an accent. Many of First Direct's staff are recruited from close to its headquarters in Leeds UK, and generally from the north of the United Kingdom. Research into accents indicates that Northern and Scottish accents are more acceptable. Similar research also indicates that an upper-class English accent is prone to incite hostility among Scots. Accent in identifying service delivery is another element to consider when creating a successful identity.

Identities and the practice of identity have transformed in the last 20 years. While the old backbones of graphic design, orderly systems and hierarchies, visual consistency and strong colour ownership continue, the role of a great identity also transformed into being about expanding relationships between the company and its customers.

British Airways 're-brand' in 1997 is case in point. In the early '90s BA appreciated that its image had become associated with pomposity, superiority, stiffness and nannying. There was a snootiness that while authentic in portraying an ingrained British character defect, was not a good way to build global likeability at a time when other world airlines were starting to fight for control of the skies. Armed with the knowledge of this time bomb and instead of continuing to promote its old heraldic logo that many saw as detached and uncaring, and also referred to as the 'flying fag packet', BA went all out to express a new global and caring attitude. This is a case where an *identity* change became the most fundamental and immediate carrier to interpret the big, new idea of global and caring. Had BA not changed its identity but only communicated its new poise via a new advertising campaign then it would not have worked. Why? – because total identity change uproots an organization. It is an extreme act that can't be ignored. Identity change like the one BA went through created a new platform to brief its organization about the need for change. BA's change touched every part of its organization. When the airline redesigned its fleet and advertised this change by applying art to its tailfins created by artists from communities of the world, it was reinforcing its wish to be seen as a citizen of a modern world and not as an imperial relic. By changing identity, BA opened the door to the re-training of staff, to the recruitment of staff who spoke at least two languages and many other demonstrations of internationalization. Through its identity programme, BA countered perceptions that it was 'past it', and instead said it was ambitious and ahead of the rest. For those who observed this, it was easy to also see how powerful an identity change could be. Indeed, for many in the United Kingdom, BA's move to a 'global Britishness' caused uproar. But the episode also drew some of the biggest opinion formers into the story. Simon Jenkins of *The Times* captured part of the mood of the day – excitement and pleasure that a new identity could be an optimistic sign for business as well as sadness that for so many UK companies this state of creative exuberance could hardly be imagined. He concluded his piece with the following observation and advice:

> Tailfins are not the end of all business. They do not make planes fly faster, safer or smoother. They do not make food taste better, nor can they silence the insufferable cockpit patter that noise-pollutes the start of every BA flight. But they have exploded a burst of joy over the landscape of air travel, a landscape of inexpressible tedium. They are the human made global. They are a flourish of personality, creativity and fun. And they are British. Stick with them, BA.

Readers may ask why some of the examples in this chapter are 'oldies'. Hasn't identity moved on, aren't there better new examples all around us? Yes, there are thousands of great examples in recent years of striking and original identity creations to be inspired by (Belkin, Firefox, Adani, Nixon Peabody, AOL, to name a few), but in terms of defining the value of a strong and differentiating identity then history does the job properly. Orange, First Direct and BA are examples where it's possible to see the elements of identity at work years after their creation. One of the criticisms of identity arises from a misunderstanding that identity is only concerned with a change of logo and the tedious consequential upheaval of hundreds of printed and expensive materials to replace communications. Identity is who we are today, which has to be managed anyway regardless of our logo. If our identity is about surprising people, being light, creative and positive then that has to be managed in detail through all the touch points of our brand. The true test of a great identity is seeing that careful management play out over time and the examples I've given all do that. First Direct is honoured today for customer service and France Telecom rebranded as Orange 13 years after the French incumbent bought the mobile operator and gradually adopted its identity. Even BA, who were forced to capitulate against a storm of media-whipped pressure to ditch their ethnic tail-fins, used that bold identity change to transform their service standard, product brands and global status. Take South West Airlines too as another popular stop on a tour of interesting identity stories. When South West acquired a landing slot at LaGuardia its announcement used the language style so typical of this Southern challenger – both its blog and beer mat trumpeted 'We've got a gate and we're not afraid to use it. Now serving LaGuardia' – a brilliant demonstration of the use of language and carrying forward a consistently pacey identity.

So, we've answered what identity is and why it's needed. Every brand has one and needs one; the questions are, does it do the job well and is it being managed well? Through famous examples we've explained that identity is multi-dimensional and that the process of creating an identity is and should be spirited and full of imagination. Chris Moss by the way, the one who pushed for Orange, also worked for a time at Virgin Atlantic where he tried to persuade the powers that be that 'Middle Class' would be a far better name for Virgin's Premium Economy. He's right.

We've also looked at an example of a sonic identity with SNCF, although we haven't yet covered the point about the role of *taste* in identity, and yes, that too can create a strong identity. Here we travel to Peru to meet with the Jesuits. Agostino Salumbrino, a Jesuit brother and apothecary living in Lima in the 16th century, observed the Quechua people using the bark of the Cinchona tree to extract quinine for use in the treatment of malaria. Quinine is an alkaline with fever-reducing, anti-malarial, analgesic and anti-inflammatory properties. It occurs naturally in the bark of the cinchona tree that is native to Peru and Bolivia. Centuries after this discovery, English army officers put quinine in their tonic water for the same anti-malarial purposes and gin and tonic was born. Schweppes is famously connected to the quinine-induced bitter taste branch of the larger soft drinks family, especially through its famous Indian Tonic Water and Bitter Lemon brands. In an expansionist era in the '90s, Schweppes used its identification with bitterness to create a new range of interesting adult soft drinks that would stand as diametrically different alternatives to the sweeter flavours of younger and globally available famous names. This initiative was all about taste being marketed as the identity of a brand. Look no further than 'Bitters' in Wikipedia to enjoy our long history with taste.

Other questions that remain about identity are:

- *How do you define an identity for a brand?* Brand and identity exist in a virtuous cycle where each spurs progress in the other. Often, and especially where new technology is concerned, the role of the physical identity is to launch and be the out-rider. The identity plants the flag for where the new service wants to go and sets up the customer expectation. The identity surrounds the launch with the right imagery, visual excitement and inspiring experiences. These enable the brand to stabilize and become established. As the brand's owners push out new service additions then the identity needs to respond again with its firepower. This could be the creation of new sub-brands or service names. Examples abound in airlines – eg re-launched business class services, new seats, the creation of a low cost cousin, code shares, young travellers, new lounge designs, new destinations. As the meaning of the brand modernizes its identity transmits the desired messages. As businesses proliferate and diversify, brand hierarchies can sometimes become messy and clean up strategies are fixed into place that use identity elements to kill off rogue brands and errant communication streams. This is identity acting as corporate signposting.

- *Where do you place the emphasis in an identity? Which components are most important?* The role of brand tells us what to emphasize. Others will deal with role of brand fully in this book. Suffice it to say here that not all brand categories are created equally. You need to take account of this when creating the physical identity – the look and feel of a brand. Luxury crystallizes an intense concentration of associations. Name, the styling, global consistency, calibre and quality re-state this time and again. Luxury is a pure form of identity. Conservatism is an ingredient of luxury because luxury should not appear uncertain. In professional services marketing the emphasis is different. Decisions about the kind of physical identity that's needed are driven partially by practical usage. When Price Waterhouse and Coopers & Lybrand merged, the internet was in its infancy and the new firm could exist with a long name – PricewaterhouseCoopers. However, it was clear from the start that the brand would need to be shortened to PwC and that at some point the firm should rebrand. This happened in 2012. 'PwC' is far more user friendly in an online environment.

Retail identities work on façades where restrictions encourage identities to adapt to horizontal and vertical shapes.

Physical identities for transport services, trains, planes, ships and soon spacecraft use logos and colour systems that can be applied to a myriad of inexpensively produced 'identity carriers' – cups and saucers, antimacassars, work wear, tickets, fuselages, carpet designs and so on. Many transport operators buy from the same suppliers so templates for these items tend to be standardized.

Identities for B2B industrial companies need to work well in PowerPoint, in presentations to analysts, CSR reports and the occasional advertisement in *The Economist*. They need not be too exuberant – the look of durability and precision are often more important properties for business models based on long-term investments in serious assets and facilities.

Identities for media companies show off by being animated or morphing. Their platform is fluid so they can deploy more tricks in execution – something that's expected of these kinds of brands.

It's easy to see that the world of identity adapts to the world around it. That's why we have a term called identity cues. Why soft drinks, car badges, pharmaceutical companies, media businesses, ad agencies, branding companies, fashion houses, sports brands, rail operators, telcos, government agencies, NGOs, charities look like the category to which they belong.

But should they conform or break the rules? Your editor asked for this final area to be addressed, the need to dare and the rewards of doing so.

Identity at the frontier

Great identities of the future will share properties with those of the past and present – an abundance of instinct, focus, timing, money and talent.

Identity guidelines provide focus. Money buys talent, but instinct and timing are the killer principles. They come from deep down. From understanding what's right, what's creative, what's tired, what is leading and what is supporting. Great champions of identity are often owners of businesses who feel the life and personality of their company and relay this to the world in the actions they take. Sometimes the driver is the hired architect, a Paul Rand, an identity Svengali who through an intense interest in his patron and dedication, supplies decades of creative originality to his or her sponsor.

Identities are influenced by nature and nurture. Market forces cause companies and brands to position to avoid or beat other brands. Companies that start life as purveyors of luxury services launch lite versions to capture new emerging groups of affluent consumers. The whole world of brands and identity is in a state of flux, observing, reacting, leading and following. And in this sea of what can sometimes seem sameness, star companies, led by star individuals, do emerge.

Textbooks stress the need to differentiate to be successful. This is true but there may be another way of looking at things. Companies, as people, are not created identical. The quest for identity is to find it and not to lose it. The greatest companies, brands, football clubs, cities, songwriters, supermarkets, travel experiences and everything we value are different to us, precisely because they have succeeded in being ultra confident about their own identity, not someone else's.

The role of an identity and the reason identity remains a very big deal is that identity is deep, true and the source of authenticity that people value. Identity in the true sense creates loyalty – from employees, shareholders, customers, suppliers and partners. Where might we go next? Anything was always possible. Now it's possible in a blink. Don't lose it.

Biography

After studying Physical Anthroplogy at Cambridge University, **Tony Allen** joined McCann-Erickson Advertising and spent four years working with famous brands including Coca-Cola, Kodak, GM and Nestlé. This led to a position in the new emerging world of corporate design at the London firm of Newell and Sorrell and from there to a 14-year period where Tony worked in the United States, United Kingdom and Europe, setting up N&S' business in Amsterdam where he was based for four years. As the world of branding expanded, N&S was acquired by Omnicom and merged with Interbrand and Tony became MD and then CEO of Interbrand's UK business before starting his own company Fortune Street in 2004 which joined forces with Dragon Rouge the global design and innovation business, in 2011. For most of his career Tony has led major international brand strategy and identity programmes in banking, law, pharmaceuticals, telecommunications, industry, retail and country branding. He is a contributing author of *The Economist* book *Brands and Branding*, and Dragon Rouge's book *Business is Beautiful*.

Brand innovation
Embracing change to innovate your brand and accelerate growth

PETER FISK

I love Nike.

Not the company, but the idea. It's not about the founder Bill Bowerman and the story of his waffle iron, much more about the adrenalin and inspiration that I felt tingling down my spine on the night when Steve Cram broke 3 minutes 30 for 1,500m in Nice.

FIGURE 3.1 I love Nike ... not the company, but the idea

I've worn Nike shoes and clothing for 35 years, and never considered any other brand. Products have come and gone, trends and technologies. It's not about technical quality or superficial image, it's about the confidence and confirmation that I get from wearing the iconic 'swoosh'. It's about me, and how I feel.

Brands have come a long way. From their origins in the 'brandt' of a farmer's mark on his cattle, to the reassuring symbol of ownership, and even premium value. But today, everything is a brand. So the best ones need to be more. They are a reflection of customers, uniquely shared value, and potentially your most valuable business asset.

Brands capture an irresistible idea, compelling and intuitive, engaging and inspiring people in ways that companies and products cannot. They build platforms and connections through which customers and business can achieve more. A great brand captivates people emotionally and irrationally, about them and what they want to achieve, and ultimately to make life better. Brands are also your bridge to new products, catagories and markets, to sustaining and growing your business in a world of relentless change.

'Brand innovation' is perhaps the most important capability in business today. If your brand is your core asset, then innovation is about how you evolve and leverage this asset in changing markets. Products, manufacturing, and the majority of business activities can be achieved in partnership with others. As Christian Audigier, designer of the Ed Hardy brand says, 'you don't need lots of people'. In his business, there is him, an accountant and licensing manager – just smart thinking. Success is not about managing your brand as it is, but how effectively you use and evolve your brand to achieve more.

Innovating your brand has a number of steps – some around how you innovate the brand concept itself (why it exists, who it's for, how it's manifested, and articulated), but also around how you innovate the branded business (what it brands, how it's delivered, how it can extend, and what difference it makes). We explore each of these aspects, and how they can be achieved in smarter, more innovative ways. But to start, it is important to consider the context, the world around us. Brands need to be agile and responsive, reflecting the changing environment. In the same way, this will be the most important starting point for you in thinking how to achieve more with your brand.

Brands in a changing world

We live in the most incredible time.

These are days of exponential change. We are now in the middle of a decade when the global population is growing faster than it ever has or will, when technology fuels unimaginable possibilities, from 3D printed organs to driverless cars. We see power shifting from west to east, north to south, business to customer, and few to many. We see youthful passion outwit venerable experience, and small companies topple the big ones. The question is, are you riding these waves of change ... or hanging on to the past?

Between 2010 and 2020, the world's population will grow from 6.9 to 7.7 billion people, mostly in megacities of the fast-developing world. Most significant for marketers will be the rise of a huge 'new middle' consumer class, neither rich nor poor, driving global GDP from \$53 to \$90 trillion. But this growth is not a linear extrapolation of the old world. It is a fantastic 'kaleidoscope' of changing markets,

FIGURE 3.2 Kaleidoscope world: A decade of exponential change, new opportunities and growth

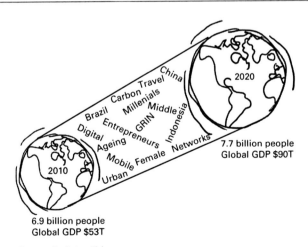

SOURCE *Gamechangers* by Peter Fisk

new customers and priorities, new capabilities and aspirations. A tectonic mash up.

The turmoil of financial markets, collapsing banks and defaulting nations, was the dying pains of an old world order. Amid the shake-up there are new winners and losers. In 2014 China's real GDP growth will be 7.1 per cent compared to 0.9 per cent in Europe. However, some markets, including Ghana and Nigeria, Brazil and Colombia, Indonesia and Vietnam will grow even faster. As Samsung launches its smart watch and Beijing is recognized as the world's leading city for renewable energies, we realize that the best ideas in business are shifting rapidly. The big investors are in Shenzhen, the most sustainable innovators in Nairobi, the best fashion designers are in Buenos Aires, the best digital engineers in Hyderabad. No longer are these emerging (wrong word, I know!) markets the source of low-cost supplies, and low-budget consumers. They have youth, education, disposable income, fast growth and ambition on their side too.

More than half the world live inside a circle based 106.6°E, 26.6°N, and within 4,100 km of Guiyang, Guizhou Province, in southwest China. Fifty-five per cent of all products are now made in more than one country, and around 20 per cent of services too. Twenty-four per cent of the world's adults have a smartphone, typically checking it 150 times per day, spending 141 minutes on it. Seventy per cent of people think small companies understand them better than large, 55 per cent trust businesses to do the right thing, but only 15 per cent trust business leaders to tell the truth. The majority of the world's business value is now privately owned. Over 40 per cent of companies in the Fortune 500 in 2000 were not there in 2010, and by 2020 over 50 per cent will be from emerging markets.

It is a period of awesomeness, of opportunities limited only by our imagination. A world where impossible dreams can now come true.

The power to change the world

From Alibaba to ZaoZao, Ashmei to Zidisha, Azuri and Zipcar, a new generation of brands are rising out of the maelstrom of economic and technological change. These are just a few of the companies who are shaking up market structures and customer expectations. They are disruptive and innovative, start-ups and corporates, in every sector and region, reshaping our world.

These brands are more ambitious, with stretching vision and enlightened purpose. They see markets as kaleidoscopes of infinite possibilities, assembling and defining them to their advantage. Most of all they have great ideas. They outthink their competition, thinking bigger and different. They are like speedboats, fast and flexible, outthinking and outplaying the supertankers, steady and stable. They don't believe in being slightly cheaper or slightly better. That is a short-term game of diminishing returns.

Next generation brands – I call them 'Gamechangers' – capture their big ideas in more inspiring ways that resonate with their target audiences at the right time and place, enabled by data and technology, but most of all by rich human experiences.

Gamechangers recognize that people are more emotional and intuitive, different and discerning than ever. They know what they like and who they want to be with. Social networks drive reach and richness, while new business models make the possible profitable. They collaborate with customers, and partner with other businesses, fusing ideas and utilizing their capabilities. They look beyond the sale to enable customers to achieve more, they care about their impact on people and the world.

People trust the best brands more than any traditional institution – more than governments, lawyers, sometimes even more than religion. Brands connect with them, shape their attitudes and aspirations, connect them with people like them, to give them a platform to achieve more together. Ultimately, brands have the power to change the world – not just to sell products and make profits, but to make life better.

However, this requires a more enlightened approach to branding – to challenge our conventional wisdoms as to what a brand is, and how to manage it; and to be innovative in the ways in which we innovate the brand. There are nine steps to brand innovation, ensuring that a powerful idea can create and sustain profitability and growth.

We consider each of these in turn. However brand innovation is ultimately an integrated process. Improved clarity of purpose drives everything else. It is also a reinforcing, virtuous cycle. A better

FIGURE 3.3 The nine steps of brand innovation: each one valuable, together transformational

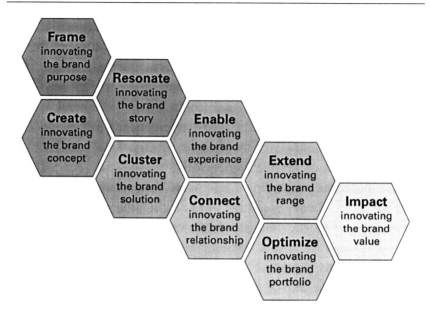

understanding of the economic value potential of a brand, gives us the mandate to do more.

Step 1: Frame . . . innovating the brand purpose

Brands are not about what you do, but what you enable people to do. Brands are about people not products. Brands are about customers not companies.

A great brand is one you want to live your life by, one you trust and hang on to while everything around you is changing, one that articulates the type of person you are or want to be, one that enables you to do what you couldn't otherwise achieve.

Brands were originally developed as labels of ownership. They were factual and introspective – the best cosmetics company in the world, the most innovative technological solutions, or the original hand-made shoe company. They relied upon their names and logos,

Conventional brand thinking	Gamechanger brand thinking
Brands are about products and companies. They articulate ownership, heritage and functional differences. They seek to build awareness of mass audiences, but are limited by their defined function and domains.	Brands are about people and passions. They articulate what people want to be and achieve. They are emotional and relevant to their target audiences, and unlimited in what they can deliver.

articulated through superficial taglines, and delivered through generic service.

Just like internally motivated mission statements, this does little to engage customers; it doesn't reach out to them, it doesn't describe their world, it doesn't cut through the noise of crowded markets, or gain the trust of sceptics. It can also be limiting to the business, with less ability to flex and stretch into other markets and applications.

Brands are engaging to customers when they are about them, when they reflect who they are, or want to be. They define what customers want to do – or be, become, or belong to – rather than what products do. They capture the dreams and aspirations of customers, or at least the applications and benefits to them.

A brand builds on the purpose of a business, articulating and visualizing it in a clear and compelling way, relevant and about customers, standing out from the crowd and touching people more deeply.

Brands can become 'anchors' around which customers live their lives, representing something familiar and important, while everything else is changing. Yet brands must also evolve as markets and customers evolve, with the portability to move easily into new markets, and glue to connect diverse activities.

A great brand is not designed for everyone, but for their target customers. In reflecting these people, they seek to build affinity and preference, encourage purchase behaviour, and sustain a price premium. They seek to retain the best customers, building their loyalty, introducing new services, and encouraging advocacy.

The brand identity, communication and experience is designed to reflect the target customer. Look at the typography of the Build a Bear

TABLE 3.1 What are brands about?

Brands are not just about	Brands today are more about
Image	Aspiration
Promise	Experience
Difference	Resonance
Values	Spirit
Consistent	Coherence
Awareness	Participation
Personal	Shared
Engaging	Enabling
Like	Love
Relationship	Movement

Workshop logo, the layout of its stores, the programme of activities – all designed to be child-like. Consider the design of Apple – from its logo to its typography, the black T-shirts of its people, and industrial design – they all capture modernity, coolness and simplicity.

If a brand seeks to reflect its target audience, then this also means that a brand must be prepared to alienate other people.

As Scott Bedbury, the man who put the 'just do it' into Nike, and the Frappuccino into Starbucks says, 'a great brand polarizes people – some people will love it, and others will hate it.' FC Barcelona can never be everyone's favourite sports club, but it is everything to its fans. McDonald's is heaven to some, hell for others. Some people adore their Mini Cooper, other people think it is ridiculous.

To find a brand's purpose, we must see the world like customers do, capturing aspirations and priorities as they see them, and in their language. However, the customer's perspective is usually very liberating. Customers don't live their lives in categories, defined by products. They exist in a bigger world, where they live and work in more joined-up ways.

FIGURE 3.4 Reframing brands from a customer perspective creates more opportunities to innovate.

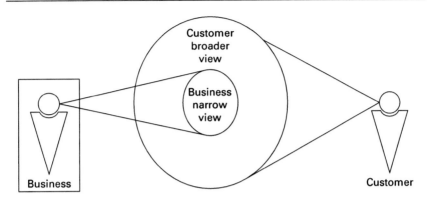

SOURCE *Customer Genius* by Peter Fisk

This 'reframing' creates a bigger space in which to define the brand, and what it seeks to achieve. Take a mobile phone company. Instead of being in the communication business, we reframe as entertainment for one customer, being close to family for another, and mobile working for another. Having reframed, we have to find the core idea. This depends on whether you want to be all things to all people, or special to some. The latter is easier.

At the heart of the brand is this core idea, or brand purpose, which becomes a guiding direction for everything else we do, why we exist, how we make the world better. Having found it internally, it is often articulated in a more creative and memorable way.

- Coca-Cola's brand is about happiness: 'Happiness is anything that can bring a smile to someone's face. We're in the business of spreading smiles and opening happiness every day across the world'... or more creatively, 'Open Happiness'.

- Crayola's brand is about creativity: 'We believe in unleashing the originality in every child... Helping parents and educators raise creatively-alive kids'... or more creatively, 'Everything Imaginable'.

- Patagonia's brand is about environment: 'Use business to inspire and implement solutions to the environmental crisis'... or more creatively, 'Nothing should be made that can't be fixed'.

Brands are about more than words and slogans, images and colours, more than businesses and their cultures, products and their functional benefits. Brands are about people, their hopes and dreams, and enabling them to achieve more. For consumer brands, the people and emotions are obvious, but for business brands the same applies, helping people to succeed individually and together, driving growth, innovation and success. Brands are ultimately, in one way or another, about making life better.

CASE STUDY   Dove, a brand about me, the real me

Dove's 'Campaign for Real Beauty' began in Brazil, back in 2004. A forensic sketch artist draws several women, first based only on their descriptions of themselves, and then based on the descriptions of a stranger who has observed them. The women, seeing the resulting sketches side-by-side, realize that the sketches inspired by strangers are much more flattering than the versions from their own self-descriptions. 'You are more beautiful than you think.' The first two versions of these videos each received over 35 million views within two weeks of being posted to YouTube.

Led by Unilever's VP for Brand Development, Fernando Machado, the 'campaign' has many components. Advertisements showed real women, older or heavier than the 'ideal' but still beautiful. Passers-by were invited to vote on whether a model was 'Fat or Fab' or 'Wrinkled or Wonderful', and results updated live. The brand seeks to engage 15 million girls by 2015. It partners with Girl Scouts to promote self-esteem and leadership with 'Uniquely ME!' and 'It's Your Story – Tell It!' An annual Self-Esteem Weekend aims to inspire mothers to talk with daughters about beauty and confidence.

Dove is a brand that makes life better, connecting with deeper issues in a relevant way, challenging itself and its industry, building a movement among its customers, with new attitudes and purpose. Insights came through extensive immersive research; an advisory panel guides the campaign, in collaboration with consumers and specialist groups. One of the ads, 'Evolution', showed how much effort goes into creating a 'model look', winning unpaid exposure estimated to be worth over $150 million. The platform sought to create a debate about the meaning of beauty, with products ranged from 'Nutrium' body washes and 'Weightless' moisturisers, through to Men+Care, and has spread across 80 countries.

Step 2: Create . . . innovating the brand concept

Brands are much more than a name or logo. These are just symbols of a much richer experience, uniquely delivered through stories and activities, products and services.

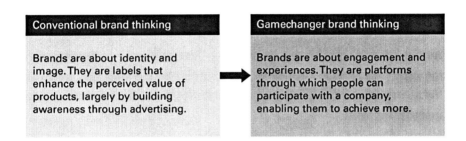

Conventional brand thinking	Gamechanger brand thinking
Brands are about identity and image. They are labels that enhance the perceived value of products, largely by building awareness through advertising.	Brands are about engagement and experiences. They are platforms through which people can participate with a company, enabling them to achieve more.

Renova is a Portuguese brand of toilet paper. It asks why all toilet paper is pretty much the same. White. After all it is one of the most personal products we use. Why can't it have emotion and be colourful, playful, lively and even sexy? Renova launched black toilet paper and found it was a big hit. Others liked lime green or raspberry. While most of the competitors were discussing personal hygiene and convenience, the relative benefits of three-ply or four-ply paper, Renova was talking about 'the sexiest bathroom on earth'.

Brand concepts are bigger ideas. Names and logos are just shorthand ways of representing this bigger idea. Products and services can make the ideas tangible, but so can packaging, pricing structures and retail displays, service style and communication stories. These are all part of the brand entity. The Apple Store says as much about the brand as the iPad. The friendly Starbucks barista is as important as the coffee. The cabin scent of Singapore Airlines is as distinctive as the logo on the head rests.

There are many complex models of brands. However a brand is fundamentally not about description, but enablement – what it does for people, rather than what it is. This is described in three components: rational, comparative and emotional:

- *Rational:* What does the brand enable customers to do? [Nike is not about great sports shoes or apparel, it's about people doing sports, such as running.]

- *Comparative:* Why does it enable them to do it differently or better? [Nike is not just about running, it's about running faster or further than you could ever before.]

- *Emotional:* How do people feel about the brand as a result? [Nike is an attitude to doing more, doing it better, and winning – just do it, no finish line.]

At the heart of the brand, connecting these different components is the core idea, which should be very similar to the business purpose for a corporate brand, but perhaps articulated in a more creative and memorable way.

FIGURE 3.5 Innovating the brand concept around what it enables people to do better

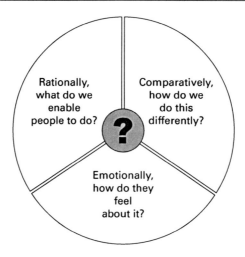

SOURCE *Marketing Genius* by Peter Fisk

CASE STUDY   Red Bull's brand is a deeply immersive experience

Red Bull 'gives you wings' ... it's a brand that gives you the adrenalin to be extreme, incredible. Of course there is a functional benefit to the caffeine-maxed soft drink that is sometimes called 'liquid cocaine' but the

brand is as much about emotional attitudes, demonstrated by its connection with extreme sports, people and teams, and global events.

From the Red Bull Air Race, with stunt planes spectacularly flying along the Danube, to the Red Bull Flugtag, where the amateur teams launch their home-made contraptions in the hope of flight, the Red Bull X-Fighters freestyle motocross and Red Bull Cliff Diving in Boston Harbour, from fun Soapbox racing to music events, to high performance F1 and soccer teams, the brand engages audiences in spectacular experiences. The brand is the event organizer and team owner, not just the sponsor; it has full control of the immersive brand experience, the enormous PR which spins out of it, and all the IP which sustains the stories further. The *Red Bulletin* magazine with 4.8 million copies sold monthly, sustains the interest, as does the brand's Facebook page with 40 million followers.

It seems a long way from 1987 when Dietrich Mateschitz was in Bangkok selling photocopiers. After a long flight he collapsed into the chair of a hotel bar. 'I know exactly what you need, Sir' proposed the Thai waitress. She quickly returned with a glass of *Krating Daeng* (daeng means red, krating is a guar, or very large bison). While the original ingredients were said to contain bull's testicles, Mateschitz was soon energizing, returning to his native Austria with a plan to modify the recipe, and launch his new brand.

Of course, 'extreme' keeps going further. In October 2012 over 10 million people watched Felix Baumgartner rise 38km above the New Mexico desert in a huge ultra-thin helium 'Red Bull Stratos' balloon, jump off, and reach 830 mph during a nine-minute fall, setting records for the height and speed of descent. Thirty-five million have since watched the YouTube video, read news features, and watched broadcast documentaries. Despite costs of around $40 million, in one way or another over a billion people have engaged in the branded event.

In fact, Red Bull Media House has become a profit centre, a media company, and an interesting example of emerging brand companies. While many large brands have set up their own brand-owning companies within their corporate structures, a specialist business unit which then licenses the brand to other business units for a royalty, this had been initially for tax benefits. As these diminish, the real benefit comes in building a brand beyond products, in a way that has focus. In a world of 'ideas and networks', business structures, brands and the ideas that they capture can become distinctive and incredibly valuable entities.

Step 3: Resonate . . . innovating the brand story

Advertising doesn't work. The old idea of a mass-market ad campaign, that interrupted your favourite TV show to try to sell you a new car when you don't need one, just doesn't work.

Conventional brand thinking		Gamechanger brand thinking
Brand communication was about pushing messages to build awareness around mass-market advertising campaigns, driving people down a sales funnel.	➡	Brand resonance is about storytelling plus real-time relevance to engage people at key moments during and beyond purchase, and drive advocacy over time.

Brands need to find more relevance, more connection with their audiences. In a world where we are typically bombarded by 3,500 commercial messages every day, you need to find a way to connect more deeply with people. Brands are about their world, at a time and place relevant to them. Communication works across many media today – TV to billboards, mailshots to e-mails, events and sponsorships, online and mobile.

Of all these, mobile is probably most disruptive. It harnesses the potential of 'big data' to personalize communication, based on your time and place. Encouraging you to buy your favourite brand as you walk into the store, interacting with you as you watch sports, gaining advice from friends at the moment of purchase. Mobile also becomes a glue that brings together other media: responding to a TV ad by text, voting by phone at a branded event.

The dynamic is about pull not push. Customers connecting with brands on their terms. Or more likely, interacting two way. The points of influence change too. In the past, brands spent most of their budgets seeking to build awareness, measuring success by ad recall. Now it is much more about influencing at the time of considering and making the purchase, the time of usage, and the time when they tell others, or decide to repurchase themselves. Advocacy is far more powerful than advertising. People believe a recommendation from their friends far more than they believe anything a brand says.

The message changes too. It's about starting from the customer's context – where they are, what they're seeking to achieve, looking at why it's currently not possible, and building appetite for something better. And then introducing the brand, and how it can do more. It's

FIGURE 3.6 Brand resonance is focusing around influencing customers at key moments

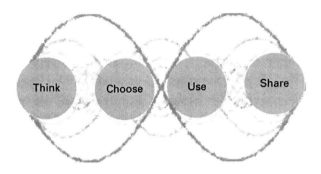

SOURCE *Gamechangers* by Peter Fisk

like an inversion of the old 'what I want to tell you about' sales pitch, but makes a far more compelling story.

When outdoor clothing brand Patagonia advertised its latest $500 goose-down jacket with the campaign slogan 'Don't buy this jacket' its sales grew by 30 per cent. When Unilever's Persil laundry brand (known as Omo in some markets), knowing that kids want to live life to the full, proclaimed 'Dirt is good' people were confused, but then it slowly dawned on them that this laundry powder must be really good to make such a bold claim.

When South African airline Kulula touches down it always gets the name of its destination incorrect. While first timers look confused, regular travellers have a grin on their faces, enjoying being part of the joke. When the Superbowl 2013 was plunged into darkness due a power outage, the real-time marketers at cookie brand Oreo sprung into action. Within minutes they had tweeted an image saying 'You can still dunk in the dark'. It became the most retweeted ad of all time.

These brands stand out. Their stories become contagious. And people take notice. Because they are different. Not saying we are slightly better, or worse, slightly cheaper than all the competitors. But by saying something different, about the customers' world, rather than the product. Often in a provocative or fun way, showing that they have a personality, a sense of humour.

Resonance is all about engaging with people more deeply. About them, and their worlds. In their time, and place. It is about engaging them more deeply, it's more emotional and relevant. Storytelling is a powerful way to achieve this, particularly when it is over time, progressive. This can be supported by more personal, real-time activities, for example on social media. Stories and conversations can be enhanced through collaboration, co-created content such as stories and reviews submitted by users, or user-generated material such as blogs and tweets. Brand owners find these more difficult because they no longer control what is said about their brands, but for customers it is more interesting and believable, and as a result can become more powerful and contagious.

CASE STUDY Capturing the best of Asian culture with Shanghai Tang

Shanghai had the feel of exotic glamour, a spirit of limitless opportunity and a sense of danger too. The stars of the 1920s and 30s, from Charlie Chaplin to Aldous Huxley converged on the bustling Chinese port with its cruise liners, art deco hotels, film studios and opium dens. It was a cultural melting pot, where emigrating Russians met entrepreneurial Americans, Japanese jazz was enjoyed alongside the finest French champagnes.

One of the first truly international cities, it was variously known as the 'Paris of the East' or the 'New York of the West'.

Almost a century later, Raphael Le Masne de Chermont, the new CEO of one of Asia's most glamorous luxury brands is watching the launch of his new collection. A crowd had gathered to view his latest examples of Chinese elegance in a contemporary style. With spotlights on, the music turned up, the stunning Asian models make their way down the red catwalk, oozing sensuality and the distinctive Shanghai style.

What would the ancient Chinese warriors have made of it? How would the Emperor have reacted to such female exhibitionism? Would the communist party have allowed such an event even a few years ago? Unlikely. But the modern, discerning audience of today loved every moment.

'Shanghai Tang is the best of 5000 years of Chinese tradition, exploding into the 21st century,' says David Tang Wang Cheung, the British-educated son of a wealthy Chinese entrepreneur, who launched the brand in Hong Kong in 1994.

While the fashion label certainly represents the new China – one in which style, creativity and wealth is quickly replacing an image of much tradition, cheap production and widespread poverty – it has not been an easy ride for Tang and the brand that bears his name.

In its first year, Tang's store attracted a million visitors, rising to 4 million within five years. The focus was on luxury, tailor-made clothing, employing some of the best Shanghai tailors, and he quickly expanded into ready-to-wear ranges targeting international visitors. The ranges were derived from traditional Chinese costumes and handicrafts – rows of vibrant *qi paos* 'Suzie Wong' dresses to velvet lined Mao jackets for men, silver rice bowls and painted lanterns.

In 1997 he sold a majority share in the business to Richemont, the Swiss-based luxury goods company that also owns Mont Blanc, Chloe, Dunhill and Cartier. Tang wanted the investment to take his brand into the Western capitals, and most urgently to take on the designer labels of Madison Avenue. He opened his store in typically flamboyant style. But the United States did not buy it. With low sales, high rents, the Asian financial crisis, SARS, and demanding new owners, the founder was in trouble.

Le Masne de Chermont, with a classic French training in luxury brands, was brought in by Richemont in 2001 to set the business back on course. He scaled down the US ambitions, and dropped many other international plans. He refocused the business back on China. While the visitor market is growing rapidly, with US visitors there soon to outnumber those that visit Europe, the Chinese own luxury goods market is the real opportunity.

He also recruited a brash, self-confident Asian-American from Cincinnati as his marketing and creative director. She immersed herself in Chinese history, culture and society. She was enthralled. She felt the existing ranges were overpriced, impractical and had little credibility with local people.

Joanne Ooi refashioned Shanghai Tang as modern and relevant. The brand needed more authenticity and depth. She dug deep into Chinese culture to find a theme for each season. She roamed art galleries, museums and antique markets to find inspiration. And pop culture too.

The clothes had to be luxurious and prestigious, but also wearable. She ditched all the tourist trinkets. Her designs were subtle and sophisticated, highlighted by mandarin collars or knotted buttons, designs from traditional dragons or even the emperors' robes. Every piece, she argued, should also be easy to wear with jeans.

Le Masne de Chermont and his team are on a high. The Chinese economy is booming, and its people are embracing designer fashion as if there were no tomorrow. David Tang is happy too, that he has created China's first significant luxury brand.

Step 4: Cluster . . . innovating the brand solution

The brand is much more than the product, creating a higher level of engagement and a platform on which to introduce a wider range of products and services.

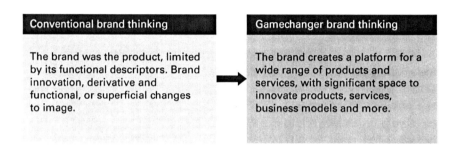

Conventional brand thinking		Gamechanger brand thinking
The brand was the product, limited by its functional descriptors. Brand innovation, derivative and functional, or superficial changes to image.	→	The brand creates a platform for a wide range of products and services, with significant space to innovate products, services, business models and more.

IBM's 'Smarter Planet' brand concept is a great example of a broad and enduring brand platform that allows the brand to build a rich story. It can be accessed in different ways by different audiences, making it relevant to many segments. It can support a diverse range of products and services, because it is not about them, but the higher purpose which they support. It inspires and accelerates ongoing innovation, creating a context in which to add new themes, and helps new ideas enter the market quickly.

Narrower brand platforms like Vaio for Sony's range of laptop computers again creates a platform about smart and stylish hardware which comes and goes in its models and specifications. People engage in the idea of a Vaio rather than a specific product. Similarly, car brands like BMW's Mini can have a diversity of models for different audiences, but promoted together with a bigger idea.

Brand platforms are more strategic, more emotional and more engaging to audiences. They create the 'air space' under which a wide range of products, services and experiences can evolve. These can be clustered and configured into personal solutions for each customer. Business models, through which the brand works with partners, and through different price points and revenue models, can be flexed. And the overall experience can be adapted too.

FIGURE 3.7 Brand solutions are typically a cluster of many different hard and soft ideas

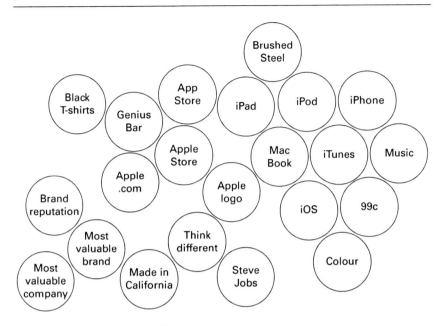

SOURCE *Creative Genius* by Peter Fisk

Ultimately brands are clusters of many ideas and symbols, with a coherent 'big idea' theme. These ideas might be aspirations and stories, products and services, channels and pricing, affinity partners and distribution channels, business models and service styles, distinctive content and ways of participating. They form brand molecules. Indeed an alternative 'bottom-up' way to develop a platform is to map out the molecule, and then find the richer theme in it. Different molecules can be shaped for different audiences, with the component elements coming and going over time.

CASE STUDY   Method in the madness of homecare products

Adam Lowry and Eric Ryan were childhood friends, who became (in their own words) 'brainparents' of one of the US's fast-growing consumer goods brands. Adam trained as a designer and marketer, while Eric studied chemical engineering. Method emerged out of their maddening frustration with cleaning products – poorly designed, environmental pollutants and many just didn't work. They declared war on dirt, and dreamt of a cleaning world that was eco-friendly and non-toxic, stylish and exciting.

They started by mixing soap formulas in beer pitchers labelled 'do not drink'. In 2001 they got (slightly more) serious, and launched the Method brand as 'people against dirty', and declared themselves 'superheroes' for seeking to rid the world of dirt. Adam's passion was to produce cleaning products that people would be proud of, displayed like fragrance bottles, which smelt as good. Eric knew how to make them. In their own words, they 'set out to save the world and create an entire line of home care products… Gentler than a thousand puppy licks … Able to detox tall homes in a single afternoon'.

Mollie Stone, a Californian grocery store, was their first customer, stocking a range of cleaning sprays. They were good, but didn't stand out. Packaging design was their response, starting with an hourglass-shaped bottle of washing-up liquid, and within a year they were being stocked in Target supermarkets across the nation. By 2003, their designer, Karim Rashid, started winning awards, particularly for his tear-drop bottle of hand wash.

They articulated their distinctive attitude as 'the Humanifesto', which includes 'we look at the world through bright-green coloured glasses', 'to get out and fight dirty, take deep, satisfying breaths all day and sleep easy at night', 'we're entranced by shiny objects like clean dinner plates, floors you could eat off, Nobel peace prizes and tasteful public sculptures', and 'above all we believe dirty, in all its slimy, smoggy, toxic, disgusting incarnations, is public enemy number one'.

Within four years, the brand was ready to go international – launching in Canada and the United Kingdom, now also with a concentrated laundry liquid. They focused on their environmental credentials, winning awards from PeTA and ensuring their bottles were 100 per cent biodegradable. Growth followed rapidly, as did their product range. *Inc.* magazine named Method one of the fastest growing private companies in the United States.

A year later, Adam and Eric set up B Corporation, a non-profit network of organizations, collectively committed to 'solving the big social and environmental challenges through the power of business'. Alongside Method, they attracted brands as diverse as Ben & Jerry's, Etsy and 750 others to join, sharing best practices and resources, creating a standard certification and a shared platform for promoting a better way to do business.

Step 5: Enable . . . innovating the brand experience

Brand experiences are the totality of interactions, real and perceived, which a customer has in buying and using the brand, and are as important for product as service brands.

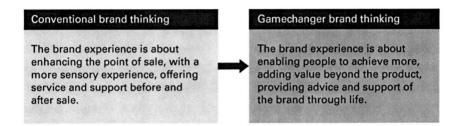

Conventional brand thinking	Gamechanger brand thinking
The brand experience is about enhancing the point of sale, with a more sensory experience, offering service and support before and after sale.	The brand experience is about enabling people to achieve more, adding value beyond the product, providing advice and support of the brand through life.

Walk into an Abercrombie & Fitch store and you are immediately struck by the scent. It's a classic but youthful fragrance designed to capture the casual, West coast styling which is accentuated by the store interiors, typographies and clothing range. Walk along the mall to the chain's next brand Hollister, and it is an entirely different smell, look and feel. You are now in California. The brand logo is different, but many of the clothes are actually the same, but seeking to engage a different audience with different aspirations. Walk a little further and another branded sensory experience awaits you at Gilly Hicks.

The brand experience is an immersion into the personality of the brand.

For a café or store, bank or airline this is about joined up thinking. Everything that the customer experiences, hard and soft, real and perceived, is part of the brand. From the store design, decoration and ambience to the lighting, sounds and smells. From the merchandise layout and shelf fittings to the staff dress and service style. From the typography on the store signs to the small print on the check-out receipt. This is all part of the brand experience.

It is retail theatre – everything you see, feel, think and do shapes the perception of the brand in the customer's mind. But it is also an opportunity to do more – to educate, to entertain, to coach, to collaborate. Look at the workshop space at the back of the Apple Store, where you learn how to do amazing things with the MacBook you've bought. Look at TechShop, where you go to make things, buying the components then constructing them in-store like a workshop. Look at Adidas stores with changing rooms and shower cubicles where you can go for a run with like-minded shoppers.

If you manufacture products, it's much harder to create a great brand experience. You have a physical product, you are distanced from your end customer. This is why retail brands, even private label supermarket brands, have an opportunity to engage people much more deeply. But the reality today is that there is no difference between a product and service brand. Every product can offer a service that helps people do more with what they have bought. Be this in terms of cooking or nutritional advice from a food brand, a theme park that brings to life a children's breakfast cereal, a home cleaning service by a laundry brand, or a virtual lifestyle manager – that ultimate lifestyle enabler, your mobile phone.

A great example comes from Colombia, where the nation's largest group of coffee growers were tired of selling their great coffee at low commoditized prices to branded packagers or coffee shops: 2 cents to them became $2 to the brands. So they decided to create their own branded coffee, Juan Valdez, which is now the leading brand of coffee in the country. It was authentic, local and distinctive. They

FIGURE 3.8 Brand experiences that enable customers to achieve more are much more valuable

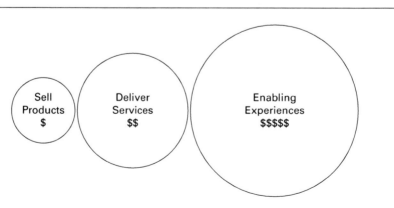

promoted it themselves, wearing their ponchos, with their donkeys in their coffee plantations. Then they went further, creating coffee shops, Juan Valdez Café, with Colombian interiors and music, and a donkey outside. People love it. Far more than Starbucks.

Brand experiences are increasingly collaborative too. In fact it is the customer's experience, not the company's experience, that matters. This might be about helping the customer to make choices, acting more like a curator, in the form of Amazon's recommendations, or premium clothing brand Jaegar, which actually brings competitor brands into their own stores to help shoppers choose. It might be about co-creating the product, like the Nike-ID studio inside Nike stores, with customers paying a premium to choose colours and add their name. It might be like Threadless, where customers submit online new T-Shirt designs and vote for the best ones. The top 50 winning $2,500 prizes, seeing their designs made and sold for one month only, before it starts again.

Every brand can deliver a rich, human, enabling experience. Enablement matters most. Branded experiences were originally designed to drive more sales, build an added-value aura that supported a price premium. Now, brand experiences are more focused beyond the sale – helping people to use the product or service, to get more out of it, to achieve what they want to do. The purpose? Research typically shows that a retained customer is 7–10 times more valuable than a prospective customer. Not only because they buy more, but because they tell others like them. It is retention and advocacy that provides the ROI of experiences.

CASE STUDY Welcome to Umpqua, the world's greatest bank

'Fall in love at Umpqua Bank ... We want our customers to be really really happy' is not the proposition you'd expect from a serious bank, particularly in tough economic times. But this bank is different. There's more. 'Spread some good (the world always needs more).' And 'Reinvest in yourself' as a rework of taking out a loan. People really do love Umpqua Bank. Is there any other bank in the world where you would consider buying a branded T-shirt or baseball cap?

The River Umpqua weaves through the deep forests and rugged canyons of Oregon State. This is the land of lumberjacks, and in 1953 the South Umpqua State Bank was founded to serve the people of Canyonville. In 40 years it grew to a mighty six branches with assets of $150 million, until the logging industry fell into decline, and the CEO died.

Ray Davis, a former management consultant who believed he could do something special with the bank, applied for the job. He told the board of directors: 'If you want things to stay the same, I am not your man. If you want wholesale change that will create shareholder value, I might be.'

In 1994 he set to work, famously taking all his staff to learn from the likes of Gap and Starbucks what it means to deliver a great retail experience in today's world. He reinvented the branches as stores, or even meeting places, with relaxing sofas and magazines, coffee and cookies. He replaced cashiers behind bars with a concierge desk, long queues with a 'relax, sip, surf' and staff that come to you.

Over the last 16 years, Umpqua has won more admired-company and best-places-to-work awards than anyone else, and also managed to stay ahead of competitors, in a time of severe turbulence and an industry generally considered not to work.

Davis believes the challenge is to 'find the revolution before it finds you'. The bank now has over 200 stores, stretching from Seattle to San Jose, assets of $11 billion, and a strategy to build as a lifestyle brand – about people rather than their money.

Umpqua's 15-year track record of growth has little to do with the products it markets, which are virtually identical to any other bank, although there is a strong focus on ethical finance. It's much more to do with how they're marketed. They start with people, human and simple, inspiring and aspirational.

You might notice large colour-coded wall displays of the latest financial services – 'your green account', 'in your prime', 'the business suite' (themed to the audience, not just standard products promoted on their per cent APRs). You might be inspired by the successful local restaurant owner, whose story is described this week on the Hero Wall.

Umpqua *looks* different… bright, colourful, modern (the Gap influence), products are cleverly packaged on shelves, and there are book clubs, movie nights, neighbourhood meetings, 'business therapy' gatherings, even 'stitch and bitch' sessions.

Umpqua *sounds* different… the bank signs indie bands to its Discover Local Music project and invites customers to listen to songs on in-branch kiosks, sells compilation CDs of the best songs, and hosts live gigs on a Friday night.

Umpqua *smells* different… freshly brewed coffee, Umpqua Blend (which it also sells by the pound), and they end every transaction with a piece of gold-wrapped chocolate served on a silver platter (which is the *taste* bit!).

Umpqua's Innovation Lab goes further. A more experimental store on Portland's Waterfront, it is packed with new technologies, for banking and beyond. It includes the largest Nintendo Wii bowling alley you have ever seen. People, usually office workers in their lunch break, come along wearing their bowling shirts, ready to play.

Umpqua wants to be different, to create a different relationship between the bank, customers and the community; to be interesting when most banks are boring, to be a brand that shares a passion for improving people's lives.

Davis argues that banking doesn't just need a paradigm shift, but the whole industry needs to be rethought, reinvented and rebuilt. While most banks feel they have little to say, or compete on, except who has the cheapest interest rates, Umpqua plays a different game. Back in 1994, Umpqua's market value was $18 million. Today, despite the difficult economy, it has risen to over $1.5 billion.

Step 6: Connect . . . innovating the brand relationship

Brands actively seek to build relationships with their customers. The reality is that customers are more interested in connecting with other people like them.

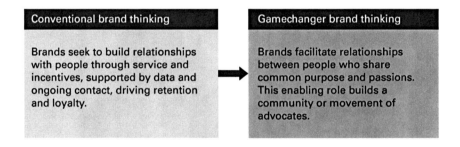

Conventional brand thinking	Gamechanger brand thinking
Brands seek to build relationships with people through service and incentives, supported by data and ongoing contact, driving retention and loyalty.	Brands facilitate relationships between people who share common purpose and passions. This enabling role builds a community or movement of advocates.

Brands invest millions of dollars seeking to build relationships with their customers, in search of the holy grail of loyalty. Recognizing the huge potential lifetime value of an ongoing customer, they want people to trust them, and be loyal to them. The rise of big data encourages them to do this even more, to profile customer behaviour, to predict and incentivize what they do.

But people rarely want this, and increasingly resent the one-sided attempts of brands to gain loyalty. Coupons, loyalty cards, mobile offers actually drive more promiscuous behaviour, the opposite of what brands intended. They make choices more rational, and less emotional. They commoditize rather than enhance brands.

Customers trust and are most influenced by their friends. And then by other people like them, people who are in a similar situation, who share their ambitions and passions. Look at the way in which Trip-advisor has replaced holiday brochures. People want authenticity, the good and the bad. A brochure is unlikely to tell them the truth. It also makes it hard to compare, to understand the inevitable trade-offs involved with every brand.

Brands can build much better relationships, even loyalty, by focus-ing their efforts on connecting people with others like them. This rarely happens. Look at how many people wander around a similar store, particularly a specialist store, in pursuit of great wines, or new mountaineering gear, but never speak. Imagine how many more this

FIGURE 3.9   Brands connect people who share similar purpose and passions

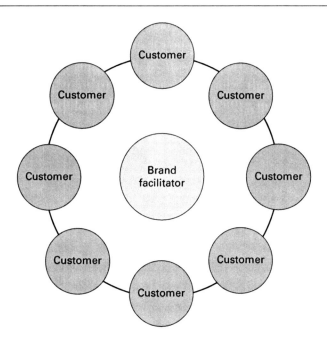

is likely to be online. People are social by nature, they enjoy sharing their passions, learning from each other, and doing more together. It's time for brands to connect people.

Community building, however, is a delicate art. In society communities evolve over time, finding their own values, rituals and structures. These cannot be imposed. When Coke tried to create a youth community called 'Coke, My Music', young people rejected it as too commercial and manipulative. When Pampers provided an online platform for new Mums to share their experiences and advice, Mums loved it, and Pampers for making it happen. A community has to be people, not brand-centric. And the more focused, niche if you like, the more relevant it can be. If a brand has defined its purpose well, about what customers want to be able to do, then there should be a good fit. The trick is to provide the right tools for the community to build itself.

The best brands go even further. When people really care about something, they start to promote their passion – be it spiritual enlightenment, the joy of running, belief in a better society, or a protest against something. Participants become activists, crusading to achieve something more. Dove achieved this, creating a 'campaign' not by the brand but by the millions of real women who believed in real beauty. Challenger brands are naturally good at this, built around the desire to change something, to make it better. Positive Luxury, an online lifestyle brand community, mobilizes its participants to demand more from brands, in particular that they are more sustainable in their impact, and then curates those brands that are.

Brands become movements of people with passion. They create a platform for what they believe in, to come together, and to have a voice.

CASE STUDY   How Nike Women built an inspiring movement

Nike. The Greek goddess of victory – a fabulous, powerful and beautiful woman.

Yet through much of the history of Nike, the company had been about loud, masculine, testosterone-fuelled success. Phil Knight first met coach Bill Bowerman while at the University of Oregon, as he tried to make it as a middle-distance runner. After an MBA at Stanford, Knight returned with an idea to bring low-priced, technically superior running shoes from Japan. They each invested $500 to establish Blue Ribbon Sports and import running shoes made by Onitsuka Tiger, which later became Asics.

The two men knew what runners wanted, so Knight focused on selling the shoes at local track meets, while Bowerman constantly worked on ways to make them better. In 1972 their competitiveness drove them to set up their own brand, and Nike was born.

They rode the seventies jogging boom, and in many ways created it, and gradually embraced more sports. With his passion for success, and marketing flair, Knight took Nike into sports like basketball, soccer and golf. With the support of the likes of Michael Jordan and Tiger Woods, Nike stormed the world of sport. By 2006 Nike had revenues of $15 billion and profits of $1.4 billion.

But the business needed to change. People were more sophisticated and discerning in their sporting appearance, wanting technical excellence in their shoes and clothing, but also fashion and style. Long-term rivals Adidas had acquired Reebok, and while Nike was still the choice of champions it was becoming less popular on the street.

The organization needed to get closer to its customers, the many diverse people around the world who choose Nike because they believe it will give them an edge, or just look cool. New CEO Mike Parker recognized that they needed to be much closer, and much more responsive to the changing needs of their customers. 'There is no question that today customers have the power in business,' he said.

Nike's existing structure – with business units focused separately on footwear, apparel and equipment just wasn't working together. Integration between the units was inconsistent, customer insight was fragmented, while innovation and design were too technical and product-centric. It was only at special moments like the Olympics or the World Cup that Nike came together.

Parker wanted Nike to align itself to its distinctive customer types and their specific needs. He identified six market segments in which the business could expect to see 90 per cent of its future growth. Running, men's training, basketball, soccer, women's fitness and sportswear formed the six new categories around which Nike would focus its resources, innovation and marketing. Smaller categories such as golf, tennis and children could be incorporated later. 'Nike Women' was the most remarkable of the new businesses.

To understand Nike's approach, you should watch the Mel Gibson movie *What Women Want.*

Nick, playboy and advertising hot shot, thinks that he is God's gift to women. After a little accident he discovers that he is suddenly able to hear what women really think. At first Nick is pretty disappointed when he discovers that his beloved macho behaviour does not exactly contribute to being desired. Then it emerges that the job he has dreamed of is being given to a new team member – Darcy is not only a woman, but a man-eating one, and a very talented marketer too. So Nick decides to sabotage his new boss by reading her thoughts and selling her ideas as his own.

Understanding women, and selling their thoughts has made commercial sense for Nike too. It found that women typically spend around 40 per cent more on sports apparel than men, and will pay a higher price for the most fashionable items too. They buy more items, more frequently, and coordination is important too. Nobody wants to be seen with shoes that don't match, or in last year's tennis range.

Back at Nike's Beaverton campus, Heidi O'Neill had been pushing for years to get separate functions to work together, and offer a more coordinated approach to women. Her cross-functional team had delivered success, but had had to compete against the system, challenging processes and leadership, breaking through the silo-driven product-centric profit centres. At last, in January 2007, she became head of Nike's global women's fitness business, with a team responsible for everything from product development and operations to marketing and profitability.

With top global athletes such as Maria Sharapova, Nike has been sharpening its focus on women's fitness, emphasizing running, walking, cardio, yoga and fitness dance. Nike Women stores have opened around the world, with a very different interior to the noise and adrenalin of traditional Niketowns. The annual Nike Women's Marathon, launched in 2004 in San Francisco, has become one of the largest women's running events in the world. Nike's dance fitness events, such as the globally popular RockStar Workout, and innovative clothing and footwear products such as the Zoom Dansante have deepened connections with women and driven significant growth.

They maybe didn't realize it back in the seventies, but Knight and Bowerman chose a good name for their business.

Step 7: Extend . . . innovating the brand range

A brand defined around customer aspirations rather than product functionality, can stretch across categories, providing a faster, less risky way to grow your business.

Brand extension is a disciplined yet creative process. Caterpillar's stretch from heavy engineering to clothing and footwear was not obvious but makes sense once the core brand is recognized for its

Conventional brand thinking	Gamechanger brand thinking
Brand extensions follow product adjacencies, extending to categories with similar capabilities, turning product brands into range brands.	Brand extensions follow customer adjacencies, extending to help them achieve more, built around a coherent and relevant brand purpose.

FIGURE 3.10 Brand extension at increasing distance, and risk from the core idea

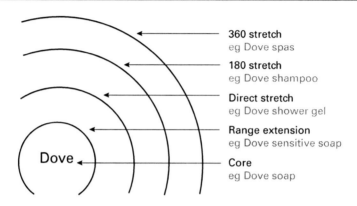

360 stretch
eg Dove spas

180 stretch
eg Dove shampoo

Direct stretch
eg Dove shower gel

Range extension
eg Dove sensitive soap

Dove

Core
eg Dove soap

strength and durability, rather than its technical machines. Dove's extension from soaps into shower gels and shampoos worked well, but an attempted stretch into spas and clothing were steps too far.

Starbucks is a great brand story, turning great coffee into brand experience, the 'third place' between home and work. Once they'd saturated our cities, they wanted to go further, extending on supermarket shelves, and into new segments. Their Via microground coffee showed how a brand can extend with the help of an innovation, bringing a new level of performance to the adjacent category, and justifying their premium gained through providing an experience. When they identified juice bars as an adjacent sector, an alternative for their health-minded customers, they had problems. Starbucks was too identified with coffee, rather than as a place. Instead they created a new brand, called Evolution, seeking to create a new third place.

A strong brand core, built around customer aspirations is far easier to stretch into new categories than a famous but functional product brand. A brand about refreshment can easily work across drinks categories. A brand about travel can extend from airlines and hotels to travel guides and tours. While it is often useful to have manufacturing capability to support an adjacent category, this can be sourced through partners, and is secondary to adding to the customer's experience.

Licensing is often a more effective way to extend into non-familiar categories, relevant to the customer but not your existing expertise. Virgin is the ultimate licensed brand, finding partners in every sector – from airlines to space travel, banking to communications – who can deliver a Virgin brand experience effectively. This requires careful understanding of the brand equity, to find a way of operating an airline, or a bank, that is true to the brand. How are Virgin phones different? What is better about its banks? It also requires a smart business model, to ensure continued influence over the brand and its activation, as well as IP ownership and financial reward.

In planning brand extensions, it is essential to plan the move carefully. While new categories might seem attractive, it is important to strengthen or shift the core brand concept first. Once ready to stretch, the migration needs a logical order, the right sequence of categories, and innovations to support entry into each. This is a brand and innovation journey, the sequence of which can ensure success or failure. Sometimes it can even mean shifting the core, as IBM effectively did, moving away from low-margin hardware into high-margin services. Whatever, the strategy, it needs a structured and thoughtful execution to protect the current brand and business, while also realizing the best new market opportunities.

CASE STUDY   Camper is much more than a poor man's shoe

In Catalan, camper means peasant.

You will find the whole story of the company and its value inside every pair of colourful, quirky and distinctive Camper shoes. The shoe company from the beautiful Spanish island of Majorca likes to do things differently.

Look at its shoes – in some styles, left and right shoes are intentionally mismatched, while in other models there are philosophies and quotations on the soles.

The shoes are rustic and authentic, unlikely to be called fashionable. They are inspired by the unique culture and traditions of the tiny Mediterranean island where they are still designed, and many of them manufactured. Most people of the island worked on the land, and so they wanted tough, durable shoes that could withstand the extremes of weather.

'Imagination Walks' goes the advertising slogan.

The story inside the shoes tells you that the business was founded in 1877 by a shoemaker called Antonio Fluxa, while the Camper brand was introduced by his grandson Lorenzo, 98 years later. In an interview with Fast Company, Lorenzo said: 'When people call us a fashion brand it offends me. We don't like the fashion world at all. We're trying not to take ourselves too seriously.'

Not fashionable or serious, maybe, but certainly popular. Camper's sales reached almost €100 million in 2007, making it a market leader in Spain, and it continues to grow rapidly with over 250 stores across the world, from Beijing to Buenos Aires, Victoria to Wellington.

The brand is much more than the shoes, becoming an alternative lifestyle, an attitude that challenges conventions.

'Camper Together' stores are designed in partnership with local artists and architects to offer customers far more than a shoe shop. In Barcelona, for example, the store is inspired by Jaime Hayon, one of Spain's most provocative graphic artists who designs furniture and toys. Bright and bold, the store is as much a quirky art gallery as a place to buy comfortable shoes. Meanwhile in Paris the store seems to still be waiting for a designer, encouraging visitors to draw on the walls, and express their own feelings and creativity.

There are Camper hotels and restaurants too. Casa Camper offers 25 simple but stylish bedrooms in the heart of Barcelona, with free wifi and DVD players in every room. It has a help-yourself, 24-hour snack galley, a vertical garden, a recycling centre, and free bikes to explore the great city too. Down the street you can eat at FoodBall, Camper's vegetarian restaurant, specializing in macrobiotic foodballs, made of rice and numerous natural and surprising ingredients. You can sit on the floor cushions, listen to the karma music, and drink the local organic beer too.

Go to the website and you can do all of this in a virtual world. 'Take a walk' enables you to test walk the camper shoes, and as you walk down the Barcelona street, you might pass a Camper Together store, pop into FoodBall for some new recipes, and then arrive at Casa Camper where you can book your real accommodation and pay for your new shoes too.

Most brands are designed to support or encourage the frenetic pace of our lives – with pocketfuls of electronic gadgets racing against the clock and against each other. Yet experience and expression are increasingly valued above money and materialism. Camper urges us to wake up and smell the flowers rather than the Starbucks, to enjoy those moments of quiet as we wait for the internet page to download.

Camper is a brand at peace with itself, its purpose to enjoy living life, rather than anything with numbers attached. Sebastian de Grazia captured the attitude of the Catalan shoemakers in his book *Of Time, Work, and Leisure*, saying 'perhaps you can judge the inner health of a land by the capacity of its people to do nothing – to lie abed musing, to amble about aimlessly, to sit having a coffee. Whoever can do nothing, letting his thoughts go.'

Step 8: Optimize . . . innovating the brand portfolio

As a business grows, its range of products and services become more diverse and complex. Brand portfolios need focus and brand architectures based around customers.

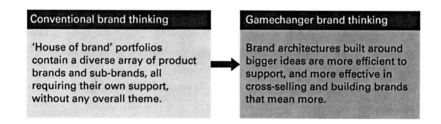

Conventional brand thinking	Gamechanger brand thinking
'House of brand' portfolios contain a diverse array of product brands and sub-brands, all requiring their own support, without any overall theme.	Brand architectures built around bigger ideas are more efficient to support, and more effective in cross-selling and building brands that mean more.

Large companies struggle with complexity. This is mainly because they have grown through diversification and acquisition over time, adding many entities to their original theme. From a customer perspective, customers associate with individual brands with little understanding of the company behind them, or what more they do. In an age of transparency, people want to know where products come from. From a business perspective, the cost and complexity of building 100 product brands, is far more than say building five range or concept brands.

Some companies, like GE, seek a 'monolithic' approach, where everything is branded under the corporate umbrella. The difficulty with this is that the corporate brand needs to stand for something, have purpose, which is not easy with so many different technologies. Stories and propositions become important in creating relevance to different audiences. Consumer product companies like Unilever, seek to enhance the endorsement of their corporate brand, like a seal of approval to their product brands. Others like Nestlé seek to create platforms, for example around healthy eating, that bring together their wide range of breakfast cereals.

When seeking to optimize a brand portfolio, there are two distinct tasks. One is to optimize the portfolio of products – ranges, products, or variants (SKUs). The other is to optimize the portfolio of brands – names and concepts, trademarks and designs.

When seeking to optimize a product portfolio, you will typically find the 80:20 rule at play: 80 per cent of the revenues will come from 20 per cent of the products (and 90 per cent of the profits from 10 per cent of them). Some companies label these most important products as their 'power brands', deserving of most investment and attention. As with all types of focus, putting more effort in some places means less in others. It is not uncommon to find that around 30 per cent of the products are value destroying. That is, when full costs

FIGURE 3.11 Brand portfolio analysis enables a business to optimize brands for better returns

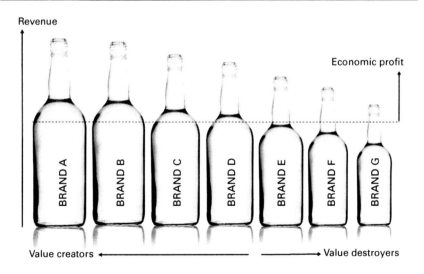

SOURCE *Gamechangers* by Peter Fisk

are allocated across the portfolio, a significant number of them are unprofitable, and selling more of them will just become even more unprofitable.

When drinks company Diageo evaluated its portfolio, it found that a number of its largest brands based on revenue, actually destroyed value (they didn't deliver a sufficient return on the capital employed). One of these brands was Bailey's, requiring the business to rethink the brand, from its positioning to its bottling process. They found that by refocusing the brand on a younger audience, portraying it as a sophisticated cocktail with ice, and sold in miniature bottles through specialist channels, it was able to transform the image and economics of the brand.

The second challenge is the brands themselves. Consumer goods companies have huge numbers of functional brands, often with supporting ingredient brands, and usually executed differently in local markets across the world. This can create huge cost and confusion. The challenge is to find focus and coherence. Global and local branding are both good, but need to work within a system.

The biggest difference can be made by bringing together brands with a similar purpose, and for the same audience. Volkswagen's portfolio – from Bugatti and Audi to Seat and Skoda – is not a diversity of technologies, but a carefully planned spectrum of brands to address different audiences, each motivated differently. Technological platforms then work across these brands to ensure product efficiency, while being relevant in different ways.

CASE STUDY   Making sense of GE's complex portfolio

Tommy Lee Jones, all in black, describes how GE's technology is providing hospitals with data software that connects patient to nurse to doctor to machines, reducing down time and turning waiting rooms into just rooms. GE has become a storyteller, helping people make sense of emerging possibilities and how they change all of our lives, and helping them to do it.

CMO Beth Comstock describes herself as a market maker: 'To be an effective marketer, you have to go where things are, you have to see what's happening and be a translator. You have to immerse yourself and not be comfortable sometimes.' She talks of rural doctors in China and farmers in Africa, where she sees the future GE making most difference, and money.

She sees her job as engaging people in a brand that does more for them, 'connecting the dots' between products and businesses. Brand platforms such as 'Ecomagination' engage people in GE's vision of a more human, responsible future.

Connecting the dots is also about making sense of fast-changing markets, looking for the patterns, the opportunities. She sees marketers as the people to do this, saying a great marketer 'translates observations into insights that can move a business or product forwards'. However that is not just about brand and communicating what exists, 'Marketing is now about creating and developing new markets; not just identifying opportunities but also making them happen'.

Customer innovation centres across the world drive this innovation within markets. In the Chinese city of Chengdu, for example, local and global marketers and researchers collaborate on new initiatives in mobile, affordable healthcare, and green energy. Other sources of ideas come from new types of open partnerships and innovation competitions.

Communicating ideas in more human, intuitive ways is important. While advertising still matters, it is more diverse media such as videos, social media and events that engage people more deeply. Facebook is used as GE's social 'hub' for engaging both business customers, and end consumers. There are over 30 GE pages, including social health and fitness apps. Google+ relates more to its technical audiences with videos and articles, while Pinterest is more female-focused, pinning more lifestyle photos and quotes. Twitter is for business users, keeping stories topical and drawing people in. YouTube is more of a video library, complementing TV ads.

GE sees this media as convergent. 'The idea of an ad as a separate entity is fading fast. Brands are content publishers and consumers are, too,' says Comstock. GE track engagement metrics to assess whether each new medium is relevant and scalable. Instagram passed the test, with around 150,000 people now following GE's photos of engines and power modules on the mobile social network, engaging tech geeks and business decision-makers alike.

One of the company's biggest growth strategies is based on the 'industrial internet' or to most of us, the 'Internet of Things', applying digital and social technologies to machines – MR machines to wind turbines – to improve their connected effectiveness. The emerging data will help to tell better stories, as well as use the machines better. The point is that business markets are becoming as social as individual consumers. GE's new storyline is about 'Brilliant Machines', with ads, for example, featuring Night Rider's KIT supercar getting a 21st century upgrade.

Step 9: Impact . . . innovating the brand value

Brands create value for customers and shareholders, but also have an impact on society and other stakeholders too. A brand's value is much more than its revenue or profits today.

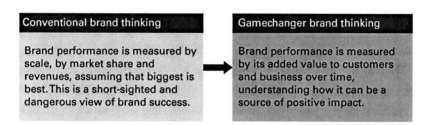

Conventional brand thinking	Gamechanger brand thinking
Brand performance is measured by scale, by market share and revenues, assuming that biggest is best. This is a short-sighted and dangerous view of brand success.	Brand performance is measured by its added value to customers and business over time, understanding how it can be a source of positive impact.

Brand equity was described by David Aaker as the 'brand assets and liabilities linked to a brand name and symbol', which add to or subtract from the value provided by a product or business. This radically changed the marketing function, articulating the direct impact it can have on the business, rather than as a support function to selling. In a sense it's the amount of 'positivity' in the brand to elevate a product or business beyond a commodity.

Of course a brand creates value for customers and business. This requires a balance, which can sometimes seem like a compromise. The reality is that brand building takes time, building equity with customers, which gradually amplifies into equity for the business.

For the business, brand equity is driven by awareness (how many people know about it), perception (how they feel about it, and are prepared to pay more for it), preference (how different is it, do people prefer it, will they stick with it?) and agility (how far can it extend and evolve?).

For the customer, brand equity is driven by relevance (is it for me, both in terms of function and aspiration?), confidence (do I trust it, and feel good using it?), connection (does it connect me with others?) and enablement (can I achieve more because of it?).

While this might sound obvious, it is surprising how many businesses, and brand agencies, still see brand as a labelling device to communicate their difference. Brand 'positioning' is often seen as how visible and different you are, as opposed to focusing on the brand's primacy in an audience's mind, based on perceived relevance and value.

Brand value is often quoted as the financial outcome of the equity which has been built in a brand. Business leaders delight in telling others that they have a 'billion-dollar brand'. What they probably mean is the sales volume of the brand, which is not always profitable.

However, when *Businessweek* announce Apple as 'the world's most valuable brand' (worth $98bn in 2013, ahead of Google $93bn, and Coca-Cola $79bn) they are actually seeking to measure the amount by which the brand enhances the market cap (capitalization) of the business. In other words, the way in which a brand increases the future revenues, the price premium that people will pay, and the certainty of them buying.

What matters is the business value, measured by the sum of future profits. Brands add to this by creating a premium on these, as well as making them more likely and less risky. By understanding the value drivers of a brand, that is, which brand actions most positively affect the business value, then we can make better choices about brand strategy.

FIGURE 3.12   Brand innovation can transform the potential for business to succeed

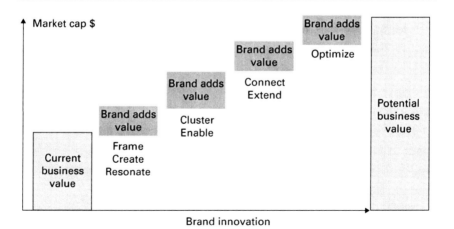

SOURCE *Gamechangers* by Peter Fisk

Each of the nine steps of brand innovation is an opportunity for the brand to add more value to the business. Understanding upfront the value potential of such actions creates much stronger commitment and secures investment. Together, the innovations can have a dramatic impact on the bottom line, the future health of the business, how much it is worth.

CASE STUDY Getting started: A roadmap for brand innovation

Innovation in each of the steps is most effectively achieved by a similar process, but with different topics and tools. The process is typically workshop-based, bringing people and ideas together in an accelerated, collaborative environment. The 'diamond' approach involves opening-up (stretch and explore, challenge and extend) then closing-down (connect and combine, filter and focus) for each of the challenges.

FIGURE 3.13

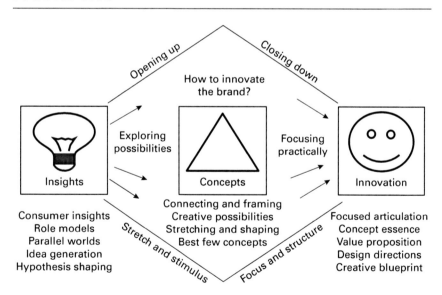

While there are nine steps, they are most effectively considered together to ensure their mutual dependence and impact. There are typically five phases in innovating your brand, deploying the diamond at each stage, combining analytics and intuition, creativity and discipline, to develop the right strategic approach:

1 **Intent:** The starting point is commercial, understanding the best market opportunities in the medium to long term, where the business can most effectively create and sustain profitable growth over time. This should align and shape the business strategy.

2 **Insight:** Deep understanding of potential customers in the identified markets, maybe through collaboration, enables the development of brand purpose and concept, opportunities to innovate the solutions, communication, experiences and portfolio.

3 **Ideation:** Creatively articulating the brand concept, from which flow appropriate solutions, by bringing together new and existing products and services, partners and resources to design an engaging brand experience. Ideas are visualized and evaluated.

4 **Innovation:** Making the strategic choices in each of the nine steps, from brand story to brand solutions, brand experience to brand portfolio. Underpinning this with a smarter allocation of resources, aligned culture and organization.

5 **Implementation:** Planning and executing the agreed strategy over a sequence of horizons, over which the brand evolves and grows in the market and commercially. Supporting this with effective leadership, appropriate metrics, staying agile to change.

The result will be a winning brand with a better strategy to drive future growth, in a way that is positively disruptive in the market and drives a step change in value creation for the business.

Biography

Peter Fisk is a best-selling author, inspirational keynote speaker and expert consultant, helping leaders to develop innovative strategies for business and brands.

He is a professor of strategy, innovation and marketing at IE Business School, and is CEO of GeniusWorks, a London-based consulting firm, helping clients around the world. He features on the Thinkers 50 'Guru Radar' as one of the best new business thinkers.

Having trained as a nuclear physicist, Peter moved to managing brands like Concorde at British Airways, helping Microsoft to adopt a value-based marketing model, and Virgin to launch into new markets. He was also CEO of the world's largest marketing organization, the Chartered Institute of Marketing.

GeniusWorks helps companies as diverse as Aeroflot and Coca-Cola, M&S and Mars, Philosophy and Red Bull, Sabre and Santander, Tata and Virgin, Visa and Vodafone to think bigger and smarter, develop innovative strategies, bolder brands, and accelerate growth.

Peter's best-selling book *Marketing Genius* explores the left- and right-brain challenges of success, and is translated into 35 languages. Others include *Customer Genius* on customer-centricity, *People Planet Profit* on sustainable innovation, and *Creative Genius* – defining what it takes to be Leonardo da Vinci in the 21st century.

His new book *Gamechangers ... Are you ready to change the world?* is based on extensive research into the 100 companies that are making sense of changing markets, shaping the future in their own vision, innovating strategy and brands, business models and marketing, to out-think competitors and win smarter.

Email: peterfisk@peterfisk.com
Website: www.theGeniusWorks.com
Twitter: @geniusworks

Bridging the gap between brand idea and delivery in a move-faster-but-be-certain market

Why the traditional process of building a brand needs a reboot

ALLEN ADAMSON

Part one: Let's set the foundation

In 1995, Pixar produced its first feature-length film, *Toy Story*. The film won an Academy Award and was nominated for three others. It set a benchmark in terms of animation to which other film companies have since aspired. The success of this film led the company to release two sequels, the second of which, *Toy Story 3*, (2010), the 11th Pixar production, became the highest-grossing animated film of all time worldwide (until it was surpassed by *Frozen* in 2014).

I bring this up, not to flaunt my skills at cinematic trivia (which are pretty paltry), but to set the context for the two terms critical to building a strong brand (that's what this book is about) – and to set the foundation for this chapter's subject: *The new challenge of launching brands in a marketplace that demands both speed and certainty*. Please hold that Pixar thought for just a moment.

First, let's get the two terms out of the way: *brand* and *branding*. A brand, for all intents and purposes, is something that lives in your head. It's a story, a promise, an idea that links a product or service to a consumer. Brands are mental associations that get stirred up when you think about or hear about a particular car, camera, bank, beverage, a website, an app, organization, celebrity, or even country. When the brand name comes up in conversation, or you have an experience with the brand, the associations you link with the brand are set free. You feel something. You react in some way – positively or negatively – based on how these associations make you feel. In order to have any chance for success, the idea on which a brand is based, what it means to people, has to be both unique and meaningful. Those in charge must identify something to convey about their brand that's authentically different and that they know people will care about. Oh, yes, the idea must also be absolutely simple and clear-cut. It can't be about two or three things, but one sharply focused idea that is easy to grasp and remember. I'll get to why in just a minute.

Branding, on the other hand, is how you go about establishing your brand's relevantly differentiated meaning in people's minds. It's about signals – the signals people use to decipher what you stand for as a brand. Branding signals generate associations. The most inspired and inspiring signals transmit exactly what they should be transmitting with no question relative to their intent. It is critical for a brand idea to be simple and sharply focused so that those responsible for the branding know exactly what it is they're supposed to be conveying; so they can *be* inspired to be inspiring. Branding is advertising, promotions and public relations. Branding is product design and functionality; it's taste and smell. It's social media, websites, customer service, store design, events, packaging, logos, product placement, you name it. Branding is anything and everything that makes up the customer experience. Establishing a simple, differentiated and relevant meaning for your brand, which leads to brilliant and effective branding signals is, in essence, what makes for brand success.

So, back to Pixar. The folks at Pixar had two fabulous insights, both of which made my life as a dad exponentially better, and which make the company a perfect example of what makes for a great *brand* – and great *branding*. The first insight was that kids were becoming a whole lot more sophisticated than in prior generations. They were no longer falling for cute mice and fuzzy bunnies but, rather, falling under the influence of more visually and conceptually stimulating diversions, digital and otherwise. The movie entertainment choices for the ten-and-under crowd were not reflecting that. The second Pixar insight was that even though seven-year-old kids were too cool for dancing mice and bunnies, they didn't go to the movies by themselves, either. The simple brand idea? Create movies that parents would want their kids to go to, that kids would *want* to go to, and even movies that adults would go and see on their own. Pixar saw a gap in the marketplace and figured out how to fill it with a categorically relevantly different offering.

As for the *branding*, the signals, Pixar continues to look to its simple and focused idea as inspiration for everything it does, from its storylines, to the lovable characters, to the famous folks employed as voices for the characters, and to decisions about investments in its amazing technology. Pixar knows that staying focused on what it stands for in people's minds will enable it to send exactly the branding signals required to connect with children and parents of all ages worldwide. Even Pixar's partnership with Disney, which bought the ingenious brand in 2006, was a brilliant branding signal. Disney has been weaving magical family entertainment into the fabric of life for decades and Pixar was able to put a new buzz in Disney's creative portfolio. It was – and is – a smart partnership.

A brand, to sum it up, is your story. It can be a story about what you do or make, who you are, or why you do what you do. For a brand story to be effective it has to be based on one singular clear idea, whether it's animated movie entertainment that appeals to the whole family, à la Pixar, or GE's 'Imagination at Work', or FedEx's absolute certainty in overnight delivery, or BP's story of going beyond petroleum to make the world a more energy efficient planet, or Annie's wholesome, organic kid-friendly foods that are win-win delicious and nutritious. Branding, again, is how the story gets told. It's all the things that help consumers understand and experience what makes the brand unique and meaningful. Branding is the actual proof of concept brought to life across multiple touchpoints. Okay. Foundation set, let's move on.

Part two: So, what's the problem?

While it's still true, and always will be true, that success in building a brand is a function of having a simple, focused idea that's different and relevant, telegraphed with brilliant and appropriate signals, there is a problem. Actually a few problems, a function of the world as we know it: transparent, accessible, global, and very, very noisy. To begin with, remember a few paragraphs back I stated that Pixar had 'found a gap in the marketplace'? Well, it's getting harder and harder to find a gap in the marketplace. The ability to identify something new and different and that people care about is not easy. Way back when, Maxwell House coffee could say it was 'good to the last drop' and didn't have to worry too much about there being more than a cupful of other coffee manufacturers with which to compete. NBC executives didn't have to plan their fall season with any networks in mind other than CBS and ABC. If people were thirsty, they'd reach for a Coca-Cola or a Pepsi or, if they were into un-cola, they'd reach for a 7 Up. Shampoo, cereal, insurance, automobiles, kids' toys, online shopping sites, gaming sites, news sites, reading sites, apps of every application, have multiplied exponentially. To say the marketplace, across every category, is hyper-cluttered and hyper-competitive is an understatement.

Problem one: Coming up with the shiny new object that people want and can use is a tough assignment.

The second problem for marketers today is being able to develop branding that breaks through. In the age of *Mad Men*, Don Draper and his troops would create a 60-second TV spot with the knowledge that people across the United States would all be sitting on their couches at the same time, watching one of the three basic network television stations, and – with no remote control in sight – be forced to see this 60-second TV spot. They'd pick up one of a few magazines or newspapers and see the accompanying print ad reinforcing the brand story – say, 'Dove is one-quarter cleansing cream', or 'Gimme a break of that Kit Kat bar', along with a coupon or two. It was, for the most part, how the brand story was delivered and received. As we all know, there are myriad new media channels for channelling a brand message, be it cable television or any number of online venues. More than this, there are myriad other ways consumers interact with brands and receive branding messages, from social media sites (word of mouth on steroids, as it were), to product and service review sites, to product placements in every conceivable entertainment setting, to customer service and retail situations, to, well, you get the picture. And it's not just that there are more brand points of touch than ever before; to exacerbate the issue, consumers have more control of what they see, hear, do, turn on and turn off.

So, to summarize problem two: Getting your brand story out there in a way that breaks through and sticks is a tough assignment.

But wait, there is, of course, more. Problem three: Marketers continue to think about building brands via, what I call, the conveyor belt approach, a long-standing formulaic approach that is no longer relevant.

In this linear process, which was, in fact, developed as a manifestation of the traditional manufacturing assembly line (think Ford's Model T), one department hands off a piece of the initiative to another. Strategy people come up with an idea. They pass it along to the research department who take it into focus groups with a series of white cards on which are written possible positions for the idea. An idea is selected. It goes to the creative team. They come up with ads, and logos and signage, and colour palettes for all the collateral material. The media department is consulted. The client weighs in and changes a lot of components. The creative team goes back to rejigger. The below-the-line agencies are told to come up with their direct marketing, their digital marketing inclusive of Facebook pages and YouTube videos, their crowd-sourcing scenarios, pop-up stores, and other public relations events. The customer service people are told what's going into market and to become familiar with the service-call script. The retailers are given their hang tags and in-store materials. One stage-gate step after another, down the line. Whether all the piece parts come together in a coherent, cohesive way in alignment with the brand idea is the hoped-for outcome, but not necessarily the certain outcome.

Concurrent to this is the client activity, also stage-stepped. Their researchers and developers research and develop a product, a factory is tricked out to produce it, a packaging team to wrap it (or if it's an airline, a financial services product, or some other experiential brand, a mixed bag of teams to design and get it to fly), after which it's introduced to the sales and marketing teams who are told to go sell whatever it is. Add to this the hierarchical nature of big companies, the pecking order of buy-in, one level after the next, as well as the silo-like nature of a lot of businesses today (you do your job, I'll do mine and we'll all push for funding and accolades for our respective departments) and you've got a pretty unwieldy situation in terms of being able to get things out the door and into market before the next guy does.

Suffice it to say, in today's pinball marketplace, consumers simply don't experience brands in a linear fashion. They ping from one interaction to another, on their terms and in their own due time. There's media fragmentation, for sure, but also rampant experiential fragmentation. Add to this, as I said earlier, the fact that things are moving a whole lot faster than ever before. Companies don't have the luxury to do the copious in-and-out-of-market research they used to be able to do. Whether it's a technological device, a car, a granola bar, or a laundry detergent, you can bet some other company is working parallel to your efforts to get out first. By the time your shiny new object is ready to go, well, the cheese, as they say, will have moved. The reality is that you have to consider all the practical implications quickly. It's a new, open world that brands live in. Another reality is that it's a world in which everyone's a critic. In brand building today there is the paradoxical need for both speed and certainty as well as consistency across all brand touchpoints. Whatever you've got to offer had better be right, right out of the gate.

Bottom line: The world has changed. The conveyor belt approach to brand-building encumbers thinking, is cumbersome, and takes time and money. It may have worked in *Mad Men* days, but it's neither efficient nor effective given current marketplace conditions.

Part three: So, what's the solution?

Okay, so how *do* you launch a brand faster and with greater certainty of success knowing that the guy with the possibly better mousetrap is in lockstep with your efforts? How do you launch a brand faster and with greater certainty knowing that, even in the best-intentioned focus groups, consumers can't always tell you what they want, or that they'll actually end up buying it? How do you launch a brand faster and with greater certainty of success knowing you have multiple constituencies creating the branding, often in silos, as well as multiple levels in the client buy-in process? How do you launch a brand faster and with greater certainty of success knowing consumers will quickly weigh in and share their input with the world the minute your new whatever hits the market?

The answer, in brief, is to work on the brand idea and the potential branding ideas *concurrently*. Think about the story you'd like to tell and, *at the same time*, think about the best way to tell it, getting the cross-functional team together in an open forum. Evaluate the idea *and* a breakthrough way of activating it simultaneously. Determine the point of touch, the signal you can send, that will optimize, maximize, leverage in the best way possible the brand idea *and* the proof that it's different in a way people care about.

It's kind of like taking a page out of the technology business playbook; *prototype* the product or experience in a way that brings it to life for the decision-makers. Build something people can see, touch, experience, and interact with as a way for them to determine if the idea makes sense, has legs, can go the distance, and can take on the competition. Sure, you could write up the idea on a whiteboard, put it in a PowerPoint presentation, and then create an ad to get your message across. But doing this will never have the oomph needed to get the reaction, and subsequent action, needed to get to market quickly and with as much proof of concept as possible. Think about Virgin airlines, for example. Sure, its founder, Richard Branson, could have telegraphed his idea of 'Let's not be ordinary' by way of a print ad, but instead, he and his teams initially brought the idea to life by promoting the limo service to and from London's Heathrow Airport, by the funky design of its cabins, and the airline's very funky on-board safety video, which has since gotten a gazillion hits on YouTube. These branding touchpoints made the brand point and made it fast.

For years, prototyping has helped consumer businesses better integrate a number of related variables – get the right combination of variables as close to the real deal as possible in order to gauge consumer reaction as speedily and accurately as possible. Steve Jobs, as has been very well documented, used the prototyping approach to successfully grow and manage the Apple brand, assessing every component of his magical machines, from logo design to user interface. From the get-go, the multiple disciplines involved in a project, be it the battery team, the research and design team, the app team, or the antiglare glass team, work as a unit to ensure all separate lines of activity come together, fit together, and work together to pull off a brilliantly executed product. (If you don't know how this little brand turned out, I can suggest a few books.)

The notion of using this prototype approach for all sorts of brand-building projects is logical because the same dynamics apply: lots of moving parts – people and otherwise; lots of brand experience touchpoints; lots of competition; lots of time constraints; and lots of public scrutiny and commentary at the ready. Yes, I know, not every brand is a touchable, tangible product, but the general mindset – create the most effective, efficient, accessible proxy brand experience possible, with the greatest degree of agility built in – still holds true.

Building and testing the brand experience via prototyping is not formulaic but, rather, enables – and encourages – a team to determine the best way to introduce a specific brand idea. It prompts them to identify the most optimal branding vehicle given the idea, be it a breakthrough package design, an event, a different retail approach, say a 'genius bar' or pop-up store, or a social media initiative. (Yes, it may even be a television ad, but it had better be a great one.) The operating word here is 'breakthrough'. Is the brand idea, itself, breakthrough, and is the branding breakthrough enough to get people talking about it?

Working concurrently on the story and its telling allows the team to evaluate the idea and think about the relevance and potential success of the branding within the context of the entire user experience. Assessing a possible positioning statement while simultaneously looking at how it could manifest itself in market lets those involved, agency and client-side, better determine where and how to invest time and infrastructure costs. Here's a super example from my agency, Landor. Thomas Ordahl, our Chief Strategy Officer, was working with a team on a new product for a national oil company that has gas station franchises country-wide. The challenge the team wanted to solve was to create a branded packaged food offering, akin to convenience store offerings, at these franchises. It was to be a 'grab-and-go' selection for a target market consisting mainly of construction guys, tradesmen, blue and grey collar workers who want to get something good to eat quickly and get back to the job.

'We were struggling with how to position this,' Thomas told me:

> Not just what is the value proposition, but we wanted to actually develop the concept for the product, itself. It wasn't just the positioning, but the menus and the evolution of the product. We were strategically circling three ideas, looking at three different strategic territories we could occupy. One was to focus on convenience, food that's easy to eat, to place in your vehicle's cup holder, easy to throw away. If you think about anyone who eats in the car in a rush, it's a pain to unwrap a messy sandwich. So simple and easy was one direction.

Another potential position, Thomas told me, was the food, itself. Maybe come up with a unique food offering, like the Slurpee at 7-11, or a signature sandwich. The third position the team considered was event-driven related to the target audience, focusing on game food, or afternoon snacks.

'When we discussed this with the clients, they, themselves, were struggling with the three options,' Thomas explained:

> What we did was create concept prototypes for each position. What would they actually look like, and what would need to be developed to bring each to market? For the convenience positioning, we created packaging concepts that looked almost like a Bento box into which people could quickly pick out the items they wanted and place them in the box. The box was not only easy to eat from and throw out, it helped keep the pricing model simple. The second concept was built around the idea of regional food and a regional food truck which would drive around to key locations. We had an app that would tell the potential audience where the truck would be, whether it was a work site or a baseball game or state fair, and what would be on the menu. For the third concept, we came up with a variety of event ideas and created promotional material that might appeal to the target group.

In terms of the process, Thomas and his team first studied the analytics around food trends and each of the potential concepts, almost from an account planner's point of view, and then created a framework for evaluating each concept. 'The client totally got what we were trying to accomplish,' Thomas said:

> They got that it wasn't a matter of choosing purple over pink, the color palette or visual identity, but that we used the prototypes to help them see what the concepts would look like as in-market initiatives, and the inherent financial and timing factors involved. They picked two to take into research, focus groups wherein the participants were also able to look at the ideas made tangible. We found that the convenience positioning was the leading idea. The prototyping was an incredibly valuable process. The client had a good sense of where to make their investments and why.

How does this prototyping process actually work?

It's important to think of the prototyping process as an 'all together now' approach. Consider an orchestra working literally and figuratively in harmony. Each musician must play his or her part brilliantly, but each is dependent on the others for a melodious outcome. If you can't hear what the other musicians are playing, your ability to create a harmonious result is diminished. Creating and assessing the branding signals in a holistic, integrated way lets you quickly see if your storyline makes sense, how each of the consumer's experiences aligns with the story, and which is the most powerful application relative to the story – which one has the power to bring it to life most effectively.

As for the details, here's how we do it where I work:

- We start every 'all together now' prototyping session by getting all our strategists, our insight team members, the verbal team, the visual team, and the activation team together in one room to talk about, first, the brand story – to make sure it's an idea that is as relevantly different as it is simple and focused. (Analogy: For anyone who has ever written a piece of ad copy, an essay, an article, or a book, if your headline isn't sharply focused your content won't flow naturally or effectively.)

- After we've defined the brand story, ensured that it's different in a way that people will care about, we develop two or three alternative ways to frame the story. We do this to see which one might offer up a greater and more effective variety of consumer brand experiences than another.

- We then brainstorm the specific brand experiences that will bring the idea to life, how the story will manifest itself in the marketplace and across multiple points of touch, from logo and store design, to customer service, online applications, events, advertising, and so forth. One of the telltale signs that the storyline may not be as sharply focused as it should be is if the branding experiences are less than brilliant, if they don't feel as if they can be executed with authenticity.

- As we define the story, we concurrently match it not just to the brand experiences, but to the brand personality itself. Is this something that feels genuine and credible? Will consumers find it believable and, equally important, is the experience or any given touchpoint actionable?

- Another dimension of this session is that as we set out to determine tried and true touchpoints, we also charge ourselves with coming up with new or unexpected points of interaction. Let's touch the consumer in a way they're not being touched by the competition. We look for things that didn't exist before. It should be noted that there is not one set of customer experiences, but that each set is defined by the storyline, the brand idea. The objective is to achieve that 'yin and yang', the perfect symbiosis of strategy and execution that couldn't happen in a linear process.

- Finally, we assign team members the responsibility of identifying ways to prototype the individual branding signals, be they tangible, as in logos, packaging, store design, website, Facebook page, YouTube video, etc, or less tangible, as in a customer service script, or a reservation desk scenario.

Why is the prototype process better than the traditional linear process?

Good question. Here's the answer:

- Things happen faster on the branding agency side and the client side when people have something to react to. I'm not talking about a PowerPoint presentation, or a whiteboard with a positioning statement, but something that crystallizes the story and the branding and brings it as close to real as possible. I like to say that words are a mile wide and an inch deep. Ask a consumer – or a client – what the 'friendly, contemporary, innovative' insurance company means and you'll get as many answers as there are people to ask. Show or illustrate to consumers – or clients – exactly what you're talking about and you'll get a much more constructive response.

- Once you can crystallize an idea and show how it manifests itself as the customer experience, it will be easier to manage the multiple layers of both agency-side teams and client-side management. You will be able to get much more definitive responses to 'I love it' or 'I hate it', and why, which will foster more open communication about next steps. You will know what to tweak and why. In the end, this will save both time and money. Simply put, prototyping enables you to cut to the chase faster. People absorb and process information in different ways. When everyone is looking at a prototype, when the vision is in front of them, there is less chance of misinterpretation or a budget gone awry.

- Prototyping allows people to see the future. (Very few people are like Steve Jobs who could see the future, envision the experience, and tell us why we'll love it.) A prototype helps people to understand the business implications more clearly, to understand what will be required to execute on Plan A or Plan B, the investments required in both personnel, infrastructure and financing. By fully understanding the various implications of a given branding scenario, business decisions are easier to make and support. There will be less surprise when something hits the market.

While there are these essential benefits to a prototyping versus the traditional linear process, there are some qualifications to keep in mind. First of all, it's very easy to get lured into the nuances of an execution and lose sight of the core idea. Not seeing the forest for the trees, as it were, requires diligent focus on whether the basic concept is right or wrong given the strategic objective, and not whether a specific colour or word or creative detail is right or wrong. It's critical to keep the conversation centred on the inherent strength or weakness of the idea. There is a natural tendency when evaluating creative output to say 'I don't like that', but this often refers to a subjective like or dislike of an irrelevant detail. Don't get lost in the weeds of executional elements when determining the value and validity of an idea.

Another qualification in the prototyping process is that, yes, the upfront financial investment may be greater than that in the traditional approach to branding. You will be pulling in your creative resources sooner, and you may even see some ideas left on the 'cutting room' floor. Like anything else in marketing, there are trade-offs. The trade-off here, making bigger upfront investments, will be mitigated by a process that is more efficient and effective in the long term. That key decisions can be made faster and with a greater degree of certainty earlier in the process, thereby speeding up time to market, is a definite plus.

Consumers don't experience the marketplace in a linear fashion, nor the brands with which they interact. The traditional branding approach was a linear one. This new, prototyping approach takes into account the way that consumers actually experience brands and branding, and the fact that the brand story must be made clear quickly, effectively and with maximum impact. It's a new way of working, yes. But it's what brand success today looks like.

Biography

Allen Adamson is Chairman, North America at Landor Associates, a strategic branding and design firm, and author of *The Edge: 50 tips from brands that lead, including Apple, Zappos, GE, P&G, and even Justin Bieber.* His previous books include *BrandSimple: How the best brands keep it simple and succeed* and *BrandDigital: Simple ways top brands succeed in the digital world.*

A noted expert in the areas of branding and advertising, Allen is a sought-after industry commentator and writes a bimonthly column for Forbes.com on business trends and their impact on brands. He has appeared on ABC News, the BBC, CNBC, Fox Business Network, and NBC. He is frequently quoted in publications such as *Advertising Age, Bloomberg Businessweek,* the *Financial Times,* the *New York Times, USA Today,* the *Wall Street Journal* and *The Washington Post.* He regularly lectures at local and national universities and business schools.

Prior to his current role, Allen was Managing Director of Landor's New York office, where he was responsible for operations and overseeing branding efforts for a broad spectrum of corporate and consumer brands in industries ranging from technology to health care to fashion.

Luxury branding

05

JEAN-NOËL KAPFERER

Building luxury brands means forgetting most of the classic rules of marketing and adopting instead what are now recognized as the anti-laws of marketing. When a luxury brand is managed without taking into account the critical specifics of luxury it undermines its own luxury credentials, loses prestige, equity and thus pricing power. Unfortunately, this is a classic error often seen among luxury brands where strong pressures lead managers to forget these specifics. Some luxury brand owners are in a hurry to get a good return and are willing to dilute their brand by making it more accessibly priced and more widely available. This happened to Jaguar when managed by Ford. Using the wrong brands as benchmarks can also lead to making the wrong decisions. This problem arises when one includes in the same survey Coach (a masstige [mass prestige] brand) and Chanel (a true luxury brand).

The objective of this chapter is to illustrate how the foundations on which luxury brands are built determine 90 per cent of their success. Behind the fashionable blanket term 'luxury brand' there are actually a number of very different business models. At one extreme lie brands such as Coach or Ralph Lauren which are managed just as FMCG (Fast-Moving Consumer Goods) brands are. Their goal is selling large volumes of the brand and not of achieving supreme quality. If one looks beyond their nice flagship stores, one will realize that a high percentage of their sales is achieved through discount channels, factory outlets and by regularly slashing their prices. They delocalize their production outside their home country and use licences to stretch their brand.

At another extreme lie brands such as Hermès, or Louis Vuitton (the world's No 1 luxury brand valued at $27 billion according to Interbrand and Millward Brown). Louis Vuitton only sells through stores that they directly operate. They produce every product that they sell without ever licensing their brands to others, they never offer rebates, they never relocate their factories to low cost countries, etc. This is called a 'luxury strategy' (Kapferer and Bastien, 2012). For luxury does not lie in marketing but in the offering. This model is also followed by Ferrari and Rolex, Park Hyatt Hotels and Chanel.

After revisiting essential conceptual, sociological and economic issues, we will focus on how brands need to conduct themselves in order to be built and considered as luxury brands.

Luxury in question: Ending the confusion about definitions

There is a lot of confusion about the definition of luxury brands, and in fact, the word luxury itself. In a recent global survey, Louis Vuitton was called a 'fashion brand' instead of what it purports to be, a symbol of luxury. On the other hand, one reads that 'Starbucks coffee is equated with romance, relaxation and luxury' (Taylor Clark, 2008: 94). If a $4 caffè con latte is luxury, then the word luxury has truly become meaningless!

Interestingly, just as in some religions it is forbidden to mention the name of God, at Hermès one does not talk of 'luxury'. Former Hermès CEO Jean Louis Dumas Hermès used to say 'we make beautiful products that are sold in beautiful stores'.

On the other hand, Coach – a low-price leather goods competitor – uses the word luxury to describe themselves on their website. To end this confusion, it is important to distinguish between the concept of luxury, the luxury sector (a macro-economic notion) and the luxury strategy.

Etymologically luxus means overabundance or excess. This is why the concept has positive and negative connotations. To afford luxury goods, one needs to be able to do so, paying for something that over-delivers, beyond what rationality commands. Luxury is 'needlessly expensive' said Seth Godin. Why buy a €5,000 Hermès leather bag? Wouldn't a €700 Coach bag be enough? The answer is 'No!' The reason for this is that beyond the obvious differences in work, quality, tradition, culture, luxury prices are discriminatory prices, separating those who can or are ready to pay for something that is expensive beyond necessity, and all others. It is a fact that since ancient times, luxury has existed because not everybody can afford it.

To understand luxury, one must understand how luxury is recognized. Interestingly luxury producers do not define luxury the same way luxury non-buyers do. Producers emphasize the richness of details, the extreme quality, the rare craftsmanship, the cultural roots, all of which make ownership of the brand a privilege. In luxury, a bag is no longer a bag: it is an object of art that speaks volumes of the owner's sophistication and ability to appreciate the intrinsic value of such a product.

Non-luxury buyers, however, stress the highly conspicuous nature of luxury, the high price paid to convey mostly status and appearance. These actually negate the rare artistry and heritage that the product embodies. As for luxury buyers, they talk about indulgence, the highly hedonistic nature of the object and of the service that necessarily accompanies it, of an experience that pampers their senses, making them feel truly special, privileged.

The luxury strategy

How have luxury brands such as Ferrari, Aston Martin, Riva, Louis Vuitton, Chanel, Cartier, Hermès, Rolex, Patek succeeded? How have they been able to sustain and continually grow their pricing power and desirability? The answer is by learning through trial and error. The result, however, is a very robust strategy, with proven results, which should not be confused with fashion branding or the branding of premium products.

It is a common error to believe that luxury branding is just a higher form of premium branding. Luxury lies in a different realm altogether. It exists close to art, with which it shares a common worship of creativity, a grain of folly, exquisite craftsmanship, rare materials and exclusivity. Also, although luxury is fashionable today, it is not fashion.

Luxury is a creative industry that sells cultural advancement and a higher quality of life. Its products are symbols of culture, icons of beauty. Unlike FMCG and masstige brands, luxury is not a customer-driven industry that requires surveys and customer relationship management techniques. In order to create people's dreams one needs special talents and the ability to anticipate what people would yearn for.

Luxury brand strategy is different from that of premium brands. In premium brands, producers sell better performance for higher prices, but at the end of the day these brands still chase customers. The luxury strategy however demands that customers chase the brand, hence it is about creating a very strong artistic desirability in the offering. Like art, luxury has a timeless quality because its value extends far beyond performance and functional values. The goal of the luxury strategy is to create incomparability. Just as it makes no sense to compare Van Gogh and Manet, it is as meaningless to compare Cartier and Bulgari. Their roots, history, heritage, tradition, art, know-how and creativity are too distinct to make any comparison meaningful.

The luxury strategy is about building incomparability into all the aspects of the brand and thereby maintaining the gap with the many brands that try to grab market share by copying the codes and look of luxury brands.

Figure 5.1 shows the key words of each of the three core strategies (luxury, fashion and premium).

FIGURE 5.1   Comparing luxury, fashion and premium strategies

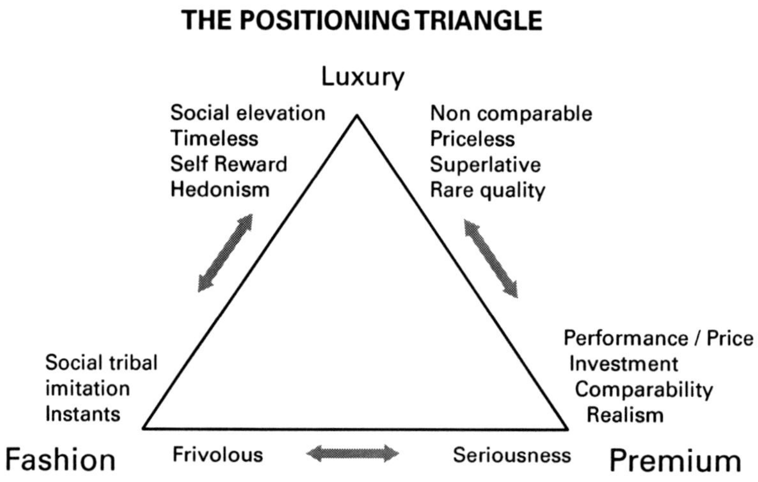

THE POSITIONING TRIANGLE

Luxury

Social elevation
Timeless
Self Reward
Hedonism

Non comparable
Priceless
Superlative
Rare quality

Social tribal
imitation
Instants

Performance / Price
Investment
Comparability
Realism

Fashion   Frivolous ⟷ Seriousness   Premium

Fashion is the process of adapting demand to supply, just the contrary of what marketing does (adapting supply to demand). Fashion sells the benefit of being fashionable. Fashion is about seduction based on permanent renewal; each season needs a new best-seller. Who decides whether a brand is fashionable? Not the brand itself but the fashion eco-system, the buzz, the institutions, Vogue, Anna Wintour, the many influencers. Since fashion does not last, product quality is not a core value of this business model. What is fashionable this summer will no longer be fashionable in a few months. There's no point in investing in quality for ephemeral products. This is why most fashion brands outsource their production to China to get as low manufacturing costs as possible. Also fashion brands have to slash prices down by 70 per cent when the season advances and demand falters. Typically, the unsold inventory is sent to discount channels, to internet sites or to factory outlets to be quickly sold off.

Fashion needs celebrities to capture the *air du temps* and look modern. Fashion brands use licences to increase their financial revenues faster; this is how they *stretch* their portfolio of activities from the core product to peripheral ones after only a few years.

However well this can work for fashion brands, this strategy cannot work for a luxury brand. Has one ever seen rebates on a Ferrari or Rolls Royce? Has one ever seen Chanel products in a discount channel, even on an internet site like Net-a-porter.com?

Louis Vuitton does not use licences: one cannot delegate the quality reputation to third parties. The luxury brand has extended its portfolio over time by investing time and money in learning how to make eyewear and watches (and soon even fragrance).

Let's understand the specifics of the luxury brand and business model that makes it so different from more conventional categories. These are listed in Figure 5.2.

This is a demanding business model carved by the most successful brands and not all industries can try to follow these principles. For instance, spirits and wines do not own their own distribution networks, they sell through bars, hotels, restaurants. They also don't meet their end clientele. The same is true of fragrance, skincare brands and watchmakers (although Rolex has just recently opened some exclusive stores).

FIGURE 5.2   The specifics of the luxury business model

* Worshipping creativity and quality, passion for detail, craftsmanship

* Always keeping supply far less than demand

* Total control of the value chain upstream to ensure the highest level of quality (Hermès own their own crocodile farms as opposed to most other brands who buy skins at the best price from wholesalers; Chanel owns flower gardens for its fragrances.)

* Total control over downstream quality in order to guarantee personalized one-to-one service and keep direct one-to-one contact with the end customers

* The recognition that luxury is built at the retail level, hence having highly selective distribution

* Highly experiential directly operated stores where customers can experience not just exceptional service but also the brand culture

* A fine combination of rare know-how, craftsmanship and an appreciation/respect for tradition

* No licences

* No rebates

* Recognition of the significance of brand provenance, country of origin

* Keeping affiliation with art and avant-garde contemporary artists

* Giving to charities as an obligation

It is important to recognize that luxury is not a technique or a set of rules; it is a culture of quality and art that has to be shared from the doorman of the company to the CEO and from the salesperson to the craftsman. By promoting rare products which are made by craftsmen, locally, and will last a long time, luxury shares the ideals of sustainable development.

Luxury is not a more expensive version of premium but a completely different mindset

A comparison of whisky and cognac illustrates the difference between luxury and super premium. Whisky producers follow a *premium strategy* wherein the price charged must always be justified by some product characteristic. This can lead to tricky situations, for example if an eight-year-old bottle of Chivas is sold at €30 then how old should be the whisky that is sold at €300, or even €3,000? The problem is that beyond 21 years, the quality of a whisky does not get better and so an age-based claim of product superiority only allows price extension to a certain extent.

Cognac producers have been more clever, and their prices are far higher. First they restrict the use of the name 'Cognac' only to those spirits made in the Cognac region. All others are called brandy. Also they keep the age of the product a mystery on purpose: XO means Very Old; VSOP means Very Superior Old Pale. There is no quantification of age, for it provides a basis for price comparability, thus preventing a significant increase in price. Cognac also leverages history smartly, for instance with 'Napoleon' being a specific quality, 'Louis XIII' another quality.

Skincare brands too illustrate the difference between a luxury strategy and a premium one. Although most skincare brands found in high end department stores *look* luxurious on the basis of the classic attributes of luxury brands (high price, selective distribution, pursuit of perfection, very attentive salespeople, many small details, aesthetic packaging, donations to charities and foundations, etc), however most of these brands actually follow a premium strategy and not a luxury strategy.

In a premium strategy, brands compete on the basis of proving their product superiority and are constantly trying to establish that they have the best product in the world by comparing themselves with other brands. Conversely, a luxury strategy builds incomparability and timelessness. It is based primarily on implied superiority and does not even acknowledge competition. Brand authority is based on faith thereby endowing the brand with symbolic authority.

Let us analyse how true luxury brands (La Prairie, La Mer or SK2 in Asia) talk about themselves on their websites and in their stores. The structure of their storytelling is as follows:

- I have an incredible 'magical ingredient'.
- There is a fabulous story behind it.
- It can deliver much more than one could expect.
- This is a magic formula against ageing, against death.

- This can be found in our 'star product', our long seller (time).
- The naming of this star product sets it apart, beyond comparison ('Caviar Illuminating System' or 'Platinum Collection' of La Prairie, 'Crème de la Mer', 'Miracle Broth' for SK2).

Lancôme, Clarins or Biotherm don't have a beautiful story with a hint of magic in them. Why is Clarins not considered to be a luxury brand? Their brand storytelling takes on a very humble approach with humility as a virtue. It says that it takes the active principles of its product simply as they are in nature. Clarins wants to be sincere and state things as they are without indulging in exaggeration or overpromises. As a result there is no real Clarins dream. This does not mean the brand has no loyal clients and fans worldwide, but its symbolic authority is weaker as is its pricing power. There is no magic intermediation that creates a gap, an element of incomparability with other brands.

Building incomparability and value in the brand

When creating a new luxury brand, two classic mistakes are made. The first one is to believe that quality will be enough. Even if a brand has exceptional quality, such as in the case of some start-ups, these may just remain a respected craftsman's brand and never grow enough. This is the case in India where so many remarkable craftsmen exist but hardly any Indian luxury brands. They forget that luxury brands are made by their myth-making clients: Audrey Hepburn made Tiffany just as Grace Kelly made Hermès. The Kelly bag gained star imagery from a star. Grace Kelly, both a Hollywood star and a princess, made it the everlasting icon of elegance.

The second mistake lies in believing that luxury is only about logos, communication, influential marketing, PR, and opening an e-commerce site as fast as possible. The Kelly bag by Hermès is sold in limited supply because it takes 18 hours for each bag to be made by one single talented rare craftsman who embeds French know-how, culture and magic into the bag. All women with class and culture in the world think of 'Kelly' as soon as they are luxury 'aware' and hope that they will possess one, at least once in their life. This is exactly how the luxury strategy operates; a timeless desire is nurtured around iconic products encapsulating the universe of iconic brands. Unlike fashion, which destroys the value of its products after each season, luxury builds timeless icons which become the milestones of each individual's personal progress. Many men say 'Someday I shall own an Rolex Oyster Perpetual, or a Porsche 911, or a Cartier Tank watch or Jaeger Lecoultre Reverso watch'. It is extremely profitable for brands when profits come from everlasting SKUs (stock-keeping units). Luxury brands entering fashion is only done for appearance, it creates hype but not much more than that. Designer Marc Jacobs' clothes sold at Louis Vuitton represented 1 per cent of the sales but 50 per cent of PR visibility. However, the gigantic profits of Louis Vuitton – that make it the world's No 1 luxury brand – come from its iconic leather timeless bags (Monogram, Epi, ...) that act as a long-term fixation for people, a measure and reward of their own advancement in life.

This is why brands' role in the creation of value is of paramount importance. Clients enter the store of a brand. They do not dream just of a leather bag; they want the Christian Dior one. Just as an artist's name epitomizes value, luxury brands are aggregators of value inherited from tradition, heritage, DNA, visions, cultural references. We shall see below that even new brands must start by spending enough time defining their heritage. This is how they will make themselves comparable to none. You cannot compare Petrus and Château Latour, two iconic Bordeaux wines sold at prices above €1,000 a bottle. You cannot compare Lamborghini and Ferrari, two different legends!

The importance of heritage

Recent research has demonstrated that without heritage there are no luxury brands, no dream (see 'the dream equation', later in the chapter, p 116). This should be a matter of concern for all luxury start-ups that do not spend enough time working on their heritage, values, culture, for this is the main source of their long-term incomparability and coherence. A new luxury brand cannot be launched as an answer to a SWOT analysis or to a market study identifying a business opportunity; it can only start through an authentic, passionate desire to create objects for today which embed higher values and culture.

Thus Bell & Ross, a watch brand, looks as if it always existed. Yet it was created just 25 years ago by two young men, an HEC graduate and a designer, sharing the same passion for military aviation instruments. They did not care about the presence of competition, giants such as Breitling, Breguet, Tag Heuer, who were already selling aviation watches. In luxury, passion and authenticity are intrinsic qualities and not rational responses to competition aimed at building differentiation from other brands. As one of the luxury anti-laws states, 'think identity, forget positioning'. Tod's – also a recent brand – is the modern expression of the classic eternal Italian elegance, that of Firenze, highly cultural and aloof.

Luxury does not lie in marketing but in the offering: The anti-laws of marketing

Luxury brand building is about creating and remaining the dream of the target consumer. It is also about sustaining a symbolic gap from opportunistic brands that copy the luxury brands while following another business model, a masstige one, also called fast-moving luxury goods (FMLG). Finally, it is about selecting one's clients.

Luxury is not a set of techniques, of codes; it is a complete culture; everything the brand does should aim at making it incomparable, from the products themselves, the stores, the service, to each single act of communication …

Luxury that, until recently, was limited only to the richest people, today targets the middle-class – people also known as 'excursionists' – who will buy luxury only occasionally. One should not forget though, that there are two main drivers of value for a luxury brand: the perception of luxury for oneself (self-indulgence) as well as relevant others' perception of the offering as luxury. Without this second driver of value, these products and services are merely hedonic supreme artisan work manifested through nice offerings. They will however not create the implied social stratification that their consumption indicates, nor be the marker of sophisticated tastes and cultural elitism. An analysis of many young luxury brands and start-ups indicates that many fall into the trap of being overly product-focused and losing sight of the sociological role of luxury brands in our society, which is to elevate and endow the buyers with class, elegance and refinement. To be a statement, a luxury brand must be recognized as such by others. This is why it is said that counterfeits raise the brand awareness too, thus paradoxically contributing to the brand prestige.

Luxury represents more than products – it is the taste of the elite. Nowadays there are many types of elite (old money, new money, creative elite, internet elite, sport elite, intellectual elite, etc) and hence there are many dreams. Consequently there is room for many luxury brands. Since luxury's extension from the happy few to the happy many, luxury brands moved from 'the ordinary of the extraordinary people to the extraordinary of the ordinary people'. As a consequence, the challenge for luxury brands is growth – how to grow while maintaining salience with extraordinary people? How to remain aspirational to them?

In order to do this, luxury brands must maintain a careful balance between some critical yet opposing aspects of their business:

1 Inclusion/exclusion: luxury brands must look at being accessible in order to sell their products, yet remain only for the chosen few. This explains why selling on the internet can be a problem, with anyone being able to buy the brand as opposed to traditional retail where the brand 'selects' the patrons.

2 Accessibility/inaccessibility: too many accessible products create sales but kill brand equity, dream and pricing power. On the other hand, significantly overpricing may lead to the business failing if there is insufficient demand. Also, those clients who can afford extravagant prices may lack aspirational power (the luxury brand image is made by its clients).

3 Unlocking the power of the past/preparing the future: worshipping the heritage, the DNA, yet often being *transgressive* to be relevant today.

4 Cultivating craftsmanship/developing sales (to answer the mounting demand from the world).

5 Praising objective rarity of production (as Ferrari, Aston Martin, or Kelly bags) but practising more and more virtual rarity (high priced limited editions signed by artists).

To retain their premium clientele while extending the customer base, luxury brands must use Veblen's law, ie permanently raise their average price level, especially if they have introduced a few accessible

FIGURE 5.3 Some anti-laws of marketing: How to build a luxury brand and avoid destroying its value

---

Do not start with the client; instead start from the House and pay extreme attention to the product.

Do not try to be modern; creativity and style will make you timeless and contemporary.

Don't try to be fashionable; the flipside of being fashionable is going out of fashion.

If a product or design takes off too fast, discontinue it.

Spend a lot of time adding value; spend very little time on saving costs.

Do not relocate your production to countries that pay low wages.

Do not try to build Group synergies.

For true luxury brands, it is never too late to enter a market or country.

Forget about 'positioning', luxury is not comparative, so think identity instead.

Always go back to your roots, to your cultural heritage, but do not hesitate to reinterpret it in a surprising, disruptive way.

Dominate the customer, do not pander to all his or her wishes.

Make it difficult for clients to buy by restricting supply and distribution.

Sell small volumes on the internet.

Luxury determines the price; price does not determine luxury.

Raise your prices as time goes on in order to increase demand.

Never sell luxury products with discounts, for you are selling timeless value.

Never license your brand; lending your reputation is dangerous as it is your long-term treasure.

The role of your advertising is not to sell but to fuel the dream.

Keep celebrities out of your advertising.

Cultivate closeness to avant-garde artists.

Luxury branding is about being fantastic; testing and building consensus only dilutes this process.

Beware of consultants: through benchmarking they promote one dangerous idea, 'do like other brands do'.

items for luxury 'excursionists' – those clients who only occasionally purchase luxury goods or services (like going to a Michelin three-star restaurant once a year).

The second solution lies in dual management – creating specialized labels with their own lines, own price level and own distribution (Giorgio Armani stores vs Emporio Armani stores vs Armani Jeans stores). This is why Louis Vuitton introduced high-end jewellery with special unique pieces designed by artists (a €1 million necklace) or leather bags in limited series signed by Takashi Murakami that distract the rich from the fact that the brand is selling large volumes to the middle class. Instead, the rich focus on the joy of buying art that is co-produced by Louis Vuitton.

To manage the equilibria discussed earlier, successful luxury brands have carved very specific principles which are the opposites of the classic laws of marketing. They are called the anti-laws of marketing; for luxury does not lie in 'marketing' but in the 'offering' of creative, disruptive and hyperqualitative realizations. We have identified these anti-laws. Some of these are mentioned in Figure 5.3. In the following pages we shall elaborate on some of these, along with examples.

Anti-law: When one product sells too much, discontinue it

Building a luxury brand requires that one does not look for 'best-sellers' but for 'long sellers' – products that will sell for years. Sometimes, unpredictably, one particular product becomes very popular and everyone wants it. While this is a blessing for any other category, in luxury this is a mixed blessing because this means that both the product and the brand are becoming 'fashionable'. There is a contagion of desire as René Girard demonstrated (2005). The flipside of being fashionable is that there will be a day when the brand is unfashionable. This does not matter for fashion brands that keep producing new fashions, but for luxury brands that compete on being pieces of timeless art this can undermine their image of timelessness. The fact that 75 per cent of all Rolls Royces are still running and able to be repaired by the company is because the brand is consciously keeping these timeless works of art alive. Luxury brands typically do not wish to become too fashionable. Hermès, probably the most profitable luxury company, is a great example of this anti-law. Hermès produces new designs of its famous silk scarves every year. If any one design sells too much, the brand withdraws it immediately. The brand recognizes that the game is not about volume but the feeling of privilege and this has to be protected even at the cost of sales.

Luxury brands pursue a value strategy that determines their pricing power and this explains why beyond the significant differences in quality, Hermès bags sell at four times the price of Coach's bags. Even Hermès makes an exception to this rule for products that are sold through wholesale distribution (watches and fragrances) or through multi-brand retailers where it is difficult to react immediately.

This anti-law explains why despite its explicit naming (Lexus is not far from Luxus), this premium brand of Toyota is not pursuing a luxury strategy. In the United States, Lexus often reiterates that its goal is to become the No 1 imported luxury car brand in volume. Contrast this with Rolls Royce's target of selling just one more car in 2014 than they did in 2013 and the difference is apparent. Rolls Royce follows a bespoke strategy of selling a personalized dream. The personalization of each Rolls Royce sold creates much more value to the client and to the company too than selling more cars.

Anti-law: Price alone does not define luxury, it is luxury that defines price

A classic mistake is to equate luxury with being overly expensive. One can adopt a strict luxury strategy at quite accessible prices too. Take champagne for instance: it is one of the strongest luxury brands in the world. One can find champagnes at €12 in France, coming from very small producers, who do not have the means to build their own brand. However, they operate under the magic of the umbrella brand Champagne, which unlike any other sparkling wine in the world represents luxury and celebration.

Statistical studies show that champagne consumption is correlated with GDP growth. This is typical of a luxury product. Economic growth creates more occasions to celebrate. Champagne is a collective brand that can be used by any company if their wine comes from the very strictly defined geographical area of Champagne. Some hundred kilometres east of the Champagne region, one finds famous German sparkling wines called Sekt (they cannot use the word champagne). So would a German Sekt brand that tasted exactly like champagne and sold at €120 be luxury? The same question applies to an Italian Lambrusco or Jacob's Creek sparkling Australian wine sold in the United Kingdom at say £100.

As stated by the anti-law, price is not enough to determine whether a brand is a luxury brand or not. Price can help qualify a product as premium or even a strategy as a super-premium strategy. Producers can argue on the grounds of length of maturation (how many years in the cask), the quality of grapes used, the soil, the special techniques applied, the grade obtained from judge and critic Robert Parker, all the other efforts leading to the creation of this rare wine. All this is typical of a premium strategy but it's not enough to be considered luxury.

The question then is why does the word champagne alone mean luxury? And the answer is simply that only champagne *evokes a dream*. Customers can buy part of this dream for as little as €12. In contrast, at €120, a Sekt is a very superior product but conveys no dream. The same is true of all sparkling wines of the new wine countries. They promise a tasteful experience, but no dream.

This prompts the question, what is the dream that champagne is made of?

Champagne evokes associations of royal courts, of Louis XIV, also known as the Sun King, queens of the UK, the tsars of Russia. It calls to mind a region of the world that is known for history, art, savoir-faire, culture. Champagne is known for its connotations of exclusivity. Its consumption is like a staging, a ritual, and is conducted with almost sacred fervour. The thought of champagne always conjures thoughts of celebration, success, exceptional people and defining moments. Champagne evokes magic and how it is made seems miraculous and not just superior technique. It has a magical touch in its effect, changing bad moods to good. In the liquid, one finds euphoria, seduction, freshness, vigour, effervescence, a subtle mix of tangible and intangible added values.

Interestingly when one talks about Champagne, taste comes last. People hardly speak of the taste. The imagery comes first and this is normal as all dreams primarily have a visual effect. These visuals stage a privileged experience, sharing a legend, absorbing this legend and its magic effect. A dream of exception, exclusivity.

Anti-law: Anchor the brand in its roots yet surprise by transgressing the normal

While champagne as a category has a collective dream, each champagne brand however has to build its own dream. The Dom Perignon brand is quite recent. Certainly the name itself (that of a monk born in 1638) is part of the legend of champagne. It was owned by the Maison Mercier who had not used it so far and sold it to Moët & Chandon who launched it in the late 1950s at the occasion of the coronation of Queen Elizabeth II. But their main target was elsewhere, the US market. The brand used a special glass for the bottle to make it look visibly different and very old, and its label looked like an ancient *blason*. It also spoke of the legendary recipe of champagne and length of maturation. Dom Perignon sells only vintage wines and its quantities, while important, are limited.

As a rule, new brands must capitalize on sociological or technological disruptions and this holds good for luxury brands too. To penetrate the US market, Dom Perignon aimed at the emerging ruling class in the United States, the nouveau riche of the booming post-Second World War economy. It was the champagne of meritocracy, sold at twice the price of Krug, which was the reference of high-end champagnes at that time. Its arrogant pricing matched the psychology of the new class of rich people, the capitalists. Interestingly, despite its mythical anchoring in a legend, Dom Perignon did not hesitate to break the rules, just as the nouveau riche themselves do. Instead of following the personalized communication approach of all champagnes of that time, Dom Perignon chose to be very visible – far beyond its real target – by sponsoring the very first James Bond movie in 1961 and some others since then. Dom Perignon focused on showbiz and the jetsetting corporate executive. As a result, it became a legend, known and recognized by many, drunk by a few. Ironically James Bond gave a sexual connotation to this monk brand.

Then came Cristal Roederer, a different brand with a dream resulting from a different disruption. It used a crystal bottle associated with a legend. Roederer was a respected maison de champagne and supplied champagne to the court of the tsars. According to the legend, Tsar Nicholas II was displeased at the thought of drinking the same champagne as the members of his court. In order to please him, Roederer created a very unique and rare blend that would be served in a crystal bottle. The end of the reign of the tsars meant the decline of the maison. As did all other champagne houses, Roederer tried to emulate Dom Perignon by launching what is called a Special Cuvée and for that they used their forgotten Cristal bottle but that didn't work. A 'me too' strategy is never sustainable in the long run. Why would anyone drink a copy that lacks the prestige and magic of the original brand?

Tired of their poor results, the local US importer took the bold decision to overprice the laggard, Cristal, pricing it at $160. This was close to 50 per cent more than 'the king' Dom Perignon, that sold for $120. This worked brilliantly as suddenly Cristal was on fire in the United States! The brand had just tapped another sociological disruption, the emergence of a new flashy hedonistic rich class. Cristal was a success in Miami as well as among the rappers of Los Angeles because of its provocative yet legendary identity. Cristal's success repositioned Dom Perignon as a 'classic' champagne.

The former 'choice of the tsars' is now the icon of Russian oligarchs who consume it by the hundreds of bottle at conspicuous celebrations across the world. Cristal has seduced people with the bling bling luxury mindset.

Anti-law: Beware of celebrities

Browsing through glossy magazines, one is struck by the presence of celebrities in the ads of all so-called luxury brands. Yet the luxury strategy demands that one be very careful about the use of celebrities. In such a strategy it is the brand/the House that is the hero and not the celebrity.

You may therefore ask why Hollywood stars Nicole Kidman and Brad Pitt were hired to endorse the mythical perfume Chanel No 5, which is soon to be a century old.

Firstly, the fragrance market is no longer a luxury business, with most brands adopting an FMCG approach to marketing. All the leaders in this market apply mass-marketing principles. Marketers in the United States (where Chanel is now headquartered) have traditionally believed strongly in using celebrities for marketing, whether to sell soap (Lux) or a perfume like Chanel. They apply mass marketing to all categories, which explains why Coach and Ralph Lauren too are run somehow like FMCG companies.

One will never see a Hermès ad in a magazine with a celebrity promoting a Hermès leather bag. As mentioned earlier in the luxury strategy, the brand is the hero and not the celebrity.

Hermès iconic bags are called Kelly (named after Princess Grace Kelly) and Birkin (named after actress Jane Birkin). Interestingly, both stars already owned Hermès bags, demonstrating how celebrities themselves dreamt about Hermès quality, beauty and distinction. This is very different from hiring a celebrity in a commercial to push the sales of a product: that is a sign of weakness. Finally, this does not mean that brands cannot hire ambassadors to represent the brand on official occasions.

In the famous 'core values' advertising campaign of Louis Vuitton, one sees a Keepall beside Mikhail Gorbachov, former President of the Soviet Union, as he is travelling to negotiate on the fall of the Berlin Wall. In another ad, one sees an LV bag in U2 leader Bono's aeroplane as he flies to Africa to promote his fairtrade brand EDUN. These are the heroes of our modern times and are examples of 'the ordinary of extraordinary people' who are changing the world. These brands have used them as symbols and not as salesmen.

When Porsche hired Maria Sharapova as their brand ambassador in 2013, they did not use her to sell the brand, but used her charm, prestige of being the ATP world no 1 woman tennis player, to represent the brand values at major events, around the world.

Returning to the champagne example, since the new millennium, two champagne brands have been launched in the United States, with celebrities owning a stake in these companies.

Jay Z, the famous US rapper, has committed to the new brand Armand de Brignac, and Mariah Carey to the brand Angel Champagne. Both are aimed at a new class of rich people in the United States, hailing from the African American community. Angel focuses more on women, and is a potential competitor to Veuve Clicquot.

Armand de Brignac was an old brand from the 1950s that was recently revitalized to tap into the new class of wealthy African Americans. The $300 bottle of champagne with a gold plate designed by Courrèges uses the famous designer's name as a way of positioning the brand as art. Jay Z's personal symbol, the ace of spades, is used for the brand too. The beverage is made from Pinot Meunier, a most expensive ingredient, but also one that does not age well.

Mariah Carey's brand starts at €960 a bottle, but there are masterpieces, of 12 year vintage (Krug is only six years old), and some 24 magnums (with limited stocks) that have sold at €286,000 each. Each new year brings with it a new product.

The media exposure of these celebrities has given these two brands immediate visibility and brand awareness. This is an extremely powerful strategy in a country like the United States where the masses look to celebrities for inspiration and the world in turn copies what Americans do. In Google, click on 'preferred champagne of celebrities' and you will find that the results position these two brands at the top of the list.

This extremely active PR strategy, leveraging the cult of celebrity among those with little knowledge about champagne explains the success, so far. These two interesting brands have approached their business in a manner similar to a fashion brand that looks at capitalizing on the present fame of these two stars and leveraging their extensive media exposure. These brands are not focusing on creating an enduring brand and therefore despite the many classic signs of luxury (gold, diamonds, limited quantities, high price, restricted distribution), this is not a luxury strategy.

Enduring appeal over a period of time is the essence of luxury, and celebrities and their fame are ephemeral. However, although this is not a luxury strategy, it is a very profitable business model when one compares the gap between the cost of goods and the very high retail selling price.

Anti-law: Advertising is not here to sell

For any young MBA or hard-nosed marketer, this anti-law defies logic, but then it applies only to luxury brands.

As mentioned earlier in the chapter, luxury is about selling a dream. Recently, extensive statistical work (Kapferer and Valette-Florence, 2014) on 60 luxury brands has confirmed findings from earlier research studies that brand awareness boosts the brand dream, thereby driving sales. However, sales (measured by brand penetration) diminish the dream. Heritage too boosts the dream.

The dream equation

DREAM VALUE = .3 BRAND AWARENESS −
.4 BRAND PENETRATION +
.5 BRAND HERITAGE

SOURCE: JN Kapferer and P Valette-Florence, 2014

In other words, the more a brand is diffused, the more it dilutes the dream. This is why the dream must be permanently refreshed and this is why luxury ads have such a fantastic look to them. These ads are not to be tested as they are artistic statements, just as every piece of communication from a luxury brand is supposed to be. Luxury advertising is characterized by excess as this is the DNA of luxury. This does not mean bigger media budgets; however luxury advertising must itself reinforce the gap between normal brands and luxury ones: hence luxury TV commercials run for two minutes or more instead of the standard 30 seconds. There is no limit of time and creativity on the internet. Even in print advertising, luxury brands will do better by buying 10 successive pages in the same issue of *Vogue* than one page in 10 successive issues. When Chanel spends $30 million for Chanel No 5's latest spot, it is done to create a buzz and reinforce the symbolic authority of Chanel in the whole fragrance world.

Conclusion: To endure, luxury must learn from religion and art

In these modern times there is a saturation of ordinary, standardized objects. Luxury, however, stands out as a way of escaping the ordinary and becoming extraordinary. This can be achieved by possessing objects or accessing exceptional experiences in places. The price paid for these is not a burden or deterrent, but the access fee to a better world that is enduring and built around pleasure, craftsmanship, artistry, beauty and culture. The virtues of this world have somehow made what could be considered superfluous, to be something that is necessary.

Luxury shares a lot with two other major elevating forces – religion and art – and luxury management is close to them. Like any religion, to make their customers reach a higher plane in life than simple materialism, luxury brands need to develop:

- myths and legends;
- heroes or prophets (often the founder, or the creative designer);
- mystery, magic, avoiding rational explanations;
- icons, symbols (each brand should develop a chest of symbols);
- celebrations (occasion of setting up major events);
- temples, churches (called flagship stores); and
- community management to nurture the faith, hence the importance of social networks.

Similarly, to elevate consumers to a higher plane and justify their prices, luxury brands should learn from art, the prices of which also go up with time. This is why luxury brands are always searching for more creativity, beauty in all that they do, uniqueness, exclusivity, singularity.

Talented people form the key assets of these companies. Luxury designers are as important as CEOs in building long-term brand equity and hence they must be celebrated as pure artists whose signatures convert anything they write into gold.

By approaching luxury in these ways, luxury brands gain legitimacy and put at a distance the classic criticisms about discrimination on the basis of wealth. By being positioned as art, luxury brands elevate their clients and segment the market not on the basis of money but on their clients' capacity to value art and thus understand the price of beauty.

Biography

Jean-Noël Kapferer is an internationally renowned expert on branding. With a PhD from Northwestern University, and MSc from HEC Paris where he has taught for many years, Jean-Noël Kapferer has brought to the field many innovations, such as the concept of brand identity, the brand identity prism, the importance of brand architecture and the concept of managing by the brand.

Author of *The New Strategic Brand Management*, *Reinventing the Brand* and *Rumors*, and co-author of *The Luxury Strategy*, he consults extensively around the world. He is now strategy adviser to the President of INSEEC.

References

Girard, R (2005) *Violence and the Sacred*, Bloomsbury Academic

Kapferer, J-N and Bastien, V (2012) *The Luxury Strategy*, Kogan Page

Kapferer, J-N and Valette-Florence, P (2014) The paths of the luxury dream, Research paper presented at the INSEEC/IUM Luxury Symposium, April 10th, Monte-Carlo

Taylor Clark (2008) *Starbucked: A double tale of caffeine, commerce and culture*, Back Bay Books

Retail brand management
Perception, performance and improvement

06

JESKO PERREY AND THOMAS MEYER

In one form or another, all consumer organizations must address their brands. And, to at least some degree, there are brand considerations that apply to all consumer industries. When it comes to retail, however, marketers and brand strategists must contend with a set of organizational, consumer and competitive realities that make building a brand in this industry a uniquely challenging proposition:

- *Branding without borders.* There is really no 'behind the scenes' part of retail. So many of its elements are customer facing. While branding may begin with the customer and market insights that formulate brand strategy, it extends into product assortment and sourcing, format strategy, store design, consumer engagement, and (in many cases) the creation and supply of private label products. H&M and Zara in fashion, as well as the growing market share of private-label brands in food and other retail, are examples of how product and store can be increasingly linked in the consumer's mind.

- *Loyalty is the goal.* Some industries may be able to get away with convincing shoppers to make a single purchase of their goods or services. Given the structure of an industry like durable goods, repeat business may be ideal, but there is still success in the 'one-off' purchase. This is not the case in retail, where customer loyalty is the real bread and butter. Strong retail brands are created with a recurring shopper journey in mind and with the objective of achieving long-term customer loyalty.

- *Little room to manoeuvre.* Retailers' margins are typically managed very tightly. This means that their marketing budgets typically represent a much lower share of net sales than in other consumer categories. Many automotive, telecommunications and electronics brands allocate 5 per cent of their net sales to marketing, and some FMCG brands invest close to 20 per cent. This stands in stark contrast to the less than 1 per cent that is typical of many retail brands. Simply put, retailers have to build their brands with less, and this means making use of customer touch points outside of advertising to build and convey a powerful brand message.

- *Competition for attention.* Retail brands often have to compete for attention with supplier brands. Electronics retailers, for example, constantly face the question of whether they should promote the newest iPhone or iPad – thereby leveraging a strong brand of one of their suppliers – or invest in and promote their own brands.

- *Large number of employees as brand ambassadors.* Often, employees are a retail brand's most important touch point. Automotive OEMs (original equipment manufacturers) and consumer electronics companies, for example, certainly value the strength of their employees, but they do not rely on these employees to positively reinforce their brands to their customers. In retail, employees must represent the brand promise on a day-to-day basis. Retailers also tend to be large employers, with Wal-Mart and McDonald's regularly topping the list of the largest employers in the world with more than 1 million employees respectively – a scale that significantly multiplies the importance and the challenge of employees as brand ambassadors.

- *An operations-focused culture.* On the face of it, retail is about buying goods from a supplier and then selling them to a customer. Patents are much less common in this industry, and, without their protection, a strong focus on operational details is even more important. This creates a tough environment for brand thinking and management to thrive in. A shift in mindset and behaviour is often the first step in retailers moving from a goal of just 'best-in-class' merchandising to building a 'brand experience' for the customer.

- *Omnichannel and the internet disruption.* No consumer industry has been more transformed by the internet than retail. The earliest e-commerce successes were retailers – Amazon and eBay – and today, almost no retail brand can truly be competitive without embracing the online and/or mobile channel. This shift in paradigm has changed the role of brick-and-mortar stores from the focal point of all brand building activities to just one of several touch points in the customer's journey, and it forces brand managers to take a multichannel approach to their work.

As the line between retailer and product blurs, consumers are becoming increasingly mindful of not just what they are buying but also from whom. Price remains important – shoppers are still price-conscious in times of austerity and are searching for deals and value for money – but what really makes shoppers spend more is something that captures their imagination or attention. Whether it is the 'Foodie Heaven' aisle display at Whole Foods, Apple's unique experience-based store layout, a friendly John Lewis assistant, or a Hollister nightclub-style store experience, differentiation is key. Today's retailers – despite (and even because of) the industry's unique brand channels – need to stand for something appealing and distinctive beyond just the products they sell.

Retail's new branding priority

The degree of emphasis that organizations place on branding varies from industry to industry. This is often a function of the perceived value that 'branding' will contribute to the organization. It appears that traditionally many CEOs in retail attached little importance to branding, and few made it their top priority.

Retail companies from supermarkets to electronics stores were known for the price wars they carried out on the battlefield of leaflets and print ads, which featured heavy discounting and emphasized 'best-deal' messaging. Conscious and systematic investments of time and effort in the organizational brand, however, tended to be few and far between, as most of the focus was on the products a retailer sold and not the store itself. Trends in the recent past, however, are compelling retail CEOs to think about their brands in new ways.

Among these trends is verticalization, that is, having more control over the entire value chain, and the brand-owned retail network is a critical part of this theme in most of the cases. This not only allows brands to have more control over retailing, but it also prevents potential contradictory objectives of brands and traditional multi-brand retailers. This larger 'brand playground' has opened the door for retailers to create a more cohesive brand image. Product commoditization has also led to the growing importance of retailer differentiation along customer satisfaction lines. Starbucks, Abercrombie & Fitch, and Amazon have become associated with a superior customer shopping experience and strong, globally celebrated retail brands.

Building and sustaining a strong brand in retail

Just like in other categories, building a successful retail brand – one that is powerful and enduring – must be approached from three ways at once: as an art, as a science and as a craft.

The art is about endowing the brand with a relevant, credible and unique value proposition that is up-to-date, consistent and creatively executed. Retail brands must strike the right chord to make them appeal to consumers and generate demand. They need to engage consumers emotionally – often a challenge for operations-focused retailers – yet their claims have to be credible and trustworthy. Strong brands always do both, although the balance between the two varies. There are hardly any strong products or services that are not at least as good as the competition regarding the perception of their practical benefits, and they usually fare better when it comes to the attributes or characteristics consumers assign to them. At the same time, real brand champions, like IKEA, H&M, Nespresso or Apple, stand out because of their emotional appeal. Although the products they offer may not in all cases be superior to competitors' alternatives, it is the *way* they make consumers feel about themselves and their purchases that differentiates these brands from others.

But the importance of the art element should not be misread as a licence to go crazy. Constant changes to a brand's positioning, target group or communication style will eventually destroy its value. In fact, consistency is an important element of artful brand propositions – particularly in retail, given its increasingly multichannel nature. Consistency is about balancing relevant innovation and originality with a brand's heritage. A now legendary example is how Burberry rejuvenated its brand over a 10-year period. In 1998, Burberry famously laid bare the traditional fabric it used as a lining and started using it as a prominent pattern for apparel and accessories. The Burberry pattern – once a solely functional element – is now the brand's most recognizable characteristic. By turning a hidden asset into a tangible brand differentiator, the company's approach was original and creative, yet fully in line with the brand's heritage. There were two main drivers of Burberry's success. On the one hand, the company managed to give a more hip and young edge to its product portfolio while sticking to the roots of the brand by keeping its signature tartan lining at the centre of the design. On the other hand, the company delivered this message through innovative channels with now standard, but then best-in-class, usage of digital platforms like Facebook. Specifically, its 'Art of Trench' campaign, where curated photos showing Burberry trench coats worn by the young and urban cool, drove massive appeal for the brand.

The science involves understanding and measuring relevant consumer needs, as well as the performance of the brand in the targeted customer segments. Many retail marketing managers and agencies still use brand awareness and advertising recall as the primary or even exclusive indicators of brand performance. While there is nothing wrong with these metrics in and of themselves, they are insufficient for capturing the specific strengths and weaknesses of a brand, let alone the drivers of its performance. In some cases, the focus on awareness and recall may even create the illusion of a healthy brand, when, in fact, the brand is in trouble, as was the case of C&A during the late 1980s and the beginning of the 1990s. C&A had high brand awareness but did not manage to catch up with consumers' evolving clothing expectations; while other competitors were designing products standing for various lifestyles in accordance with consumers' expectations and accompanying them with relevant communication, C&A's indifferent standing in the market amplified with high awareness and alienated customers from the brand. Hence, retailers need to go beyond the traditional brand awareness and advertising recall metrics. They would benefit from expanding their brand management toolbox and then using it comprehensively in their brand management decisions.

Differentiating a well-known brand from a really strong brand requires a sense of if consumers know what the brand stands for in terms of products or services and if they favour the brand over its competitors in their purchase considerations. In other words, strong brands perform well along the entire purchase funnel, from awareness and consideration to purchase, repurchase and loyalty. This is not to say that all strong brands perform equally well at each and every stage of the purchase funnel; most brands reveal slight weaknesses at one stage or another. Whatever the case, the accurate measurement of a brand's relative strengths and weaknesses in the target group's purchase funnel is the starting point for fact-based brand management.

The craft is about managing the brand rigorously in all of its individual aspects throughout the organization and across all customer touch points. It is one thing to put the brand positioning on paper, but it is quite another to make it a real presence in consumers' lives: not just in TV commercials, print ads and leaflets, but also across newsletters, store displays, loyalty programmes and personal interactions. Retailers with strong brands go to great pains to ensure a superior and consistent consumer experience of the brand's proposition at all touch points.

In terms of holistic activation of the brand positioning at all touch points, many would agree that Apple sets the standard. The company does a fantastic job when it comes to translating their brand values of stylish design, creativity and uniqueness into products like the iPod, the iPhone or the iPad, as well as into a unique experience at its more than 300 Apple Stores worldwide, many of which have won architectural awards.

Excellent execution is not necessarily limited to tangible touch points like store design. For Aldi, the discount retailer, price is key. Consumer perception of the company as a provider of good value for money has made the Aldi brand strong, and low prices are the source of its competitive advantage (its private label products nevertheless provide A-brand quality). Right from the start, Aldi stressed that every article it sold was cheaper than the equivalent found elsewhere. Based on this premise, it has turned simplicity of execution into a guiding principle, from its no-frills stores and narrow assortment of around 750 products in the spotlight, to its tight rein on logistics and labour costs behind the scenes.

As illustrated by such examples, many retailers excel at one of the elements of superior brand management: the art, science or craft. But only a chosen few master all three elements in equal measure. Inevitably, companies have different approaches to brand management, and their organizations have different strengths and weaknesses. However well a retailer might master an individual element, this will be of little use to it if the company does not achieve a minimum standard in the other two elements as well.

The elements of retail brand perception

To reap the full benefits of a thoughtfully conceived and well-executed brand, retailers – like any other marketers – will need to first understand exactly how consumers see their brands, how this perception impacts their businesses, and the steps necessary to identify and improve the elements of their brands that are not serving them optimally. The following is an overview of how this understanding can be achieved.

In the consumer's mind, a retailer's brand is the focal point of a wide range of perceptions about the retailer. The relationship between retail brand perception and consumer behaviour has been thoroughly

FIGURE 6.1 Elements of brand equity

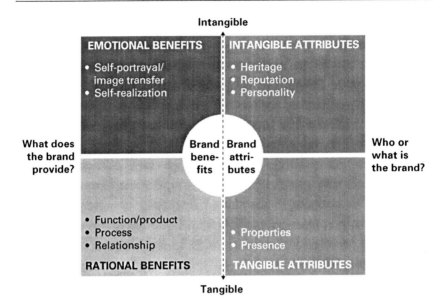

SOURCE McKinsey & Company

researched by practitioners as well as academics. To get to the bottom of how and why the brand influences its customers, retailers need to first develop a robust understanding of their current brand image. This image can be quite complex and is built upon consumer perceptions of the abstract as well as the concrete and on attributes as well as benefits (These four dimensions are summarized in Figure 6.1 and discussed further below.)

As outlined in Mazzu, Meyer and Weissgerber (2012), brand characteristics that can be perceived by consumers through their various senses are the *tangible attributes*. Within the retail arena, these attributes are usually subdivided into four categories. The store as well as its location is one category, comprised of (among other things) how many outlets there are, the in-store merchandising, the store layout, and how much parking is available. Another category is price and promotions, which describes the general pricing level or the kinds of promotions and discounts there are, and how many. The category assortment refers to the range of options available in a category, consumers making judgements about the overall amount of SKUs (stock-keeping units) in a given store, and the relative share of branded as well as private-label products. Service is the final category, including opening hours, staff size, customer reward programmes, or return policies, for instance.

The *intangible attributes* are those characteristics that together represent the retail brand identity; these could range from heritage or rituals to a distinct tone of voice. The iconic retail chain Macy's has a great heritage as one of the oldest retail chains in the world. Abercrombie & Fitch's bare-chested male greeters have become a strong part of the company's identity.

The tangible attributes of the brand form the backbone for the *rational benefits* that provide consumers with reasons to buy. Does buying from a particular retailer help the consumer save money (Aldi), stay healthy (Whole Foods), or look trendy (Abercrombie & Fitch)? Is the shopping experience itself uniquely enjoyable (Harrods and the Apple Store), or does it offer unparalleled one-stop shopping convenience (Tesco Express)? Is the level of service exceptional, like Nespresso's practice of picking up a defective coffee machine from a consumer's home and providing him or her with a substitute machine for the time it is being repaired?

While the rational aspect of consumer brand choice is significant, the *emotional benefits* should not be underestimated. Not everyone is rational all the time, and consumers are always making emotional decisions pertaining to things that affect them personally. Retailers often overlook consumers' multiple motivations – the need to feel accepted, the need to make a statement about themselves, and many more. By focusing on the rational aspects, which are more in their control, retailers miss out on an important aspect of what their brand can offer and what determines brand success.

Many customers of luxury brands, like Louis Vuitton, are buying these brands not just for their fine design, but often enough for what kind of a statement owning these brands makes for them. Pre-teen girls shopping at American Girl Place are largely doing this out of a quest for self-realization as much as pure and simple 'shopping'!

Developing a clear and comprehensive image of the brand requires identifying all the brand elements. Meticulously identifying all the brand attributes is a key part of the exercise. It is important not to take the brand's strengths for granted or to shy away from understanding the weaknesses, but to probe these too. Any additional aspects pertaining to the brand, such as consumer motivations or perceptions, need to be studied even if they are not a part of the retailer brand identity. With so many variables to be studied, market research can get very complex. The most important function of mapping brand perception along the four dimensions previously mentioned provides a great structure for developing and designing market research.

Usually, conducting a brand workshop or focus group that precedes any in-depth quantitative market research will generate a long list of statements, which then has to be narrowed down to 30 to 50 statements.

The trick in selecting these statements is to ensure that all four brand dimensions are being covered and that there are enough statements to provide depth of insight without the complexity and cost of the quantitative market research getting out of hand.

The resulting short list of attributes and benefits will provide the basis for conducting quantitative consumer research, which includes a store's own as well its key competitors' customers.

It is important to not just study the brand's customers but also its key competitors' customers, as this will help gain a true market perspective and assess the strengths and weaknesses of all the key brands in the market.

Finally, while designing the research, it is also important to cover multiple locations to identify differences in perceptions across regions. These differences are likely to occur, especially in retail, because it is a highly service-dependent and location-dependent category.

Benchmarking brand performance

While having a full understanding of how a brand is perceived on its own terms can provide the basis for a brand positioning effort, even more information can be obtained from the research. The brand's performance across the steps of the customer-decision process can provide invaluable cues for identifying opportunities for refining the brand's image.

A useful tool for retailers is, therefore, the brand purchase funnel (or the brand funnel). This tool can give retailers insights in terms of how it is performing vis-à-vis its main competitors. Like some other tools, the brand funnel is based on the AIDA (attention, interest, desire, action) model but extends beyond this significantly.

Considering that location is an extremely important aspect of retail success, it is essential to compare retailers who have stores in the same or nearby locations so that the comparison is like for like. Only including participants that have access to all the competitors' stores or inserting additional filters such as 'lives near a store' will keep the research sample unbiased. In the absence of such care in designing the research, one will find that the research will be skewed in favour of those stores that do not have competition in the vicinity.

Mazzu, Meyer and Weissgerber (2012) explain that most funnel stages can be further broken down to allow for increasing insight granularity, as shown in the example brand funnel completed for a retailer in Figure 6.2. Retailers offering products with high price tags and low purchasing frequency, for example, automobiles or real estate, will look for additional detail in the pre-purchase phases, such

FIGURE 6.2   The brand funnel in retail

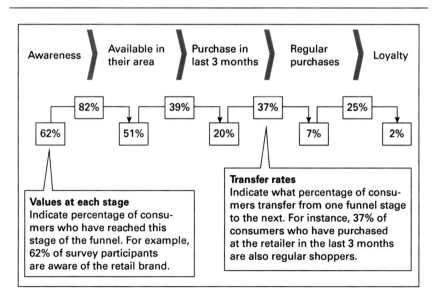

SOURCE McKinsey

as how consumers consider specific brands. It is very common that retailers will want to enhance the resolution of the subsequent funnel stages to address the fact that 'repurchase', 'favourite retail brand', or 'long-term loyalty' are often critical factors in a make-or-break situation.

At each funnel stage, values emerge that relay the percentage of consumers in the sample who have made it to this stage. So, in Figure 6.2, for instance, 62 per cent of the survey participants are aware of the brand. Then, there are transfer rates, which show the percentage of customers who transferred from one funnel step to the next. In the example, 37 per cent of consumers who have purchased at the retailer in the last three months are also regular shoppers.

Figure 6.3 provides a real-life example from 2012 of brand funnel research comparing two brands; in this case, in the German drugstore market. As the figure shows, dm and Rossmann achieve roughly the same brand strength throughout the early stages of the funnel, from awareness all the way to occasional purchase. Further

FIGURE 6.3   The brand funnel – example from the German drugstore market

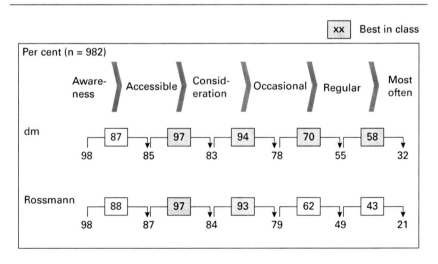

SOURCE McKinsey

down the line, however, dm pulls away from its rival, Rossmann. For a third of all consumers in the sample, dm is the drugstore at which they shop 'most often', compared to about a fifth for whom Rossmann is the default drugstore. This gap is all the more remarkable in light of Rossmann's slightly larger store network at the time, comprising some 1,600 outlets, compared to only about 1,250 for dm. In order to close this performance gap, Rossmann would need to focus on marketing activities to build loyalty rather than awareness.

An interesting analysis that can be done using the funnel data is an estimation of the incremental revenue arising from an increase in the transfer rate from one stage of the funnel to the next. This can be calculated by multiplying the customers' average transaction size with the buying frequency ('customer conversion value'). This analysis is exciting because it helps estimate possible revenue uplifts from an improvement in brand perception and subsequent brand funnel performance. However, this should not distract from the greater utility of understanding how to close these gaps. In the German drugstore example from 2012, for instance, Rossmann would want to know what it could do to improve its transfer rates from 'occasional purchase' to 'regular purchase' and 'purchase most often' in order to close the gap to its rival, dm.

Building brands; boosting business

After the brand funnel has been used to identify the brand's relative strengths and weaknesses at various stages along the consumer decision journey, the retailer can begin to manage the brand in ways that lead to performance improvement. The ideal approach to this is to leverage the diagnostic insights provided by the brand perception and influence research done earlier and to identify the specific attributes a retailer needs to address in its marketing mix in order to improve the performance in the purchase funnel.

Conducting a brand driver analysis can assist in identifying the most relevant elements in the consumer decision process and, therefore, in determining the root causes of consumer behaviour at each step of the purchase funnel. Returning to the hypothetical Rossmann question: What would be required to improve the brand's performance in the later stages of the funnel in order to close the gap to the company's main rival dm? In concept, brand drivers are those elements (attributes or benefits) that most greatly influence consumer purchasing behaviour. So, in order to answer the question, leaders at Rossmann would first need to understand what turns its occasional customers into regular ones, defined as the group that shops at a specific retailer more often than anywhere else.

There are many ways of identifying the behavioural relevance of brand elements. One straightforward way is putting the question to consumers as to what they rate as important in retail brands or the criteria involved in making a purchase. While this approach is simple and commonsensical, the quality of the answers obtained varies and can be misleading, as participants will often be unable to prioritize the elements they actually value and will state they want it all, thus, failing to pinpoint the exact elements that have an impact on consumer behaviour. Furthermore, there is often a discrepancy between what consumers say they want and what they actually want. Consider that when consumers are asked what they want in cars, their response is often safety and fuel economy. However, in-depth market research indicates that it is brand image and exterior design that consumers actually seek when choosing a car.

To overcome this lack of accuracy in what consumers actually want, it is best that brand drivers are identified not from what consumers say they are but by what statistical analysis, derived from brand perception as well as actual customer behaviour, suggests they are.

Doing this requires that the perceived strengths of a brand are looked at in the context of brand funnel performance and whether a given consumer has really made a purchase from this brand.

Figure 6.4 shows the results of the driver analysis in the drugstore example described earlier and ranks the key purchase drivers according to their behavioural relevance. 'Trust' emerged as the most important driver, but accessibility aspects, such as 'can be reached easily' and price-related attributes, such as 'store is good value for money', turned out to be similarly important in driving customer conversion.

FIGURE 6.4 Brand drivers in the German drugstore market –
trust and accessibility drive conversion

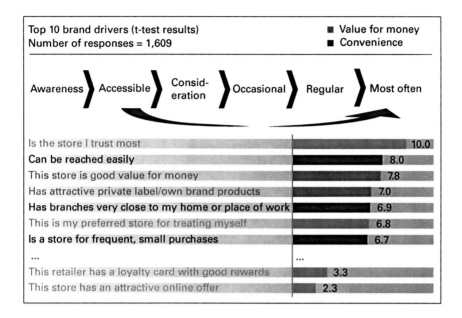

| Top 10 brand drivers (t-test results) | ■ Value for money |
| Number of responses = 1,609 | ■ Convenience |

Awareness ⟩ Accessible ⟩ Consideration ⟩ Occasional ⟩ Regular ⟩ Most often

Is the store I trust most	10.0
Can be reached easily	8.0
This store is good value for money	7.8
Has attractive private label/own brand products	7.0
Has branches very close to my home or place of work	6.9
This is my preferred store for treating myself	6.8
Is a store for frequent, small purchases	6.7
...	...
This retailer has a loyalty card with good rewards	3.3
This store has an attractive online offer	2.3

SOURCE McKinsey

Undertaking a strengths and weaknesses appraisal of the brand drivers is the next step in the process, and aims to allow the retailer to evaluate its brand performance in the key brand drivers alongside that of the market average and key competitors.

Finally, retailers can use the brand driver relevance analysis as well as the strengths and weaknesses analysis to derive a two-dimensional options matrix for identifying clear actions to enhance a brand's performance in the purchase funnel:

- *Close the gaps in critical areas of high relevance and weak perception.* Highly relevant market drivers where a brand demonstrates weaknesses often provide a natural starting point for improving the brand's performance and image. Retailers need to close these critical gaps and work on improving their scores on these in order to make the brand deliver better.

- *Extend competitive differentiation within high-relevance and strong-perceptual drivers.* Differentiation is one of the

FIGURE 6.5 Matrix of options in the German drugstore market – brand performance relative to key competitor

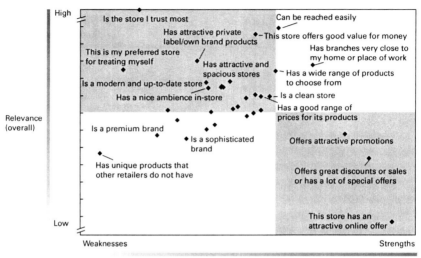

SOURCE McKinsey

cornerstones of a brand. Building on strengths in areas with high behavioural relevance can help the brand enhance its differentiation.

- *Exercise the right to not focus on elements with low relevance.* There is often no need to take action in the areas that have lower behavioural relevance if they already demonstrate satisfactory performance levels. For example, though consumers might describe sufficient parking space as a 'must-have', it is unlikely to be a decisive factor in differentiating one brand from another.

Though there will be a full matrix of options appearing at each purchasing funnel step, strategically focusing on the elements with the most potential for improvement in brand performance is recommended. In those cases where more than one stage is prominent, prioritizing actions can be supported by running a matrix of options across the entire brand funnel. The drugstore example in Figure 6.5 demonstrates such a matrix. The vertical axis shows how the brand drivers are relevant to consumer behaviour, and the horizontal axis shows where the Rossman brand features perceptually in comparison to dm, a key competitor. The matrix shows that Rossmann is perceived as a brand whose stores can be reached easily and that provides attractive promotions and has an attractive online offer. The top left-hand corner, however, reveals the brand's numerous perceived weaknesses in highly important areas, plotted relative to Rossmann's key rival, dm. For example, Rossmann's image is lagging in areas such as trustworthiness, private label offering and store design.

Brand promise and retail's organizational orientation

Much of what is described here has been diagnostic in nature. But building a brand is not just about targeting single brand elements for improvement – it also requires strategic direction setting. This is ideally done in the form of synthesizing the brand's characteristics in plain and simple terms that are realistic and easy to understand.

The essence of any brand (retail or otherwise) and its differentiation from other brands are what forms the brand promise. While the current brand performance and perception constitute key ingredients while developing a brand promise, however, there are other strategic aspects that need to be considered as well. A brand promise should not be long and meandering, but rather crisp and comprehensive. Summarizing all the brand offers into a succinct promise is easier said than done. One often sees retailers with brand promises that are equally applicable to many of their competitors. This removes the differentiating aspect from the brand. Retailers also need to be careful not to include too many aspects to the brand promise; a sharply focused promise makes the brand difficult to copy.

A brand promise that lives up to its responsibility of synthesizing and differentiating the brand will clearly meet five criteria:

- *Distinctive.* The aspects that differentiate the brand are vitally important because they make the brand stand out. Brands compete on difference, not sameness; hence it is important for the brand promise to focus on the elements that differentiate the brand from others.

- *Relevant.* Brands require single-minded, ruthless focus on what matters. By using the brand driver analysis, a company can uncover the key causes of consumer behaviour. All drivers not eliciting consumer interest should be dropped and excluded from the brand promise.

- *Credible.* A promise should be believable, otherwise it lacks credibility. The brand promise has to be plausible and somewhat in line with the current customer experience and perception. Using the brand's perceived strengths as the backbone of its promise is wise because this makes the promise credible.

- *Consistent.* Brands offer reassurance partly because of their consistency. Ensuring that the brand stays rooted in its heritage helps preserve a consistent brand identity.

- *Feasible.* Feasibility goes hand in hand with credibility. Does the promise offer something that is feasible for the brand to deliver consistently over time? Only aspects that are feasible and can be sustained should be used, as brands have a long life span, and the promise should not change easily.

A retailer brand promise can be built around the brand's rational benefits in the areas of price, assortment, service, location and in-shop experience – and then checked against the criteria mentioned above. Given that many retailers compete in these areas, it is important to focus on areas that are truly distinctive to the brand. Bundling more than two of these five areas will only serve to dilute the promise and render it ineffective.

For a snapshot of the brand promise in action, Figure 6.6 presents an example of these five areas for Lowe's, one of the largest hardware retailers in North America. Lowe's offers a fine example of a retail brand that delivers well on its value proposition. Its retail brand proposition focuses on assortment and in-store experience, and its dynamic assortment is far superior to most do-it-yourself stores. This combined with its interesting store layout makes Lowe's a fun place

FIGURE 6.6 Applying the retail pentagon – Lowe's example

Lowe's – 'Improving Home Improvement'
'Known for ...'

- Superior in-store experience
- Wide, innovative, and exclusive assortment that exceeds the typical DIY offering

Assortment
- Assortment adjusted to positioning as a 'lifestyle centre'
- Wide assortment of products that also appeal to women
- Selective listing of furniture and high-value items like consumer electronics, even at higher price points
- Exclusive deals with manufacturers of branded goods

In-store experience
- Well-lit, tidy stores with wide aisles and low shelves
- Superior signage and customer flow management
- Targeted at a unique experience, especially to attract women
- Strong network with more than 1,700 stores in 50 states

● Disadvantage in comparison to competitor   ◐ Equal to competitor   ◍ Advantage in comparison to competitor

SOURCE Lowe's Companies, Inc; store visits

to visit. This value proposition combined with successful execution has contributed to it being a more enjoyable place for women shoppers than many of its competitors. Another example of creating and delivering on brand promise is the online shoe retailer Zappos. Says founder Tony Hsieh: 'We've aligned the entire organization around one mission: to provide the best customer service possible.' The promise is delivered comprehensively and consistently, from social media to above-the-line awareness campaigns. In some of the company's most popular tv commercials, puppets act out real-life calls between customers and call centre agents, many of them revolving around hassle-free returns and exchanges. Zappos' aspiration to provide world-class service at all touch points is widely recognized and amply rewarded by shoppers. According to the company's website, 75 per cent of purchases are repeat purchases.

Once the brand promise has been articulated, retailers must seek organizational alignment. Only when mindsets and behaviours are oriented towards the brand promise can the company ensure the brand promise is delivered consistently at all touch points, from newspaper advertising and internet banners, to the stores and after-sales service. But a brand mindset, just like any other mindset, is not easy to create. It requires focus and a sustained, interested effort to establish it across the organization. Here is a four-step process that can help develop a brand mindset for employees, which will lead them to be more conscious of and, ultimately, better deliver on the brand promise at all times:

- *Inform.* There are many ways of communicating the brand promise to employees – some more creative than others. What counts though is effectiveness. Take Amazon's CEO, Jeff Bezos, as an example. The company has an objective of being the most customer-centric company in the world. Never missing an opportunity to demonstrate his obsession with service quality, Mr Bezos has been known to bring an empty chair to company meetings and ask his employees to act as if the customer (the 'most important participant in the meeting') were sitting there.

- *Get buy-in.* A brand promise that is reflected only in advertising but not in practice will not work. Employees need to understand and develop an appreciation of the brand promise. Explaining what the brand promise is and making employees believe in it are critical. The process of also making new employees 'live and breathe' the brand promise can only be done through a comprehensive communication and training programme. Encouraging internal discussions and clarifying doubts are important aspects of helping employees understand the brand promise well. Many organizations use a 'brand book', which helps employees understand what the brand is all about.

  John Lewis Partnership, the company that operates the British department store powerhouse John Lewis, has an in-house magazine, which is the oldest still being published in the United Kingdom. This magazine enables two-way communication between management and employees, as employees can write articles holding management accountable. Obviously, John Lewis's partnership structure makes it easier to foster this kind of communication, as all of the employees are partners in the company. However, other retailers can similarly establish a feedback loop to get employee buy-in.

- *Live the brand promise.* When employees understand what the brand stands for and appreciate their role in delivering the brand promise, their ability to provide customers with a great brand experience in line with the promise is greatly enhanced. Top management should act as a role model and recognize the importance of front-office staff in providing a powerful brand experience to customers. They should make sure that these staff members get the appropriate tools and training so that they can truly act as brand ambassadors. The Japanese retailer Muji, with its brand of sleek minimalism, is a prime example of 'living the promise'. Somewhat paradoxically, the company has made 'no brand' its brand philosophy, and this brand promise has been implemented so rigidly that it is widely considered a role model for brand delivery. Another example of 'walking the walk' is Amazon's tradition of having all employees (regardless of seniority or level) spend two days in a call centre as part of an annual training programme. The goal here is to provide everyone with the opportunity to get a first-hand feel for customer problems and further contribute to Amazon's customer-centric objectives.

- *Promote the brand promise.* It is everyone's job in the company to promote the brand, but it takes time for such a culture to be built and spread. Aligning the policies and processes of the company with the brand is a great way of creating a culture in sync with the brand. Incentivizing and rewarding brand-aligned behaviour help employees behave consistently in a brand-oriented manner. Take again the example of Zappos, the online shoe and clothing retailer – its brand promise entails making customers happy, so the company makes sure that its employees are happy first. One of the many benefits Zappos provides is an on-site goals and life coach. Employees can sign up to meet the coach, who will work with them to set a realistic, 30-day personal or professional goal. Setting and achieving smaller goals leads to employees setting bigger goals.

Leading retail brands refresh their brand promise regularly and in various ways, including internal communication, training and top leader-led programmes. The HR function is deeply involved with this process, as it is a significant aspect of their employer branding programmes for employees (both current and future). Recruiting employees who instinctively have the characteristics that resonate with the brand and training these employees in the ways of the brand go a long way towards developing a strong brand internally. HR, therefore, plays a vital role in retail branding because the brand is so highly concerned with service and experience.

Good intentions alone, however, do not count for much. A survey by McKinsey shows that 60 per cent of brand transformation efforts are considered failures, and the reason for this is often the lack of commitment to these efforts by senior management. It is very important for CEOs to strongly get behind programmes that have the ability to transform every aspect of the retail business and, therefore, its value.

Howard Schultz's turnaround of Starbucks is a great example of this kind of visible CEO engagement. In 2008, after being reappointed to the helm of the coffeehouse chain, not only did he famously write a memo on how the brand had lost its appeal by growing too fast, but he also invited employees and customers alike to e-mail him directly and made personal phone calls to stores across the network to see how things were going.

Branding still remains an underutilized lever for many retailers. However, in an increasingly differentiated retail and media environment, brand image becomes an increasingly important factor for consumer acquisition, development and retention efforts. A systematic, fact-based approach to measuring and managing their brand will help retailers develop this lever into a competitive advantage.

Biographies

Jesko Perrey is a Director in McKinsey's Düsseldorf office and Global Knowledge Leader of the firm's Marketing & Sales Practice. He has helped clients tackle a variety of marketing challenges across industries ranging from insurance to retail. He works in brand communications and architecture, customer relationship management, brand building and brand portfolio optimization, as well as marketing ROI programmes. Jesko is the author of many articles and essays in leading journals and compendiums on subjects such as branding, marketing ROI, and segmentation. He holds a PhD in Marketing from the University of Münster.

Thomas Meyer is a Senior Marketing Expert in McKinsey's London office and a leader of the firm's Marketing and Brand Strategy service line. His marketing work with organizations from various industries focuses on brand and brand portfolio strategy as well as marketing spending effectiveness. Thomas has published extensively in the field of marketing, including co-authoring the branding book *Mega-Macht Marke*. He holds a PhD in International Management from the University of Braunschweig.

Reference

Mazzu, M, Meyer, T and Weissgerber, A (2012) A guide to excellence in retail brand management, in *Retail Marketing and Branding: A definitive guide to maximizing ROI*, 2nd edn, eds J Perrey and D Spillecke, John Wiley & Sons Inc, Hoboken, NJ

Why brand matters in B2B

MICHAEL D'ESOPO and SIMON GLYNN

Imagine you are in the market for a new tablet. What will drive your choice – features, price or brand? Tablets offer a wide variety of features at different price points. And there are trade-offs: maybe the same basic technical specification would cost more in a Samsung Galaxy than a Google Nexus, but you might choose the Samsung anyway because of something not in this basic tech spec – something you believe about Samsung's quality, design, aftercare or upgradability.

We researched this question for our client, one of the world's biggest PC makers, among both consumers and business-to-business (B2B) buyers. We asked respondents to choose the computer they would buy, based on different sequences of simulated choices. We wanted to pinpoint the actual influence, not their self-perception or stated preference.

Our statistical results showed the relative impact of individual features, price and brand in influencing a purchase decision. Consumers' choice of computers was driven 34 per cent by features, 39 per cent by price and 27 per cent by brand. For business buyers, features again represented 34 per cent of choice, but the other two factors were exactly reversed: their choices were driven 27 per cent by price and 39 per cent by brand.

We were surprised by the results, as were most people who saw them. But should we have been? For a consumer, buying a computer is an unusual exercise in that the performance (in the form of tech specs) is unusually transparent. Why pay more than you need to for the performance you want? Hence consumers' emphasis on price over brand.

For a business, choosing technology often goes beyond consider-ations of features and price. A firm probably has, or will have, other computers. Buying more of the same will be more efficient. Today's purchase must also take into consideration potential future offerings. Technical support is another crucial element. Business buyers will put more focus on the company behind the computer, both for what it says about the device itself, as well as long-term support. Hence their emphasis on brand over price.

These considerations go beyond the once traditional, but ultim-ately negative, mantra that 'no one ever got fired for buying IBM'. That mantra played on fear, uncertainty and doubt, or the avoid-ance of potential negative outcomes. Today's B2B brands play in a much more positive territory, recognizing and responding to the real needs of business buyers, which go beyond the tech specs of a product.

B2B brands influence customer choice in many ways, each of which can be specifically managed. Brands directly support B2B sales by:

- staying front of mind for customers and landing on their shortlist to receive a tender invitation;
- winning the coin toss in close calls – making it both easier and faster to say 'yes'; and
- capturing a larger 'share of wallet' and preferred supplier position with customers once the relationships are established.

Beyond this immediate impact, B2B brands help position a company for winning future business by:

- winning permission to play in adjacent spaces and play higher-value-added roles. For example, Stanley Tools has expanded from selling hand tools to providing security solutions, with an overlapping set of customers;
- making new market entry more effective and efficient; and
- building barriers to commoditization in competitive industries.

All this is based on how customers see the B2B brand. But, as in the consumer world, the power of brand goes beyond the direct customer impact. B2B brands also create value through their influence on:

- company leadership – by aligning goals and objectives across business units;
- investors – by making superior performance tangible and therefore increasing stock multiples;
- employees, both current and future – by creating an appealing culture that attracts and retains world-class talent.

B2B brands can be very powerful. Several predominantly B2B technology brands, in particular, are among the world's most valuable – IBM, Microsoft, GE, Cisco, HP, Oracle and SAP – to name a few.

Despite this potential, many B2B companies do not manage and invest in their brands to the extent consumer-facing companies do. The disciplines of marketing and branding grew out of the fast-paced world of consumer goods, and these origins continue to influence how marketing and branding are taught and practised.

Many executives (especially those outside of marketing) believe that building a brand requires a large budget. In the B2B world, the reality is that investments are typically focused on other parts of the business, such as product development, sales support, customer service, etc.

The good news is that a large advertising budget isn't required to transform a brand. Several leading B2B organizations are beginning to treat brand as a bigger idea – one that extends beyond communications into the totality of how different audiences experience the organization.

B2B marketers need to direct their focus towards educating and influencing the organization as a whole. If the brand represents the promise of an experience with an organization, the brand becomes the responsibility of all employees, not just a marketing campaign.

In the next sections we explore how B2B brands can create the power to engage buyers. We share some specific examples, including how 3M re-established vitality around a heritage of innovation, and how CA Technologies evolved to be more relevant in the world of cloud computing.

What brand needs to do in B2B

From our work across many different sectors, we see four factors that can shape brand perception in B2B companies.

1. *Promise a customer relationship*

As the tablet example showed, part of the power of the B2B brand is what it promises about the future customer relationship. Why is this a bigger deal in B2B than in the consumer market?

First, consumers can be fickle, with little penalty for changing brands. One type of toothpaste or television is pretty much like another. But for businesses, switching brands can be complex and costly. Businesses may have to retrain staff or adapt operations to a different supplier's performance.

Second, in today's world of tightly integrated supply chains, companies must have a high level of trust with their business partners. Their own production depends on delivery from others. Companies need to know that when challenging circumstances arise, their partners will reliably deliver.

Consumer marketers often talk about 'customer relationships'. Customers do sometimes form emotional bonds with consumer brands, but very few consumer brands have actual day-to-day relationships with their individual customers. B2B companies do.

Nokia Networks (NSN), the world's specialist in networks and solutions for mobile broadband, sells to about 600 telecom operators around the world. It employs 60,000 people, more than 20,000 of whom interact directly with its telecom customers. The NSN brand may be shaped by its central marketing team, but it is reinforced primarily through the relationships NSN's people have with its customers.

We recently researched the priorities of big B2B buyers for two different global companies in the energy and chemicals sectors. We asked customers to rate a set of competing providers on 50 different attributes. We determined which attributes were most strongly correlated with customers' overall opinion of a provider. Attributes that companies often promote, such as being 'industry thought leaders', or being 'a growing and ambitious company' were of moderate importance to customers. At the top of the list was 'I enjoy doing business with this company', and 'taking a long-term perspective with customer relationships'.

So how do you empower tens of thousands of representatives to develop genuine yet on-brand relationships with various clients?

At 3M, one way is to provide client-facing representatives with lively and actionable examples of 3M innovations as part of a detailed brand guidebook. Representatives are not only familiar with the brand's innovative themes, but they have interesting facts and stories to share about the products they sell – where the ideas came from, and how the technologies are applied. These unexpected details intrigue clients, reinforcing brand perceptions and creating stronger bonds.

2. Signal a strategic shift from supplier to partner

One theme cuts across most of our B2B branding work across all industries. Companies are increasingly using brands to reposition themselves with customers. Businesses no longer want to be seen just as suppliers or vendors, selling on customers' terms. They want to be recognized as true strategic partners, working collaboratively in long-term, enlightened, win-win relationships. This shift is taking place across the B2B world. Companies undergoing the shift must take definite steps to make sure they are being perceived in the correct light.

NSN was once seen simply as a vendor or supplier of telecom infrastructure equipment. But this perception doesn't do justice to the way the business actually operates. The company's solutions often involve technology. But they also involve network design, systems integration, and outsourced operation and management. NSN's business depends on deep, long-term and collaborative relationships. Being valued as a strategic partner is at least as important as being valued for the innovative technology the company creates.

Today, NSN shapes and defines its business according to the challenges its telecom customers face as they serve the world's thirst for universal connectivity and content. This is captured in its brand essence, *for a world in motion*™.

CA Technologies, one of the largest software developers in the world, once marketed category-specific products. But the company realized that IT customers have to support changing business priorities within existing IT systems. So the company evolved its selling model to meet customers' needs. Now, instead of pushing category-specific products, CA Technologies provides well-rounded solutions that span traditional mainframe and infrastructure software to emerging cloud-computing technologies.

This strategic change is amplified through the brand positioning: *agility made possible*™. The positioning captures the company's ability to provide relevant expertise and nimble solutions while also enabling IT and business leaders to achieve evolving strategic goals.

The same story is true for Johnson Controls. The company made its name as the inventor of the thermostat more than 120 years ago. Today it is a diversified operation, capable of providing such varied solutions as the design for a car's interior, or the creation and management of intelligent building systems.

Along the way, the brand promise has evolved. It is less about what Johnson Controls sells, and more about the benefits provided – the comfort, safety and sustainability of smart environments.

Shifting the brand emphasis from product features and functionality towards broader customer benefits has had upsides in other areas. The investment community used to think of Johnson Controls as simply a component provider to the automotive industry. The company's repositioning as an environments/interiors company has led investors to compare it to companies like GE and Honeywell – companies with higher price/earnings multiples and stronger investment prospects.

3. Reach through to the end consumer

Some brands, such as NSN, are purely B2B. Every day a quarter of the world's population connects using NSN networks or technologies, without knowing they are doing so. Other B2B brands also appeal to consumers, both indirectly and directly. Few consumers know that 3M makes the product that makes a smartphone screen bright, or the adhesive that keeps the tailfin attached to an airplane. But most people know that the Post-it notes they scribble on were invented and manufactured by 3M.

Intel Inside® remains the most obvious example of a B2B brand making itself visible to the end consumer. This brand slogan complements its promise to B2B customers, while also creating pull from consumers.

Since 1991, Intel has partnered with nearly 200 equipment manufacturers on the *Intel Inside* marketing campaign. The effort propelled consumer awareness levels of the Intel brand from 24 per cent in 1991 to 94 per cent in 1995, and the brand continues to be a household name today. But success came with high costs. In the first six years, the company spent $4 billion on the programme. We often hear from B2B companies that they aspire to realize the same pull ('we should create the *Intel Inside* of our category'), although few are prepared to put the same investment into achieving it.

On the other hand, some brands act as ingredients in another company's offerings. Their business model is B2B because they sell directly to an intermediary, who then chooses or influences which products are presented to individual consumers. This is often the case for investment managers and healthcare providers. In both sectors, consumers are often faced with a myriad of largely undifferentiated options among B2B brands. This increases their dependence on the intermediary's recommendation. Brands that manage to engage end consumers, even if the consumers are not the brand's direct customers, make it easier for the intermediary to recommend them. They may also create opportunities for related direct-to-consumer activities.

BlackRock is an investment manager that sells investment products through other institutions. Even though most of the company's business is B2B, BlackRock invests in a substantial amount of advertising communications to end customers. This means that when BlackRock offers investment products to a financial adviser, who presents them to an individual investor, that investor may be more likely to include a familiar brand in their investment portfolio. The same logic holds for a corporation deciding which investment options to make available to its employees to consider as part of its retirement account.

Healthcare providers like Cigna are in a similar position. Cigna provides both health insurance policies and medical care, where insurance policies are sold to corporations and medical care to individuals. A corporation may provide employees with a number of healthcare options. If people trust Cigna as a medical care provider, they would be more likely to select Cigna for their insurance policy. This way, the B2B and B2C businesses complement each other.

4. Reconcile the B2B brand and the corporate brand

'There's a surprising gap between the brand messages that suppliers offer to customers and what their customers really want to know.' That's the conclusion of research that compares top B2B messaging with themes most important to B2B buyers (in a survey of global executives).[1]

The report explains:

> Themes such as social responsibility, sustainability, and global reach, which many B2B companies cast in a leading role for brand imaging, appeared to have a minimal influence on buyers' perceptions of brand strength. The inverse was true, as well: two of the most important themes for customer perceptions of brand strength – effective supply chain management and specialist market knowledge – were among those least mentioned by B2B suppliers. Honest and open dialogue, which customers considered most important, was one of the three themes not emphasized at all.

Our observations working with B2B brands support this disparity, and also suggest a straightforward explanation. The gap is not between what companies say and what customers care about; it's between the role of the 'B2B brand' and the role of the 'corporate brand'.

The 'B2B brand' needs to connect with business customers' needs and priorities, and set out the company's mission for serving them – just as a consumer brand does. The 'corporate brand' has a much wider remit. It must set out the company's mission as an institution – to believe in, do business with, follow, admire and forgive. It must speak to investors; local and global communities; current, future and former employees; governments and civil society; as well as to customers and prospects.

The 'corporate brand' looks beyond marketing. When most effective, it works in alignment with the company's vision and mission, and with its culture and values, to provide a beacon for what the company does.

Why is GE such an esteemed corporate brand? GE excels at humanizing its scientific work by showing how it could change the world. The company highlights this in communications, products, leadership and day-to-day practices. It ties technology and engineering efforts to visible benefits and tangible impact. While each business unit carries its own expertise, the corporate brand focuses on the big idea of *Imagination at Work*. This idea unites all lines of businesses and employees, and strengthens the perception of the brand in the minds of business partners and consumers alike.

In the fast-changing world of consumer goods, where many brand rules were written, the corporate brand was often completely separate from the consumer brand. The rise of 'own label' brands, such as Wal-Mart and Tesco, and Unilever's promotion of its corporate brand over its products, has changed that a bit.

But most B2B brands *are* corporate brands. Confusion arises because the 'corporate brand' and the 'B2B brand' are one and the same for these companies. The same brand must play both roles, connecting with different audiences. It can be done, but requires care. Here's how 3M describes itself to its B2B customers, focusing on what matters to them, but in the context of its broader institutional character for other stakeholders:

> 3M is the innovation company that never stops inventing, because we're passionate about making progress happen. We keep our customers competitive by tapping into our collaborative culture to provide a never-ending evolution of ideas and technologies to solve the world's most critical problems.

In the end, success in B2B brand building truly emanates from the ability to develop genuine relationships nurtured as partnerships – rather than vendor transactions – among both current and future clients. It requires open and honest dialogue with direct customers as well as consideration of the customer's customer. While the importance of relationship building is something often associated with B2C brands, it is even more powerful for B2B brands.

Making brand work in B2B

To succeed in B2B, a brand needs to promise a customer relationship, not just an immediate proposition. It may also need to signal a strategic shift, so that the company comes to be recognized as a trusted, collaborative partner, rather than a mere vendor. The brand may need to reach through the direct customer, and connect with the consumer beyond.

And it must do all that while also performing the role of a corporate brand, building the reputation of the company as an institution with a wide variety of stakeholders. That's a tall order. What does it mean for building a great B2B brand?

The primary rules we think about for brand-building in B2B are actually similar to the more progressive B2C brands – because B2C marketing has also moved a long way from its consumer-product roots. Much of the consumer-service economy has more in common with the B2B world than with traditional product marketing. This includes industries like banking, communications, travel and retail. Brands in these sectors often focus on the promise of a future customer relationship and experience, beyond the immediate value proposition. They also tend to integrate the customer-facing and corporate brand into one. The brands that thrive in this new world look beyond the traditional focus of marketing and successfully extend their brands in three distinct ways.

1. Beyond communications – telling authentic stories and creating inspiring experiences

Stories matter in building brands, as much as they ever did, and as much in B2B as in B2C. It's a company's story, more than its facts and figures, that inspires consumers.

Further, successful stories today are not polished, choreographed narratives, and eloquently told in television commercials or corporate videos. It's more of a folk tradition – retold by different people, each in their own way. The collective retelling instils a distinct culture and set of values. The story defines the experience – even more for B2B brands than B2C – and the experience shapes brand perceptions.

Because brand is more than a marketing communications message, the question is, therefore, whether the brand is built in a managed or unmanaged way. Conveying the brand through daily interactions doesn't work unless it's backed up by every interface and operation of the company. 'Show, don't tell.'

At 3M, for example, the corporate brand story doesn't compete or conflict with the product marketing story: it provides the way to tell the product marketing story. It complements the immediate messages that product marketers have to get across – about their product, its features and benefits, and how those differ from competitor or substitute products.

3M's brand story is not about 'what' it innovates but 'how' it innovates – the unique way the company drives innovation. '3M solves problems others cannot by harnessing the power of collaboration, internally and with customers, in a high-energy ecosystem that spans diverse technologies.'

Many new 3M innovations result from a cascade of previous innovations, using the same underlying technology platform for different ideas in different industries and applications. For example, the 'micro-replication' technology that 3M created in the 1960s to etch diffusing screens for overhead projectors has since appeared, in evolved forms, in traffic-light lenses, PC privacy screens, and as a layer in smartphone screens to concentrate the light towards the user, reducing the battery power required for a given perceived brightness.

Individual ideas may appear to come from spontaneous sparks of insight and creativity, but the system that promotes these sparks is quite deliberately managed. Telling the innovation story might seem to distract from the product story. But, the innovation story frames the product story. Here is how 3M explains the innovation behind its lightweight insulation used to protect automotive interiors from engine noise with the minimum of weight. 3M calls it 'connecting curiosity':

> How do you get from a cold-weather essential to a whisper-quiet ride?
> On developing a lightweight insulation that keeps people warm, we took 3M™ Thinsulate™ Insulation and evolved it across functions and industries to solve even more customer problems. We went from cold-weather outerwear and accessories to occupational workwear to footwear to bedding to military shelters and then to acoustic insulation in cars and boats. This voyage of ideas is not unusual and has not ended. Working together and with our customers, we continually strive to make every idea as big as it can be to help our customers achieve more.

What about other interactions that customers have – not just through scripted communications like this, but in meetings, conversations and relationships? How can the brand permeate those occasions – where no marketing people are involved?

The answer is to elevate the notion of brand beyond the marketing department, and to have the whole organization understand not just what the brand means, but what it means for every person's role.

SABIC is the world's second largest diversified chemicals company. Founded in Riyadh in the 1970s, its origins were in manufacturing commodity plastics, exploiting the hydrocarbon feedstock from Saudi Arabia's mineral wealth. Now a thriving $50 billion global enterprise, with operations in four continents, SABIC's brand vision is to enable the business performance of its customers, leveraging its expertise in materials and tailored solutions. Its business evolution is a good example of the strategic shift from supplier to partner discussed earlier.

Delivering the promise starts with understanding the ambitions of SABIC customers. The company makes a point to discover and respond to those ambitions throughout the customer experience as a part of activating its brand. For example, during discussions of materials supply, instead of having a customer order a specific type of plastic by product number, the sales team is empowered to understand what the customer wants to use the material for, and offer a range of plastics options and strategic solutions based on the customer's needs.

The brand team worked with each of the company's strategic business units – commercial managers as well as marketing – to design an ideal customer journey that defined and delivered the brand's promise. This method was derived from conversations with customers, who offered suggestions about how SABIC should listen to customer needs. This is how B2B brands are built: through the sales and service discussions, customers understand what it would be like to do business with SABIC.

2. Beyond consistency – creating a brand personality that is both authentic and vital

Ensuring a company communicates its brand consistently – across different touchpoints, different business units and customers, and around the globe – is hard. This has always been a top challenge for corporate brand teams. Hard as it is to do, it is not enough.

Strong brands today thrive on a personality that is both authentic and vital. Consistent presentation helps reinforce a brand's authenticity. It's clear why brands should come across as distinct, but internally consistent.

That way, audiences recognize whom they are dealing with, and are reassured that their experience in any one part of the business will match the expectations built up by other parts. But consistency alone is a recipe for dullness, inflexibility and stagnation. While many B2B brands have rich, long histories, placing too much emphasis on historical accomplishments may not be desirable. If history doesn't translate to meeting today's and tomorrow's customer needs, it would only reinforce the idea that the company is trading on its past reputation.

Like people, brands need to be able to adapt – to local markets, customer interests and global trends. Responding to a changing world, CA Technology moved from mainframe infrastructure to cloud computing, and 3M digitized Post-its through a partnership with Evernote. B2B brands are based on relationships, and they must be comfortable with the give and take that any relationship requires. Perfectly consistent brands, however admirable they may appear, may have trouble evolving.

Consistency has been a mantra of branding. Are consistency and freshness in conflict? Not if we think in terms of consistent principles, values and behaviours – not simply about visual assets. This deeper consistency is what we refer to as authenticity.

MFS Investment Management is a global asset manager best known for inventing the mutual fund in the United States. As a well-respected company that prides itself on home-grown expertise, lasting relationships and employee satisfaction (many employees have a long tenure with the company), MFS's brand personality is focused on being genuine, collaborative, reliable and passionate.

While this set of attributes provides consistent guidance to what MFS represents as a firm, it also enables flexibility in how it looks and acts. The brand personality provides the guidance to relationship managers to continue their friendly service, and inspired the use of digitized pitch books (tablets) in the selling process.

3. Beyond customer – inspiring internal belief in the purpose and enabling tangible action to deliver

Hopefully it will be clear from the examples above that involving employees in the brand is critical to success. This is not just 'feel-good' involvement, to get employees supportive of what's going on. It is a more active effort to recruit employees into the brand purpose and encourage them to apply the brand to their own work.

Egon Zehnder is a professional services firm that focuses on executive search and leadership consulting. Empowering consultants to become brand advocates is particularly important in the professional services business. Therefore, Egon Zehnder created a set of core principles for employees to help them bring the brand to life. They include: fostering connected conversations to facilitate knowledge and network sharing; streamlining internal processes to enable quicker responses to clients; and providing customized materials to create more personal client interactions.

Recruiting employees into the brand purpose can transform brand development. Some of the most admired brands – in B2B and B2C – have individual charismatic leaders, often founders, at the helm. These leaders provide a beacon for and unite the company behind collective effort to get there. Many long-established, highly successful corporations do not have that style of leadership; for them, brand can play a comparable leadership role, both as a beacon and as a uniting force.

That said, senior leadership must steward the brand. Human resources and marketing departments alone are unlikely to be capable of uniting the company behind a single, clear direction. Managing the brand internally is a collaborative effort, and is most effective when the leadership team members act as ambassadors, driving the effort within their own areas of the business.

At SABIC, while the communications team coordinated and drove the branding effort, leadership sat clearly with the CEO and the company's 15-member executive committee. All members were publicly interviewed about their role and what the brand meant for their respective divisions.

The SABIC brand team also worked with human resources (and the business units) in a series of workshops around the world to define the brand-led employee experience. The teams worked their way through the employee journey – from joining the company, to meeting the leadership and being managed, to how they were measured and rewarded.

At each step they asked: How should this happen at SABIC given what our brand represents? The ideas from these workshops fed into a half-day workshop with the whole executive committee. It developed a high-level set of five principles defining the global management culture that the brand required. The workshops also generated specific recommendations, which would not have been possible without the executive committee's support.

Similarly, collaborative innovation is realized in employees' daily work at 3M. Long before Google implemented the practice of encouraging employee research, 3M employees were encouraged to devote 15 per cent of their working hours to their own projects. A culture of collaboration grew within 'Tech Clubs', employee interest groups that had a proud history of cultivating the development of Post-it notes, among other ground-breaking innovations.[2] Moreover, employees are rewarded for sharing their ideas. 3M identifies outstanding employees for lifetime achievement awards based on how often their ideas are implemented by others.

At many companies, employee engagement starts during the recruiting process. Chevron, for example, faces the challenge of attracting the brightest young engineers to oil and gas when they could work with technology giants such as Google and Microsoft. Research led Chevron to create a brand based on *Human Energy*. It helped the company stand out, and supported the company's long-term global human resource growth and development.

What does this mean for the role of the CMO in B2B companies? Building long-term foundations for success requires more than a compelling story. CMOs are recognizing that brand stewardship is, more than ever, an inside job. This rings particularly true with CMOs in B2B industries. They are finding they must be catalysts for change within their organizations. Most B2B companies do not have the sort of dominant CMO role that exists in some B2C companies, but to drive the agenda we have described, CMOs must dive into the organization and hurdle internal barriers.

Brand is valuable to both B2B companies and their customers because it signifies a future relationship beyond the immediate purchase. B2B companies can secure trust by establishing genuine relationships, offering strategic partnerships, reaching through to the consumer (and/or the customer's customer), and managing the distinct roles for the corporate and B2B brands. To bring brands to life, B2B companies need to identify, reinforce and amplify brand-affirming experiences.

Biographies

Michael D'Esopo is a senior partner and the director of brand strategy at Lippincott. With more than 20 years of experience, his areas of expertise include brand strategy and positioning, customer analytics, experience innovation, and brand activation. He has addressed marketing and branding issues for a range of clients including Alcoa, Ameriprise, Citibank, HP, Hyatt Hotels, Hyundai Card, Ingersoll Rand, Intel, Intuit, Iron Mountain, Nuveen Investments, Pizza Hut, Samsung, Sun Life Financial, Tyco, Visa, and Yahoo.

Michael has spoken frequently for the Association of National Advertisers (ANA) and the Conference Board and is often quoted on the topic of brands in the business press. Before joining Lippincott, Michael was a principal in Oliver Wyman's (formerly Mercer Management Consulting) Strategic Capabilities Group, where he directed corporate and marketing strategy engagements for clients in the technology and financial business sectors.

Michael holds a BS in economics from The Wharton School of the University of Pennsylvania and an MBA from the MIT Sloan School of Management.

Simon Glynn is a brand strategy director and the head of Lippincott in Europe and the Middle East. Simon has 23 years of consulting experience for clients across 40 countries. Based in London, his work has included refocusing product and service strategies, partnering with brands to truly drive demand in their market, developing new brand positionings that connect an organization's DNA with customer priorities, and transforming large organizations through their customer and colleague experiences.

Simon's clients have included 3M, Balfour Beatty, Barclays, British Gas, Disney, DP World, Elsevier, HSBC, IKEA, Johnson Controls, London Symphony Orchestra, Nokia, Nokia Solutions and Networks, Orange, RBS, The Royal Navy, SABIC, Sainsbury's, Saudi Aramco and Standard Chartered.

Before joining Lippincott, Simon was a vice president at Oliver Wyman (formerly Mercer Management Consulting). He previously held positions with Arthur D Little, Cable & Wireless and BT. He holds an MA in physics from the University of Cambridge.

Notes

1 Tjark Freundt, Philipp Hillenbrand and Sascha Lehmann (2013) 'How B2B companies talk past their customers', *McKinsey Quarterly*, October

2 Hal Weitzman (2011) 'Man who turns Post-it notes into banknotes', *Financial Times*, 27 February

Managing media as brands
Case study – branding news organizations

WALTER S MCDOWELL, PhD

Part one: Media as brands

The study of brand management is the study of the power of a brand name to influence consumer thoughts, feelings and actions. Let's take a real-world media example. An individual wants to know the final score and see video highlights of a televised sporting event.

> Question: Where can this content be found?
> Answer: All over the place.

Using online resources, a person might do a simple Google search for this information. An alternative approach would be to go to a familiar and trusted source, such as sports-oriented cable network or website of which there are many. Basic scores and video highlights are ubiquitous across dozens of media brands, but suppose this fan desires *something more* and consequently chooses to record ESPN 'SportsCenter's' coverage of this event on his DVR. Even when the final score is obtained from another source, this person still finds time to watch 'SportsCenter'. Obviously, the programme and its parent ESPN network provide *added value*. It is an extraordinary *media brand*.

In order to cope with unprecedented competition, media firms, such as TV and cable networks, radio, newspapers, magazines and websites have looked to the highly competitive consumer goods industry for ways to create extraordinary brands. Today media trade publications are filled with headlines using branding jargon, such as 'USA Network Refreshes Brand with Premieres of Modern Family and NCIS: LA' or 'The Simpsons Is Top TV Brand of All Time, Says Survey'.

The terminology of conventional retail brand management can be adapted easily to accommodate media experiences. For instance, by changing the word 'consumer' to 'audience' and recognizing that 'purchase behaviour' can be synonymous with 'watching', 'listening' or 'reading', many retail brand concepts can serve as useful tools for the management of media brands. This chapter will give the reader a brief overview of the nature of media branding coupled with a narrower case study look at the branding challenges facing the business of journalism.

Media brands and business models

This chapter, dedicated to media branding, includes a necessary dose of media economics. At the end of the day, businesses exist to make a profit. Brand management 'experts' working for established media firms and emerging media entrepreneurs too often lose sight of this goal. Attracting engaged, passionate audiences of course is vital but successfully *monetizing* these audiences often is the bigger branding challenge. For over two centuries, the dominant source of revenue for media has come from advertising. The long-standing business model has been to first attract an audience with free or inexpensive content and then to sell that audience to an interested advertiser by embedding client messages within the content (eg ads, commercials, product placement, sponsored content etc). This two-stage business model requires two types of 'customer' brand management strategies: one for attracting audiences and another for attracting advertisers. An example would be *The Huffington Post* attracting visitors to its website using audience branding strategies and subsequently selling this acquired audience to General Motors using business-to-business branding strategies. Obviously, each has a different expectation from a media brand.

A second common approach to making money has been to charge audiences for access to a media product. Examples would be admission to a movie theatre, a monthly subscription to Net-flix or paying for a cable on-demand movie. Often a media firm will combine these approaches wherein they require a modest audi-ence subscription fee and also sell advertising. In recent years, some online programmers, such as Hulu Plus, offer two versions of the same product: a free version that has commercial interruptions and a premium pay version that is commercial free.

With so much content available for free (legally and illegally) a fee-based media business model must offer something of exceptional personal value to a consumer. *Brand exclusivity* is the key to motivat-ing audiences to pay for content. That is, audiences must perceive a brand's content to be so exclusive it is worth paying for. This demand has led to the development of exclusive original programme content by companies that initially were only in the business of distribu-tion. Netflix, YouTube and Amazon are just a few of the companies now investing in content that will require some type of enhanced subscription or user fee.

Media firms always have used brand names to identify themselves but until recently these firms rarely invested the same time, effort and money into serious brand management strategies that their advertis-ing clients have done for years. Disruptive technology fostering over-whelming competition has had a profound effect on the economics of media and consequently, many media firms have embraced brand management theory and practices as a means to survive and prosper.

Entering the twenty-first century, the internet blossomed with thousands of audio and video content choices. Within the span of 20 years or so, while the US population grew only modestly, the num-ber of media choices exploded exponentially and continues to grow. Today digital technology has been the primary catalyst for generating more media competitors creating more products distributed via more platforms to more devices catering to more unique audience groups than ever before.

The branding promises and perils of digital technology

Digital technology is both the yin and yang of media branding today. The positive and negative components are intertwined. In simple terms, the promises of digital technology are about *opportunity*. That is, economic barriers to entry have been reduced significantly, so that more entrepreneurs have the opportunity to enter markets that at one time were off limits or too expensive to even consider. Most of these changes have been the result of government deregulation and the introduction of digital technology's offspring, the internet. For decades, conventional media, such as newspapers, magazines, books, radio programmes, television programmes, movies, and sound recordings, were distinct technologies that fostered equally distinct consumer behaviours and brand marketing strategies. However, with expanding digital technology, the partitions separating one medium from another are disappearing quickly. This blurring of media boundaries has fostered the concept of *media convergence*. Furthermore, production and distribution hardware and software are now remarkably affordable, often requiring only a laptop with a few accessories. Essentially anybody with a minimal amount of money can set up an internet-based media firm. In combination, convergence and cost efficiencies have made the idea of catering to narrow audience segments (ie niches) attractive to business entrepreneurs.

The ESPN brand is an example of a media brand that thrives on media convergence. Its relentless embrace of new media has helped make it among the most profitable television networks in US history. An article from *Bloomberg Business Week* asserts that: 'The company has moved aggressively into new media and platforms, without regard for how they may negatively impact the old. This strategy allows ESPN to squeeze more revenue out of any event it carries.'

On the other hand, some once-popular media brands have been overtaken by upstart competitors. From a media distribution perspective, Blockbuster Video is an example of a well-known DVD rental company brand that failed to adapt to new technologies. All 9,000 brick-and-mortar stores are now closed. Movie rentals have migrated to cable and online – Blockbuster could have made the same journey but stubbornly refused. Instead, internet-based Netflix was allowed to capture the market. Of course, Netflix is not immune from converging competition. Comcast cable now competes with Netflix by offering movies for download and streaming through its set-top boxes and Xfinity TV website.

With opportunity comes increased *competition*. Digital technology has made competing brands far more accessible to audiences and these audiences are becoming ever more demanding. More than ever, the motivations for choosing a media brand are driven by expected *brand satisfaction* rather than by convenience. Making this competitive environment even more intense is the proven fact that, while the number of available media options has increased enormously in recent years, the number of such options actually *used* by audience members has not kept pace at all. A dramatic example is viewership of cable television today. According to Nielsen Media Research, in homes capable of receiving 200 or more channels, the number of channels actually watched by a US household in a typical week is less than 20. This is a classic business example of the law of diminishing returns, in which more product choice has not resulted substantially in more product usage.

Today people spend about the same amount of time with media as they did a dozen years ago. The media experiences may have changed considerably, such as delayed viewing (ie 'time-shifting') using digital recorders, choosing video on demand or acquiring content out of the home via portable tablets and smart phones or multitasking between these devices, but the number of hours in a day remains at only 24 and people still must go to work, attend classes, mow the lawn and sleep. Irrespective of the number of media brand choices available, media consumption remains time consuming.

The branding challenges of a zero-sum market

Imagine you open up a small pizza stand on the main shopping street of a small town and at the beginning of your enterprise, you are the only pizza vendor. Over time, however, competitors arrive on the scene, offering almost identical pizza menus and pricing. If proportionately more people were coming to the shopping area, things might work out but this is not the case. Instead, the number of pizza brands increases from one to 10 within a three-mile radius, while the number of shoppers (ie potential customers desiring a pizza snack) remains the same. You have entered a *zero-sum market*.

The 'zero' means that as the number of new brands entering the marketplace increases, the available number of customers for a product category remains relatively unchanged or 'zero'. So how does a business survive in such a restricted marketplace? It must take customers away from its rivals. Consequently, as with our pizza analogy, the name of the game for most contemporary media businesses is increasing *share of market* at the expense of your competitors. For example, adding a new 24/7 news network to the roster of available channels on a cable system is not likely to increase the overall number of households watching cable at any particular time. Instead, the new network must attract audiences that are predisposed to watching something else; another brand. Bottom line, media businesses today face massive competition for the hearts and minds of scarce audiences in an unforgiving zero-sum marketplace. Another disturbing aspect of most zero-sum markets is that the relative size of 'slices' (ie market share) among surviving brands tends to favour a few over the many. *The 80/20 rule* of business asserts that within a competitive marketplace, roughly 80 per cent of the revenue spent by consumers goes to only 20 per cent of the competing firms. Returning to our pizza analogy, even if all 10 shops somehow stay in business, probably only two or three will attract the majority of pizza buyers. This common business rule applies readily to most media markets, including radio, television, cable, print and online media. That is, regardless of the size of the market (ie New York or Fargo, North Dakota) or the number of competitors operating within that market, roughly 80 per cent of audiences and therefore, 80 per cent of revenue can be attributed to about 20 per cent of the media brand rivals. The remaining firms become scavengers, willing to discount pricing in order to grab whatever advertising dollars or subscription fees are left in the market.

Price sensitivity as a measure of brand strength

Brand researchers use an array of measuring tools to assess consumer attitudes, from surveys and focus groups to galvanic skin response and brain imaging, but often the most salient measures are the most simple. Because a prominent theme of this chapter is the competitive economics underlying media brand strategy, we will focus on a money-based metric. Price sensitivity or the *willingness to pay*

(WTP) as some business scholars put it, is a wonderfully straight-forward, yet elegant, measure of the real-world brand strength (or 'brand equity') of a media product. Whether dealing with advertising rates, subscription fees, pay walls, on-demand payments or retail purchasing, strong brands command higher pricing than weaker brands. When all brands are perceived as essentially the same in terms of customer satisfaction, the marketplace becomes vulnerable to what Professors David Dranove and Sonia Marciano of the Kellogg School of Business call 'the cancer of competition', driven entirely by pricing wars that spread throughout the entire marketplace 'like a malignant rivalry that destroys profitability without stimulating industry demand'. Brand management principles, however, can be a strong medicine that combats senseless price-slashing competition.

Strong media brands are 'platform agnostic'

A few years ago, acknowledging that more people read the *New York Times* online than through conventional newsprint, publisher Arthur Sulzberger Jr, asserted that the future of the news organization rested not on any particular distribution mode but rather on its brand reputation and therefore, he declared his company 'platform agnostic'. This attitude is underscored by other media companies, including the major broadcast networks that have struck licensing deals (sometimes called retransmission consent agreements) with all sorts of platform distributors, including cable, satellite and broadband.

Enamoured by all the new digital gadgetry, smart media professionals and entrepreneurs still realize that up-to-date technology is necessary but not sufficient to give a media brand a sustainable competitive advantage over its competitors. Rarely can one media firm possess a piece of equipment, computer software, organizational structure, business model or distribution platform that cannot be copied by rivals. On the other hand, *unique content* can be more brand exclusive and legally protected as 'intellectual property'. Regardless of the distribution and receiving devices employed, audiences are attracted and retained because of content. Stressing this point, The National Association of Television and Program Executives (NATPE) recently adopted the slogan 'Content First' as a reminder that audiences don't watch blank screens.

Strong media brands recognize the power of their audiences

Technology has had a profound effect on audience attitudes and behaviour. The media can no longer dictate when and where the audience will consume their products. In addition, online media are interactive, allowing audiences to communicate immediately with the media firm and with fellow audience members. Branding strategies must recognize and take advantage of these circumstances. Conventional news media firms, in particular, have been forced to deal with this new reality of empowered audiences. Renowned media Scholar Robert Picard asserts:

> Traditional Journalism is based on structured relationships, privacy and concealment, property, hierarchy, control, and formality. But the digital world is based on more amorphous relationships, revelation and transparency, sharing, collaboration, empowerment, and informality. Consequently many news organizations have difficulties relating to the public in the digital world and are struggling to adapt.

Another audience challenge for media brands is demographic differences. For example, younger people want their content to play on every new digital platform, especially mobile devices. In addition, research indicates that younger audiences tend to like content that is on-demand, 'bite-sized' and customized to their particular interests. Older audiences, on the other hand, still watch longer 'linear' programme content on conventional TV and cable networks. Many large, well-established media firms realize that they cannot afford to be anchored to any particular format and therefore attempt to satisfy multiple audience preferences. For instance, television programming and social media have become fast friends, transforming how younger audiences watch television. A study conducted by Nielsen Media Research found evidence of a two-way causal influence between TV programme audience size and the degree of Twitter conversation around that programme. Programme producers are experimenting with ways to capitalize on this simultaneous audience activity by participating in the online conversation.

Strong media brands rely on 'repeat business'

Brand management is important particularly for products and services purchased on a routine basis. Cultivating brand-purchasing habits is the way firms enhance *brand loyalty*. Despite the aforementioned empowering effects of digital technology on audience behaviours, researchers know that most media experiences remain habitual. From logging on to a preferred website for the latest news, gossip, scores and weather forecasts to tuning in to a weekly sitcom, drama or reality programme, audience behaviour is highly predictable. Predictability is a good thing from a business perspective. Research studies time and again have demonstrated that strong media brands provide advertisers with highly stable and therefore predictable audiences over time. Common sense supports the idea that it is far easier and less expensive to keep a good customer than to attract a new one, especially in a zero-sum marketplace! This is no less true for media brands seeking audiences. 'Repeat business' from audiences fosters repeat business from advertisers and subscribers.

Cultivating repeat business from audiences can be tricky because people have the twin desires to: (a) experience new things and at the same time; (b) experience what is familiar. Successful media brands must not stagnate but also must not change merely for the sake of change. A longstanding example of brand consistency is the *Tonight Show*. For decades the programme has won its late-night time period, attracting habitual viewers who expect new jokes but not a new format in terms of the opening monologue followed by skits and celebrity interviews, night after night, year after year. The 2010 short-lived, disruptive decision to reschedule the programme in a prime time slot was a ratings bomb. *TV Guide* declared it 'the biggest blunder in television history'.

Of course, refreshing a long-standing brand often is necessary to hold audiences. For example, MTV must cope with an ever-changing young audience that inevitably goes away as it matures. 'Unlike other brands that get a lock on the audience and age with them, we have to shed our skin and reinvent ourselves,' said Stephen K Friedman, president of MTV. The Weather Channel, with its natural emphasis on the science of weather, continues to upgrade its multiplatform presentation. David Clark, president of the channel confesses that: 'As the biggest weather geeks out there, it is totally natural for us to obsess over how weather stories of all kinds are presented and shared.'

Strong media brands cultivate a sustainable niche

At the core of all brand management principles is the concept of *differentiation*. The decades-old assumptions surrounding mass communication have fragmented into the far more complex world of satisfying esoteric needs of specialized or niche audiences. The most important advantage of developing a strong, highly differentiated brand niche is that it discourages consumers from thinking seriously about competing brands. The lack of differentiation leads to the undesirable situation that brand researchers call *equivalent substitutes* in that a customer finds many brands within a product category equally satisfying and therefore, easily substituted. In other words, the product is seen by audiences and advertisers as a commodity and not as a unique brand offering exceptional value. Perceived sameness is the antithesis for good branding.

An example of a media brand that surprisingly has yet to effectively differentiate itself is The Oprah Winfrey Network (OWN), named after the popular syndicated talk-show host. The cable network premiered with a resounding thud on 1 January 2011 and after several major changes in management and content, it remains in a slow death spiral with losses so far exceeding $300 million. Despite her strong personal brand and single-programme success, Oprah could not sustain a 24-hour network, competing with so many other female-oriented channels. Research found that unless Oprah herself was the host, the various programmes on OWN were all too similar to those already found on WE, Lifetime and Oxygen.

As will be offered in more detail later in this chapter, many news organizations are struggling today because audiences have become indifferent as to a preferred source of news.

The essential facts of a news occurrence are perceived as a mere commodity available from any number of acceptable sources.

Strong media brands know the power of intangibles

Concentrating on functional attributes at the expense of the psychological needs of customers often makes a product distant and dull; not *engaging* as some researchers would say. Considerable research addressing consumer-based branding theory has found that the most powerful and enduring brand associations are not based on utilitarian factors but rather on intangibles such as emotional satisfaction. To cultivate a sustainable niche, the expectations of an audience must be understood. Merely stating that audiences want to be 'entertained' or 'informed' is too superficial.

Despite many decades of empirical research and intuitive second guessing, predicting how people will respond to media content remains a daunting task. The source of this frustration is that different people can respond in different ways to the same media experience. Age, gender, education, race, ethnicity and dozens of cultural and lifestyle factors, from hobbies to religious beliefs, can influence the way a person will respond to media exposure. In addition, research has found that often the most important benefits a media brand offers are deeply embedded human desires and needs, such as arousal, companionship, reassurance, self-esteem, catharsis, vicarious escape and even social interaction. The emotional gratifications are as varied as the types of niche content created. Many media brands have a distinct advantage over retail products in creating emotional attachments because, unlike frozen peas or refrigerators, media 'products' typically include real-life people. It is no secret that selecting the cast members of a programme is crucial to it success. This is true even for non-entertainment content; just look at what TV and cable news anchors get paid for their services, which have little to do with their journalistic skills. For example, NBC's Nightly News anchor Brian Williams makes $13 million a year. Why? Because he is authoritative, reassuring, empathetic, approachable and most important, likable.

Unveiling the underlying audience emotional dispositions can be a challenge, typically requiring good research. Relying on purely anecdotal information or worse, the hubris of 'gut instinct' can lead to business calamities. *Bravo!* is an example of a highly successful cable network that invests in sophisticated and continuous audience feedback every week to assist programme producers in adjusting content. It's multiple *Housewife* reality franchises encourage confrontation and emotional excess among stunning and strident women, borrowing from the successful emotional formulas pioneered by scripted TV soap operas.

People often do not want to disclose or are not consciously aware of their true motivations. For example, audiences may be attracted to a particular branded news source because it makes them feel smart, hip or sophisticated in front of other people, but how many individuals would readily divulge these intimacies to a researcher? Instead, audience surveys, personal interviews and focus groups must be carefully structured and administered to tap into these hidden persuaders. The burgeoning and controversial field of 'neuromarketing' boasts that it can probe the subconscious by analysing brainwaves and biochemical activity.

An example of media creators not understanding why audiences like a product is the 2011 short-lived comeback of an iconic TV series from the '70s and '80s, *Charlie's Angels*. The new producers just didn't get it. A critic bemoaned that: 'It's just horribly wrong, with a grim, ultra-serious take that robbed whatever campy/cheesey fun you might have expected from the brand name.' On the other hand, another reprised hit crime drama from the same era, *Hawaii 5-0*, has been a huge success by exploiting the original series' emphasis on Hawaii location shooting and captivating cast members.

Brand extensions

Many companies leverage the familiarity and consumer comfort level of an established brand niche to a new product line in the form of *brand extensions*. A perfect example is the primetime TV franchise *CSI*, which originated in Las Vegas and evolved into *CSI Miami*, *CSI New York* and *CSI Los Angles*. Not all media brand extensions are successful. *The Playboy Club*, airing ever so briefly on NBC a few years ago, received widespread condemnation both from conservative family-oriented watchdog groups and from feminists. More recently, another notable men's magazine brand, *Esquire*, launched its own cable network to mixed reviews.

Another type of media brand extension is the corporate *portfolio* in which a large media firm manages several different subsidiary brands that share a unifying corporate identification. A good media example is the Walt Disney Company, which is the largest media conglomerate in the world in terms of revenue, supporting such well-known brands as the ABC broadcast network; cable television networks such as The Disney Channel, ESPN, A&E Networks, Lifetime and ABC Family, plus motion picture production, publishing, merchandising, and theatre divisions and of course, several Disney World theme parks operating around the world. In some marketing circumstances, such as the introduction of a new animated movie, the corporate Disney brand is used as a strategic selling tool for attracting family-based niche audiences, but in other cases, such as its ESPN Monday Night Football franchise, the association with the Disney corporate brand is largely ignored. This avoidance is not an oversight, but rather a strategic management decision based on a comprehensive understanding of how audiences perceive the Disney brand niche.

Beware of the overly small niche brand

For a media brand to survive and prosper, size matters. Excessive niche programming leads to a point of diminishing returns in which audiences become so small they can't offset the cost of doing business. The Golf Channel makes sense but who would invest in a proposed Chess Channel?

A common but risky branding strategy intended to attract a larger audience is to widen the niche. An example is the audience growth of The History Channel, which seldom emphasizes conventional history topics, such as the life and times of George Washington, but instead, has stretched the brand to include rather unhistorical hit programmes, such as *American Pickers* and *Pawn Stars*. The monster hit series *Breaking Bad*, which follows the exploits of an unassuming high school chemistry teacher who gradually gets drawn into the world of illegal drug dealing and the criminal underworld, aired on AMC – which originally stood for American Movie Classics – but obviously has strayed from a pure Hollywood movie network.

The widening of a niche, however, can jeopardize the clarity of a brand because the meaning or image of the brand becomes so diluted audiences are no longer sure what the brand stands for.

Several years ago, media super sports brand ESPN realized that it had overstepped its brand boundaries when it launched *ESPN Hollywood*, an attempt to reveal how athletes were venturing into movie and television roles. The fan response was dreadful and the series was soon cancelled.

Audiences may be attracted to specific programmes but not necessarily to the wider, all-inclusive network brand. This is not necessarily a bad business situation. The broadcast networks (ABC, CBS, FOX and NBC) for decades have offered a wide range of popular programmes, from scripted sitcoms and dramas to unscripted reality shows and sports, which have had little network brand cohesion.

Network executives will attempt to define an overall brand identity, which sounds very clever in an industry trade article but audiences usually fail to recognize it. A recent national study in the United States found roughly half of the participants could not correctly identify a favourite programme with its parent brand network. One can argue that this is not great corporate branding but the reasoning is more a matter of sales pressure than branding strategy. That is, at the expense of losing a strong overarching network identity, the network sales departments want a wide variety of niche audiences to sell to advertisers. Regardless of this lack of network recognition, audiences claimed to find their favourite shows with little difficulty. Electronic programme guides provided by cable systems or online sources, such as TV Guide.com, help audiences navigate the maze of programme offerings.

While some media niches expand, others contract. An example is the popular cable network FX. For many years it had the reputation as merely a source of tired reruns that aired originally on the Fox broadcast network, but from the early 2000s onwards the channel cultivated a sharper image of adult, edgy, provocative dramas, such as *Sons of Anarchy*, *The Shield*, *Rescue Me* and *Fargo*. As one TV critic once put it: 'Series on FX have balls, no question about it.'

Marketing a media niche can be expensive

The ultimate goal for a media firm should be to cultivate a niche that prospers without exhausting its energies fighting too many similar competitors for the same limited resources. Some media entrepreneurs fail to appreciate that simply occupying a newly created niche is of no value if audiences are not aware of it.

For conventional 'offline' media, such as television and cable, relying entirely on free publicity rarely delivers sufficient traction to launch a new enterprise. Instead, most media firms must purchase advertising from other branded media firms. Commenting on the resources necessary to launch a new autumn TV season, an ABC executive complained that 'It's exhausting, and it's expensive ... We can't stop buying old media, like print and outdoor and radio, but we also need to buy whatever is the new mobile experience or the new digital network.' Social media are becoming viable advertising platforms. People often do not realize that the business model underlying social media giants Facebook, Twitter and LinkedIn is paid advertising.

Aside from paid advertising inserts, social media affords media firms the ability to build relationships directly with audiences, something no amount of pure paid advertising has been able to achieve. For example, the daily news and commentary programme *The Rachel Maddow Show*, airing on MSNBC, has used social media, particularly Facebook, since its inception to engage audiences. Each morning the producers solicit a 'call' for possible stories, essentially making audiences part of the editorial decision-making process. An academic study found that indeed the programme's content is highly correlated with prior social media contributions.

Some internet-based brands, especially news brands, such as TouchVision, Fusion, Vice, and Now This News, have managed to introduce themselves to the world with little or no purchased advertising. Instead, they have exploited free social media opportunities to create online chatter, which evolved into product sampling, which in turn fostered more chatter and so on.

During certain times of the year, the highest-spending advertising clients for some media firms are other media brands, predominantly

TV networks and movie distributors. This phenomenon leads us to a brief look at the art and science of business-to-business brand management.

Strong media brands invest in business-to-business media branding

So far, in our discussion of media brands we have given scant attention to the topic of media businesses having transactions with other media-based businesses. Typically this involves an advertising business model in which the true cash-paying customer is an advertiser represented by an advertising agency or professional media buyer. Media brand expectations from advertisers often are considerably different from those of audiences in that advertisers pay media to reach *potential customers* for their products and services and yet, the brand name and all it stands for can be a powerful ad selling tool for media firms.

Savvy media buyers want more than mere audience ratings and demographic data. They want to see if their product is a comfortable psychological fit with audiences and again, we often are dealing with intangibles. Both buyers and sellers of media invest in sophisticated research designed to reveal consumer attitudes and emotional states. Given this information, media buyers often pay a premium price – beyond the usual cost-per-thousand (CPM) metric – for a highly engaged audience. For instance, Fox News has been a lightning rod for criticism from the political left, which has only emboldened the Fox brand. Craig Moffett, a long-time financial analyst who specializes in cable, maintains the key to Fox News's continued financial strength has been 'the level of passion and engagement' it inspires in its viewers.

In order not to be considered an easily substituted audience commodity by media buyers, a media brand must differentiate itself from the crowd or become victim of ruthless pricing wars among its peers. But even highly distinctive media brands may not be appropriate for certain advertisers. For instance, a chainsaw manufacturer probably will not advertise on the highly popular but female-oriented Bravo or Oxygen cable networks. By definition, branding means exclusion as well as inclusion.

Part two: Case study – branding news organizations

For the last decade news organizations have suffered dramatic losses in revenue, both from subscribers and advertisers. The sad response has been cutbacks, layoffs, buyouts and bankruptcies. Essentially, disruptive digital technology has changed the way the business of news is conducted. Massive cost cutting is not the best long-term solution for a media organization in trouble. The irony is that, while so many news organizations are in a financial tailspin, research shows that the demand for news has never been higher.

While many firms have embraced new revenue-generating business strategies in order to survive and grow, regrettably, news organizations are not at the forefront of this movement. Part of the problem is that historically journalists have distained the very idea that they were associated with a *business* that must attract readers and revenue.

Experiencing a wide-open marketplace of options, audiences are leaving many traditional news originations behind for content providers that better serve their needs, particularly new internet-based companies. Many news media brands have yet to take full advantage of the flexibility, immediacy and interactivity of content that the internet offers. The digital strategy undertaken to date by most print-oriented publishers is to simply transport their newspaper-style content to the web and to mobile devices. This uninspired warmed-over digital fare is disappointing, particularly to younger, tech-savvy audiences. Roughly half of both Facebook and Twitter users 'get their news' from these sites but we must remember that these sites and many other online news aggregators (eg Google News) are not creating news content; they are not reporters. Instead, they are linking audiences to content created by another entity, typically a news organization.

But even new online news sources are struggling to persuade users and advertisers *to pay* for having access to this content. To offset diminishing advertising dollars, some well-established newspaper-based services are experimenting with a hybrid or 'freemium' reader pricing structure in which a limited number of news items are offered free but eventually the website visitor will encounter a limit or 'pay wall', requiring a subscription or short-term usage premium. Naturally, strong brands, such as *The Economist*, *The New York Times* and *The Wall Street Journal* can make this work, but lesser brands run into problems.

Aside from desiring quality news coverage, audiences often seek out commentary from well-respected columnists or bloggers residing at these familiar brands. This exclusive content from familiar 'celebrities' contributes to a brand's journalistic stature and set it apart from ordinary competitors.

While well-intentioned professionals, scholars and pundits clamour for alternative business models, they seldom address the importance of a *brand name*. In fact, the idea of competing brands is hardly addressed directly. Instead, most of the dialogue is about saving the business of serious journalism as a total entity. They fail to appreciate that business models and brand management are co-dependent.

By definition, a *commodity* is a collection of products that are interchangeable, providing the same satisfaction. Regrettably, research has found that most audiences and advertisers today regard news as a commodity that is available from an array of acceptable sources – often for free. Furthermore, only about 35 per cent of Americans have a 'favourite' online news destination and among those who do, over 80 per cent are so indifferent that if the site charged a user fee they would find another source. From a brand management perspective, we can argue that audiences and advertisers are reluctant to pay a premium price for a particular news product because the content lacks *highly differentiated added value*. Because most news competitors are compelled to cover the same major stories, using essentially the same easily obtained news-gathering technologies, creating a viable niche brand is a daunting challenge.

Enhancing operational effectiveness, such as exploring use-generated content, creating apps for tablets and smartphones, updating obsolete reporting equipment, and other best practices are all worthwhile endeavours, but all can be readily copied by competitors. This disconcerting fact essentially neutralizes any sustainable competitive brand advantage for a news organization.

Strong news brands cope with the intertwined demands of editorial, sales and branding

For decades most respected media organizations maintained a management firewall between news content and advertising, but revenue problems are causing this wall to be breached. Today many news organizations are succumbing to the controversial practice of allowing advertisers to present their own long-form messages that look suspiciously like the regular content of the online publication or news programme. The popular jargon today is 'native advertising' and prominent news brands, such as *Forbes*, *New York Times* and MSNBC, have entered this domain. Some offer their own in-house writers and graphic artists to assist advertisers in preparing this content. The Federal Trade Commission recently hosted a workshop on native advertising titled 'Blurred Lines: Advertising or Content?'

Brand marketing professionals also are concerned about possible effects of native advertising on audience perceptions of the news product. The core issue is whether audiences truly recognize that a paid-for section of a publication or newscast is perceived as separate and distinct from surrounding content. In 2013 the highly respected *Atlantic* magazine outraged its loyal readers when it accepted an online native 'advertorial' concerning the rosy future of the Church of Scientology. Then the magazine made things worse by censoring some of the negative reaction that filled up the comments stream following the piece. Ben Kunz, VP of strategic planning at media agency 'Mediassociates', states that: 'Billions of banner ad impressions may annoy readers, but they don't misdirect users by disguising the source of the message – and this is exactly what native does. If publishers and marketers aren't careful, they are going to poison the well of digital ad communications by breaking consumer trust.'

Can serious journalism survive?

The internet has brought forth an unprecedented flowering of news and information. But it also has destabilized the old business models that have supported quality journalism for decades. Good journalists across the country are losing their jobs or adjusting to a radically different news environment. Can serious journalism survive in the digital media business world? Yes. We will take a brief look at five examples, each deploying different brand strategies but all recognizing that presenting mere facts over multiple platforms is just the beginning.

The Economist

While the weekly news magazine business in general is suffering, *The Economist* contradicts this trend by maintaining high subscription fees, high advertising rates and ever-higher circulation. From a brand management perspective, *The Economist* exudes a certain cachet that makes readers feel they are part of an elite club, yet anyone can join. As one executive stated: 'The brand's status makes those who have bought into it feel good about themselves. People want to be seen reading *The Economist*. Its wonderfully brazen mission statement encapsulates its brand image. "To take part in a severe contest between intelligence, which presses forward, and an unworthy, timid ignorance obstructing our progress."'

Politico

While *The Economist* is over 150 years old and has an international distribution, the political news source Politico began operations in 2007 and focuses exclusively on Washington, DC politics. Technically it is a non-profit organization but still accepts advertising. Going up against a dozen long-established brands, this upstart news organization quickly has become the go-to source for reliable, insightful information about Congress, lobbying, media and the Presidency. Its stated mission is 'Driving the Conversation' offering accurate, hourly distillations of what and how Washington thinks. Many readers claim they read it 'obsessively' during the course of the day because it offers exclusive behind-the-scenes insights about political power brokers. To some people, this knowledge is irresistible.

The Huffington Post

The Huffington Post is a hugely popular online news aggregator and blog founded by Arianna Huffington in 2005, offering 'a mixture of advocacy and investigative in-your-face journalism' about US politics, entertainment, style, world news, technology and comedy. *The Post* has earned a reputation for hosting dozens of well-known bloggers, from politicians and celebrities to academics and policy experts. The site also publishes columns by recognized specialists in a wide range of fields. *The Post*'s highly sophisticated computerized content management system (CMS) continually scrutinizes the internet for activity that is likely to go viral. A breaking story that appears to be the next big thing people will be talking about tomorrow probably is already presented on *The Huffington Post* today. An executive editor states that their role in publishing 'is to think fast and to be fast'. In short, *The Huffington Post*'s brand image is all about what's hot, right now.

Fox News Channel

Always controversial but always number one, at least for the past dozen years or more, Fox News Channel positions itself as the politically conservative alternative 24/7 cable news network. For almost 20 years CNN had a comfortable monopoly on cable news but in 1996 Fox News was conceived with no reputation at all for journalism. As former Fox News President Roger Ailes proclaimed: 'We had no studios, no programs, no talent, no ideas, no news-gathering capabilities... no news history... and no distribution.' The new network cleverly portrayed its CNN rival as stodgy, pedantic, passionless and insufferably liberal. Without actually using such derogatory language, Fox quickly positioned its brand as a 'scrappy underdog' in its crusade against the alleged 'elite' mainstream news media in general. And the rest is history.

ESPN

We began this chapter using ESPN as an example of a media brand and although sports are not necessarily 'serious news' in the conventional sense, ESPN does provide much-wanted information to audiences. In addition to offering exclusive copyrighted sporting events, ESPN also has earned a reputation for giving audiences a bold and often irreverent look at athletes, teams and the business of sports. The network stables a variety of distinct on-air personalities who are not afraid to have some fun as they present the 'serious' facts and images of the game. These attributes collectively, endow ESPN with intangible added value that few other sports media can match. Robert Siegel and James Andrew Miller co-wrote *Those Guys Have All the Fun: Inside the World of ESPN* claim 'ESPN changed everything, both in substance and in tone: a tone that says, "yes we're obsessed with sports, but no, it really isn't that important. We're having a good time telling you about it".'

Managing media brands is a special challenge

Most media firms today operate in a highly competitive, ever-fragmenting, zero-sum marketplace in which most technology-based innovations can be copied readily by competitors. Unlike most retail consumer goods, such as groceries, restaurants and auto parts, the consumer sampling of media brands is remarkably easy, requiring no more than a mere click of a TV remote control, computer mouse or a tap of a finger on a tablet. Within minutes, an individual can evaluate scores of media products from wherever and whenever he or she wants. And these media consumers are not zombies staring at blank screens, but rather thinking individuals seeking *content* that will satisfy any number of rational and irrational needs. To withstand the daily barrage of product choices, media brands must generate extraordinary content that transcends technology, defies imitation and engages both audiences and advertisers.

Biography

Walter McDowell is an Associate Professor Emeritus at the University of Miami, United States. Before entering academia, Professor McDowell spent over 20 years in commercial television and media consulting. After earning his doctorate in 1998 from the University of Florida, and teaching several years at Southern Illinois University, he joined the faculty of the University of Miami, concentrating primarily on media management and economics. He has published in an array of peer-reviewed academic journals including *The Journal of Media Economics*, *The International Journal of Media Management* and *The Journal of Media Business Studies*. In addition, McDowell has authored or co-authored several books serving both academia and the media industry, including *Broadcasting in America: A survey of electronic media*, *The Television Industry: A complete guide*, *Branding TV: Principles and practices*, *Troubleshooting Audience Research* and coedited *Understanding Broadcast and Cable Finance: A primer for the non-financial manager.* The Association for Education in Journalism and Mass Communication (AEJMC) awarded Professor McDowell its annual Award for Excellence and Innovation in the Teaching of Media Management and Economics.

Brand not bland
The financial services challenge

MIKE SYMES

At first glance, the financial services industry appears to be something of a paradox. On the one hand, it stands out as the most unique of all industries. On the other, it looks like a sector in danger of complete commoditization.

This chapter looks closely at financial services brands that take the road less travelled. These are organizations that are no longer prepared to settle for the me-too. Firms that are emphatically proud to stand out by standing for something. Companies with a cause. Institutions with attitude.

Before we look at individual firms whose brands are breaking the mould, let us first consider what makes the industry unique and the challenges that have shaped the financial landscape today.

Unlike a physical product, finance is *intangible*. You can neither taste nor touch it, yet it has the power to transform the macro and micro economic landscape like no other industry. From building the foundations of global economies to securing the homes in which we live, financial services is as versatile as it is vital.

The market is also extremely *diverse*. Financial services is therefore not so much a category, as a number of distinctive and clearly defined segments, ranging from retail, commercial, wholesale and mortgage banking, through to securitization, capital markets, insurance, investment and asset management, broker/dealer and real estate to mention just a few.

Each has its own individual stakeholder maps and channels. Each has its own identifiable sets of customer triggers and plays to known but discernibly different behaviours and responses.

Due to its sheer diversity, the financial services industry is often described as 'an inch wide and a mile deep'.

The wider financial market has become *polarized* between multi-jurisdictional, multi-product players for whom scale is everything and niche market operators, whose specialist focus and expertise address customer needs in ever more granular ways.

Financial transactions typically have a differentiated *risk-based* dynamic, which is mirrored in pricing and reward. As a consequence, financiers expend as much time and effort 'buying' as they do selling, eg corporate lenders conduct a thorough due diligence process before they underwrite a facility.

A reputation you can bank on?

Longevity, once a core characteristic of the industry, is no longer the arbiter for success, nor can it be considered a credible differentiator. After all, Northern Rock Building Society was formed in 1965, Lehman Brothers in 1850, Washington Mutual in 1889. The rest, as they say, is history.

Our financial system is predicated on trust and the delivery of promises. However, the severe challenges that rocked the industry to the very foundations of the fiscal cliff have resulted in a critical paradigm-shift – a fundamental change in the way firms conduct and compete for business.

Although consumer sentiment is improving slightly (Edelman Trust Barometer, 2013), disenchantment and distrust of financial institutions still lives on.

As Robert Phillips, UK CEO of Edelman, said: 'Trust is an entry that does not appear on a bank's balance sheet. As an important asset, perhaps it should.'

As a result, almost half of consumers in the United Kingdom, Germany, France and the United States feel their bank does not value them (Ipsos MORI, 2013).

From the cashier to the chief executive, every financial organization has a responsibility to live its stated values to recapture trust.

However, the values held by financial firms are often disarmingly similar. Ask 10 financial salespeople what their firm's USPs are and at least half of them will trade generalities, such as they 'believe in fostering long-term relationships' or that they 'demonstrate genuine flexibility in tailoring facilities to meet their customers' needs'.

James M McCormick, president of First Manhattan Consulting Group, certainly found this to be true from the thousands of 'mystery shops' he has commissioned with bank employees from the frontline. His researchers always ask a simple question: 'As a customer, why should I choose your bank over the competition?'

Two-thirds of the time, McCormick noted, the employees have no answer to that question; they either say nothing or, in his words, 'make something up on the fly.'

Despite the inherent diversity and complexity of the industry, financial services organizations are commonly viewed as being identical to one another.

No wonder a banking CEO once remarked that he 'could put a credit card' between his organization and his major competitors, so slim was the difference between them.

As Frank Capek once observed, 'The challenge is that most banks have a long legacy of product-centric, "everything for everybody" ways of thinking. This leads to decision-making and resource commitments that reinforce "better sameness" rather than true differentiation.'

Herein lies the problem. Merely providing 'a service' is a table stake, simply the price of market entry.

Technology continues to be a strong enabler for innovation among early adopter/challenger organizations in the financial arena. Is that sufficient to create a sustainable leadership position, however leading edge, or does differentiation demand more?

Low cost of market entry and high speed of replication would suggest not, meaning that new products can reach the high street with similar velocity to a fake brand factory in fashion week.

In financial services marketing, there needs to be something more than product and technology. And that is the *brand*.

Comply but don't conform

One would have thought that the predictable moves towards more stringent regulation and calls for compliance would stifle brand creativity. That it would make the financial services brands less vibrant. It would appear logical that the demands to increase capital adequacy, greater transparency, heightened privacy, security and reporting requirements would curb brand innovation.

Nothing, in fact, could be further from the truth.

Sameness-shunning stories

The signs are encouraging. There have never been so many sparks of change from new market entrants or so many established players looking to regain trust and market confidence as a result of ground-up reinvention.

The financial services brands that stand out achieve results by going far beyond the essential table stakes of 'flexibility' and 'tailored services' to offer a clear and inspiring purpose that lights up their customers.

Conventional wisdom dictates that the secret to successful marketing and communications is to develop a big idea for a campaign. A handful of bold organizations have been able to turn that concept on its head and develop a campaign for a big idea.

The financial industry is ripe for innovative new firms to come in and rock the status quo. It's time to meet one.

Oxygen Finance: A breath of fresh air

Very occasionally you come across a big idea that is so disruptive and has such extraordinary potential that you can't help but become absorbed by its progress.

Oxygen Finance is just such a business.

Oxygen is on its way to creating the world's largest business-to-business payments network.

Why? Because it is based on the transformational core principle that *spend* is an organization's greatest untapped asset. The new brand is wrapped with the tagline: 'Monetizing Spend' and the corporate identity conveys a next generation solution.

Before Oxygen Finance, the payables space was possibly the last place where CFOs would go looking for new ways of generating income. The act of turning a cash flow liability into a directly income-generative asset is therefore nothing short of game changing.

Oxygen solves a number of the key issues faced by organizations today – late payment to suppliers, access to new income and inefficient supply chains.

The Oxygen Early Payment programme creates a better way of doing business, enabling organizations to pay their suppliers early in exchange for a rebate, which is then returned to the buyer as additional income.

The Oxygen Finance brand is known for creating a 'win–win' relationship between the buyer and supplier that is based on a positive financial outcome for both parties – not just words of encouragement.

This has resulted in market-leading supplier adoption rates in excess of 60 per cent and the development of even closer supply chain relationships.

Suppliers embrace the Oxygen Finance solution because they value the opportunity to increase their liquidity (the key to their business health), helping stabilize and grow their business.

The systemic injection of liquidity into the supply chain generates greater confidence and business stability, improving the financial strength of the suppliers and securing a stronger supply chain.

Group CEO, Mark Hoffman, was formerly Founder of groundbreaking e-commerce company, Commerce One and Sybase, which grew to become one of the largest software companies of the 1990s.

He commented:

> The leaders in any market of the future are those who grasp the fact that supplier relationships and networked participation create sustainable competitive advantage. Shareholder value is not established by just short-term cash gain from protracted payment. It is built through close working relationships and driving value through the supply chain.'

First Direct: The unexpected bank

There are a few 'light bulb' moments that have sparked radical change in the banking industry. It's no coincidence that the same industry pioneer, Mike Harris, started two of them, First Direct and Egg.

Mike created the world's first bank without branches at First Direct, which centred on its highly responsive 24/7 customer telephone support. He followed this with the launch of 'Egg', the trailblazing internet bank designed for people who wanted to save, invest, borrow or buy insurance on the web.

Typical of any radical innovation, the media questioned First Direct's idea of 'always on' banking. One leading newspaper referred to it as 'a service for bored insomniacs'. That was, of course, before customers started signing up in their droves.

The reason why customers stayed and recommended others wasn't just that they valued the notion of 24/7 banking. It was due to the clear articulation of what the bank most wanted to be known for, creating 'heroic customer service, leaving people totally taken care of'.

Widely regarded as one of the most progressive financial providers in the world, First Direct has also been rated as the top financial brand for taking care of its customers, scoring 84 per cent and top marks for its ability to deal with issues (Which?, 2013).

The company's new tagline, 'The Unexpected Bank', reinforces First Direct's credentials as a challenger brand coming up against traditional high street banks.

A duck-billed platypus was chosen to be the 'star' of the brand's advertising relaunch. The character was chosen to symbolize a 'different kind of bank', harking back to the 'quirky' and 'irreverent' elements of the brand that the bank has fostered from its inception.

As the character says: 'They do things differently. They're not into that automated recording malarkey – you get through to a friendly human who gets things sorted.'

First Direct recognizes that it is 'difficult to imagine what makes banking with First Direct so special unless you've actually had the experience'. The website, in its instantly identifiable black and white livery, asks: 'How many other banks come with a satisfaction guarantee? We'll give you £100 if you like us, £100 if you don't.'

So certain is First Direct that its service is better than anyone else's, if you're not happy banking with them after six months, they will help you move to any bank you like and give you £100 for your trouble.

First Direct's online Innovation Lab harnesses crowdsourcing to gain deeper, richer customer insights both to fine tune the product roadmap and build brand awareness: 'The First Direct Lab is all about getting you involved. It's a place where you can tell us your thoughts on the new projects and hot topics we're working on: we might need a new release or product testing, or perhaps there's a burning research question we need answering.'

Just in the same way we are able to pick our own playlists, First Direct challenged the status quo by empowering consumers to select and define their own 'taste' in financial services.

As Mike Harris has said, the challenge for financial services brands is all 'about creating a brand experience and a culture that is addictive, infectious and, ultimately, irresistible'.

Out-local the nationals and out-national the locals

A business that knows all about engineering brand experience for its customers is Wells Fargo. From the Gold Rush to the early 20th century, Wells Fargo offered both banking and express stagecoach delivery. Today, it is the world's most valuable banking brand with a brand value of $26 billion (BrandFinance® Banking 500, 2013).

Yet this achievement has nothing to do with transactions or getting bigger for the sake of it.

Wells Fargo's vision statement is 'We want to satisfy all our customers' financial needs and help them succeed financially.' This is not simply a framed slogan pinned to the boardroom wall. It is as relevant today as when it was written more than 20 years ago and at 88 characters is as succinct enough to tweet today.

The focus goes beyond strategy to execution in building lifelong relationships 'one customer at a time'.

The line, 'We'll never put the stagecoach ahead of the horses', is evocative of the bank's traditions and clearly illustrates the principle that the bank makes money because of its focus on serving customers, not the other way around.

Customer penetration is an important factor in the bank's continued success. According to one report (Forbes, 2013), Wells Fargo's financial advisers 'on average cross-sell 10 products per household making it a leader among wealth management firms'.

Wells Fargo looks to 'out-local the nationals' with North America's most extensive distribution system for financial services, a vast 'decentralized' network of over 9,000 local stores and 12,000 ATMs, several of which are situated within community convenience strongholds such as supermarkets. The bank also seeks to 'out-national the locals' through strong product diversity, providing a breadth and depth of banking, insurance, investments, mortgage and consumer and commercial finance services at one-stop.

The bank's social media strategy is clearly aligned to its vision: 'Finding new ways to communicate and helping you to succeed financially.' This is supported by detailed public guidelines and rules of engagement for commentators to ensure that the messaging execution stays true to brand values.

Wells Fargo has been blogging actively since 2006 and has seven blogs, each of which combines authoritative content with a personal tone of voice: Beyond Today^{SM} Blog, Wells Fargo Environmental Forum, The Wells Fargo Blog, AdvantageVoice®, Guided By History®, The Student LoanDown^{SM} and Life in Balance. Wells Fargo has won the Social Media for Consumers award for the third consecutive year (Global Finance Magazine, 2013).

It really is that simple

From a long-established banking brand to a new breed of digital 'non-bank', the market is nothing if it's not diverse. Both traditional and tech finance firms have their challenges.

In a study from Javelin Strategy & Research, one in every four attempts to open an account via digital channels is unsuccessful (Bank Systems & Technology, 2013).

With Simple, however, opening an account really is as easy as the brand name suggests. Customers are guided through the process effortlessly and intuitively with screen shots, just as if they were having the process explained to them by a friend.

But then Simple's brand promise stands for a 'worry-free alternative' to banking. It has smart budgeting and savings tools built right into the account automatically, all accessible via web, iPhone, and Android.

CEO and founder Josh Reich, elaborates that Simple is there 'to help consumers worry less about money by building a new banking brand that is modern, cool, transparent, and trustworthy'.

Unusually – and this really is worth a double take – Simple doesn't profit from fees. Which means no irritating overdraft or account maintenance charges and no unwanted hidden surprises. Unlike banks, Simple just doesn't believe its right to penalize customers for making mistakes.

To understand Simple, it is important to recognize that even though it is seeking to establish itself as a banking brand, it is not actually a bank. Rather, it is an intuitive online interface that sits on top of a back-end system powered by several FDIC-insured partner banks.

So how does Simple make money? Quite simply, it shares in its bank partners' interest margin.

Simple has also reinvented reporting. Rather than showing the customer a balance, it shows them a more meaningful 'safe to spend' figure, taking into account regular expenses.

Savings aren't immune to the Simple touch, which has reimagined the savings experience through applying gamification techniques. In the 'game', the player is motivated to maintain savings goals by giving them specific names and a committed plan.

As a digital 'bank' without branches, Simple has to work harder to be engaging and it shows in a tone of voice that's breezily confident without being brash.

Customers have the ability to search their entire history to see how they are spending and what they have saved. The intuitive app helps customers manage their expenditure 'diary' and allows memos and photographs to be appended.

Simple even uses Twitter as a two-way customer service tool enabling queries to be resolved promptly – and publicly.

Somewhat ironically, the Simple proposition is complex to execute, otherwise everyone would be doing it. From the friendly brand informality that Simple has introduced to the elegant and modern customer interface, a brand vision like this isn't easy for competitors to pull off.

Turning banking on its head

Another firm, which is ploughing the digital superhighway, is Knab, which if you haven't guessed, is 'bank' spelled backwards. Knab is a new, 'socially conscious' Dutch internet bank with ambition. Backed by the global insurer Aegon, Knab is seeking to turn the banking industry on its head in Holland.

In its launch TV commercial, Knab christens a champagne bottle by smashing the bow of a boat against it, reversing the tradition. The memorable ad, which concludes, 'We see banking a different way', illustrates the paradigm shift of putting the customer – and not the product – at the focal point of all operations.

The bank has a compelling blog, 'Knab Live' but takes its level of interaction to another level by encouraging one-to-one dialogue. Knab provides its customers with a digital office, facilitating live video chat with expert advisers.

The popular 'Red Line' dashboard app instantly shows overdraft customers how they can plan more effectively and how far 'in the red' they will need to go during the month.

Knab's smart back-to-front brand thinking succeeds in making its point economically and with a distinctive style of its own.

FRANK: Cool for cash

To be totally frank, nobody would ever expect to hear the words 'cool', 'cute' or 'wild' associated with a banking brand. However, that is exactly how a bank in Singapore is regarded by the thousands of 18–30 year olds who are clamouring to sign up.

Honest, sincere, reliable, smart and stylish, FRANK by OCBC (it even sounds like a fashion label) is no ordinary bank. OCBC already looks after 26 per cent of the total Generation-Y market in Singapore and this figure is rising thanks to FRANK.

At FRANK, young people immediately enter a smart fashion conscious, ice-cool world reminiscent of an Apple Store.

Here, they are invited to explore and interact with the media on racks on the walls. Instead of iPads or music, they can select a FRANK Debit Card from over 120 exclusive designs: 'Cute, hot, quirky, retro or wild. Which one suits your personality, whim or fancy? You can even change your card to a new design whenever you feel like it.'

There are no intimidating suited banking teams here – casually dressed staff 'hang out' with the crowds and are on hand to help answer questions.

The stripped-out website doesn't even feature an 'about us' section. Why? Because at FRANK, it's all about the customer, not the bank.

FRANK's website promotes 'cash rebates all year round' and offers a range of privileges and discounts on public transport and online fashion purchases. Open an account and you get a free, designed laptop sleeve, apply for a tuition loan and you receive a voucher to the latest movie.

The central brand ethos is: 'Frank is about empowering you to do the things you want in your life. That's why is pays to be a friend of Frank.' It does pay too. Introduce your friends and you'll all get $50 worth of Ben & Jerry's ice cream completely free!

'Frank Tips' tread exactly the right balance of being friendly, helpful and educational but are never condescending: 'Everyone knows that using credit makes buying things easier, but few know that overspending could damage your credit score.'

Saving is encouraged by the use of 'Savings Jars' which enable Gen-Ys to ring-fence cash for specific goals. Interestingly, these funds can't be accessed by ATM, keeping their savings safe.

Both the offline and online environments created by FRANK didn't happen by accident. They followed months of painstaking ethnographic research. It is paying off.

Most financial institutions are good at handling accounts for high net worth individuals. What FRANK has achieved, where thousands of banks have failed, is to get young people engaged with saving, help make them more financially independent and put them in control of their finances. Now, you have to admit, that is pretty cool.

Love your bank at last

Driven by an unrelenting passion to provide unparalleled customer service is Metro Bank, Britain's first new high street bank in over a century.

The bank's founder, Vernon W Hill, II is the man who built Commerce Bancorp from scratch into a top US bank and made $400 million when he sold out.

Brand is vital according to Mr Hill, a theme that dominates his book, *Fans Not Customers: How to create growth companies in a no growth world.*

He explains: 'Great businesses create fans. To build such a business, you need three things. You need a differentiated model that is clear to the customer and to the staff. Then you build a culture that is pervasive and reinforces the model – in too many businesses the model and culture are opposed. Finally, you execute the model and you do this fanatically – and I mean fanatically.'

Mr Hill sets out to amaze his customers with a unique brand of 'retailtainment', the art of engaging customers and creating moments of magic, so every customer leaves with a smile.

The brand promise starts with being ultra-convenient. Unlike most banks, Metro Bank understands that most people have to go to work. So they open at times when it's convenient for the customer (long before and after other banks have closed their doors), including Sundays.

Metro Bank offers on the spot credit and debit cards and cheque books, free coin counting at every store (Metro Bank Magic Money Machines™), lollipops for children and they always keep a specially friendly welcome for the family pet. Customers can also use their debit and credit cards overseas without any charge from Metro Bank, whether they are withdrawing cash from an ATM or at point of sale.

Metro Bank always puts the 'Grand' into Grand Openings. Stores, as they are known at Metro Bank, are subject to a fanfare launch as customers are invited to 'Join the Revolution' with a procession of stilt walkers, a Dixieland jazz band, jugglers and buckets of popcorn.

The razzamatazz doesn't detract from the serious intent to win the hearts of the customer. As Vernon Hill says, 'This is a retail company that happens to be a bank'.

With the bold brand promise of 'No Stupid Fees, No Stupid Hours', maybe it is time to 'Love Your Bank at Last'.

The world's greatest bank

Another bank, which puts the customer experience right at the centre of its brand dial, is Umpqua Bank. There's something incredibly compelling about this brand. Maybe it's the message, 'The World's Greatest Bank' against the Google search description that catches the eye. Possibly it's the 'Slow Banking' philosophy that has so captivated and inspired its founders. Or the fact that the bank has appeared in *Fortune* magazine's 100 Best Companies to work for three years in a row.

As to whether the 'greatest bank' suffix is a reality or hyperbole, only its customers can decide. However, what is abundantly clear is that Umpqua Bank is different to the core.

Founded as a community bank in the Northwestern United States, to provide services for local loggers and farmers, the traditional roots of community prosperity are central to the brand essence.

The 'slow movement' is a fascinating phenomenon. It is a reaction to the notion that faster is always better. It's not about doing everything at a snail's pace but about doing everything at the right speed.

This philosophy has culminated in the reinvention of the humble bank branch into vibrant hubs that say more about celebrating community rather than tracking transactions.

The branches, which look and feel more like boutique hotels or smart cafés than they do banking halls, are opened up for the whole community to enjoy.

Far from being quiet, cold and uninvolving, at Umpqua Bank the humanity of interaction shines through. Here you can sit at a community table, surf the internet, read a paper, enjoy a free cup of coffee and yes – even shop for banking products. Certainly, you will see small businesses and housing associations running meetings, but you are just as likely to see groups gathering for art and yoga classes!

A brand that breathes community to this degree is unusual and unforgettable.

Extended credit

Unforgettable is certainly a word that can be attributed to the next market entrant. For the personification of a fearless market challenger you need look no further than Virgin Group boss, Richard Branson.

His Twitter feed conveys his indefatigable spirit: 'Tie-loathing adventurer and thrill seeker, who believes in turning ideas into reality. Otherwise known as Dr Yes @ virgin!'

Virgin Money timed its launch to perfection at the height of the banking crisis to provide much-needed consumer trust and by announcing it was on a quest to make banking better.

They mounted a bid to engage consumers in a category that many people find confusing and have a low interest in. Known as 'EBO' – 'Everyone Better Off', the guiding brand principle was unveiled at launch.

By everyone, Virgin Money means all of its stakeholders – from customers, staff, society and partners to shareholders. The company also gives something back by investing some of its profits in not-for-profit online fundraising website, virginmoneygiving.com, which has helped raise more than £15 million for good causes.

Advertising focuses on 'banking with a bit of soul', hitting out directly in response to significant above the line activity from rivals TSB and Lloyds Bank.

Other companies that have focused on brand extension into offering financial services include Marks & Spencer, Sainsbury's and Tesco, leveraging their brand familiarity, reputations and trust.

Above the call of duty – a mission to serve

USAA is the top performing financial services brand (Clear Brand Desire study, 2013) and is ranked as the US's 15th most desirable brand across all categories.

The company was formed in 1922 by 25 army officers who found that most local insurance companies saw military personnel as potentially too mobile and too risky. Today, about 95 per cent of active-duty US military officers are USAA members.

USAA is more than just another financial services provider. In an industry perceived for its indifference to the customer, USAA offers 'best-in-class service based on military values' and this is reflected in its cultural principles, entitled 'My Commitment to Service'.

The company has a heightened sense of mission, which is at the heart of its enviable brand reputation: 'We're committed to serving our military and veterans who have honorably served and their families.'

When the military mobilizes, USAA mobilizes. That's how they see their role when insuring fighter pilots, tank commanders and even astronauts.

Military efficiency is applied to the multi-disciplinary, cross-divisional working on Innovation Lab projects, helping to eliminate silos that are so commonly associated with financial services.

Leading edge expert systems and deployment of sophisticated image processing technology allows USAA to serve its customers better.

The success of its social media presence stems from the fact that its members want to hear from others like themselves. User-generated content facilitates the sharing of these authentic customer stories.

Niche-orientation, affinity, empathy and the ability to walk a mile in their customers' boots, marks out USAA from many other financial services brands.

That memorable meerkat

As we have established, to avoid competing purely on price, brand differentiation in financial services is critical. If you can effectively differentiate a price comparison website (whose sole purpose is to disintermediate the branded insurance market), then you can do it for just about anybody.

CamparetheMarket.com was in an unenviable space. Occupying position four in a market of four and competing for market share is challenging for any brand.

In a market as homogeneous as insurance comparison, in which the 'rate is the rate is the rate', consumer buying decisions are traditionally based on a combination of price and perception of the selected insurer's brand.

If that isn't challenging enough, people only insure their cars once a year. So how do you stay top of mind?

More particularly, how did ComparetheMarket.com become the most memorable household name brand in such a me-too market?

An appearance on TV from a little animated meerkat character was about to change everything.

Step forward 'Aleksandr Orlov' an aristocratic meerkat with a Russian accent who was to become an instant hit with the public. He complains to the viewer that his own site, CompareTheMeerkat.com is becoming completely clogged up by people trying to find cheap car insurance from ComparetheMarket.com. His website explains in pigeon English: 'Introduce the comparemabob. Our unique and innovative comparison engine. Please enjoy for compare many different types of meerkat. If you are look for cheap insurance you are in wrong place – please exit immediately! Is very easy to use, just choose which meerkat you think score highest in each comparison, simples!'

Aleksandr has not rested on his laurels. In a brilliantly executed integrated social media campaign, accounts were created in his name on Facebook and Twitter and have gained many thousands of followers.

The popularity of the collectible meerkat toys given away with insurance policies and the memetic line, 'Simples!' have become things of advertising legend that will be talked about affectionately for generations.

Shaping wealth for generations

From modest beginnings, the five sons of Mayer Amschel Rothschild founded banking houses in Frankfurt, London, Paris, Vienna and Naples. They achieved renown as the most important and most successful bankers in the world.

Today, Rothschild Wealth Management & Trust continues to serve high-profile clients with discretion and guidance based on generations of experience.

The 'Five Arrows', an enduring symbol of the Rothschild name and an essential element of the brand identity have an interesting story. Moritz Oppenheim, the 'painter of the Rothschilds' sketched the story told by Plutarch of Scilurus who, on his deathbed, asked his sons (five are depicted by Oppenheim) to break a bundle of arrows. When they all failed, he showed them how easily they could be broken one by one, cautioning them that their strength as a family lay in their unity.

The Rothschild name has long been associated with appreciation of culture and patronage of the arts and it is this that has fundamentally influenced Rothschild Wealth Management & Trust's brand.

The Rothschilds have given an estimated 50,000 works of art to public institutions and printed and digital media features art from the Rothschild archives. One of the finest single pieces of art from a Rothschild collection, Vermeer's The Astronomer, is a treasure among treasures at the Louvre.

Rothschild Wealth Management & Trust uses art and objets d'art from its own archive, to create a unique written and visual language.

The brand proposition, 'shaping wealth for generations', is both a link to Rothschild's illustrious past and compellingly engaging for wealthy clients today. As such, it helps private bankers across the world to tell the Rothschild story.

The bank that loves to prank

The last word has to go to a bank that has created such immense and intense media and social buzz that it is impossible to ignore them.

National Australia Bank, whose tagline is 'More give, less take', can't stop rolling out viral guerrilla marketing stunts to promote their brand promise of a 'fair value exchange'.

The campaigns have successfully underpinned NAB's competitive brand positioning with every new execution as part of an elaborate and sustained switch campaign.

It all started with an 'accidental' tweet from one of NAB's official corporate accounts, setting the twittersphere abuzz when the message broke: 'Sooooo stressed out. Have to make a tough decision and I know I'll probably hurt someone's feelings! Arrggghhh.'

On Valentine's Day 2011, NAB declared its intention to 'break up with the other banks'. Central to the campaign was the offer to pay customer fees if they switch mortgages from Commonwealth or Westpac to NAB.

The company's YouTube account describes the flavour of the campaign succinctly: 'It's over now. And it's out there. It really is over for NAB and the other banks and we want everyone to know. That's why we covered the front of our house with the message. At NAB we've broken up with CommBank, Westpac and ANZ. Why? Well, for a long time now we've been thinking and acting differently to the other major Australian banks. Now we've grown apart. We've just got nothing in common with them anymore.'

NAB printed a lengthy 'Dear John' letter in every major newspaper in the country and blew it up into a three-storey banner on the front of its headquarters.

Banners were flown over rivals' buildings declaring the relationship over. Pianists were hired to play break-up songs outside their offices, while actors pretending to be competitors played out dramatic break-up scenes.

In today's media saturated world, it is hard enough to gain a consumer's attention for 30 seconds. To sustain it for months, even years, is an act worth following.

Another high-profile publicity stunt saw two members of NAB's banking team tied to a lamppost in Sydney's Belmore Park and Melbourne's Southbank, illustrating NAB's 'lack of popularity' among its rivals.

NAB's website fulfils the pay-off for the campaign: 'We think our actions are driving their interest rates down, forcing them to come up with special deals, and generally making them be more competitive. So customers are enjoying better, fairer and more competitive banking. Should you break up with your bank?'

The 4 Rs of financial branding

We have seen some diverse brand stories, from trailblazing traditional market leaders to the charge of the challengers. The 4 Rs bring together the distinct and ideally balanced attributes shared by all successful financial brands:

- Relevant.
- Remarkable.
- Reputational.
- Real.

Relevant

Creating brand relevance seems obvious. However, sustaining it and staying true to the brand essence day-in, day-out can prove challenging, particularly with all of the regulatory distractions facing the industry today.

With the unrelenting mergers and acquisitions in the financial sector, it is easy for a founder's vision to get lost and become foggy along the way. Ultimately, as we have seen from the above case studies, brand relevance transcends the transactional. It's all about clarity of purpose aligned to customers' needs and consistently executed.

Remarkable

Perhaps surprisingly, for all the talk of homogeneity, there are numerous instances in which financial firms have created markedly differentiated brands as the examples have shown.

Some we have seen are remarkable for ripping up the rule books and crushing conventions, others have built a cause or big idea that they and their customers share a deep belief in, and then there are those who have shown a zeal for customer service that motivates, inspires and sometimes even makes us smile.

Being remarkable is more than just being noticed. It is about being remarked upon and letting the customers do the talking, enabling brand messages to shine out as never before.

Reputational

On the face of a dollar bill is the phrase, 'In God We Trust', on the front of a £10 note, it states the words 'I Promise'. Trust, like respect, is earned and re-earned every day through living brand values in thought, word and deed. Regain that trust and financial services firms that don't think in traditional terms (or make the mistake of measuring themselves against peers from the same industry) are capable of building substantial fan-bases. In turn, these fans will reward them through becoming active and vocal brand advocates.

Real

In this age of transparency and social networks, where all of organizations' actions and motivations are laid bare, only those companies that are authentic will succeed.

If the brand story doesn't ring true or is superficial, because the company doesn't really 'own' it, then customers and employees will see through it.

Those financial services organizations that live their brand values will win hearts, of far greater value than wallets.

Customers, partners and other stakeholders are increasingly informed, empowered and discerning about what they read and look at. Financial firms must talk to them authentically and originally at brand belief level, without the artificiality of marketing and PR boundaries. Get it right and they will tell that brand story again and again.

Biography

Mike Symes is Chief Executive of Financial Marketing Limited (www.financialmarketing.com), a multi-award winning, specialist marketing and branding agency.

Mike is recognized as a financial services branding strategist, communications expert, marketing author and international speaker.

A classically educated marketer, Mike's move into financial services saw him rise quickly to become head of communications for Woodchester Crédit Lyonnais, where he set up their in-house agency, then ultimately to become Vice-President and Marketing Director of Bank of New York Financial, before starting his own group of agencies.

Mike has a passion for branding and communications, drawing on 25 years' top-level experience in transforming financial organizations and building global iconic brands.

Mike has been awarded the Freedom of the City of London, one of the oldest surviving traditional ceremonies still in existence today. He is also Chairman of FIDES, the trusted independent networking and referral group for premier providers of products and services to financial organizations.

References

Bank Systems & Technology (2013) [Online forum, http://www.banktech .com] Javelin Strategy & Research, How To Upgrade Online And Mobile Account Opening For An Omnichannel Era

BrandFinance® Banking 500, 2013 (report)

Clear Brand Desire study, From Desire to Impact (2013) http://www. brand-desire.com/

Edelman Trust Barometer (2013) Annual Global Study

Forbes (2013) quoted in *Cracking the Cross-sell*, Andrew Starke, *Asia-Pacific Banking & Finance*, 5(10) Nov/Dec 2013

Ipsos MORI (2013) Ipsos MORI research, commissioned by GMC Software Technology

Which? (2013) Are You Being Served? (survey), October

Building a breakthrough non-profit brand

10

JOCELYNE DAW

A s the focus group seated itself around the table, there was a strong current of anticipation and curiosity in the room. The US Fund for UNICEF had brought the group together to analyse current perceptions of the organization and test emerging messages.

'We asked them to name the attributes of other like international development organizations,' explained Jay Aldous, then chief marketing and communications officer for the US Fund for UNICEF. 'They used powerful and compelling words to describe them. Then, the facilitator asked, "How would you describe UNICEF?" Silence.'

It was a profound moment. People tried to find something to say about the iconic 60+year-old organization. Finally, someone ventured a response, and others followed. While the comments were positive, they were rooted in nostalgia: UNICEF's post-Second World War founding, the Trick-or-Treat for UNICEF programme, holiday cards, and UNICEF ambassadors like Audrey Hepburn. Few, if any, participants talked about the organization's present-day work or its relevance to the world and their lives. The session was painful but galvanizing. If no one understood the modern UNICEF brand, who it served and what it stood for, how could greater commitment be built? Awareness alone was not going to be enough to help UNICEF achieve its mission. The organization needed to rethink the UNICEF brand – to succinctly define what it stood for in a manner that was relevant and compelling to its core constituents.

The branding journey took the organization back to its DNA. Looking at the track record, UNICEF was the indisputable expert on child survival and had decades-long relationships with countries, governments and other NGOs. The US Fund for UNICEF knew it could elevate its work in the global child survival movement. To seize that opportunity, it had to take its brand to the next level – moving from basic awareness to deeper brand engagement. Its cause had to become clearer, sharper, and resonate with the times. The brand needed to be the rallying flag for a community of believers committed to the childhood survival movement.

Having helped save more children's lives than any other humanitarian organization, UNICEF now articulates this leadership in child survival through its new brand purpose and supporting tagline: *Believe in ZERO*. Through in-depth research, the US Fund for UNICEF invites its supporters into a cause: putting an end to the preventable deaths of 26,000 children globally each and every day (2008 number). Current and potential supporters are called to action, to '*Believe in ZERO*' and join with the organization that does whatever it takes to reach a day when the number of children dying from preventable causes is ZERO. This is the heart and soul of the US Fund for UNICEF brand.

As the US Fund for UNICEF rolled out its brand – from a sharpened purpose and focus – it simplified its messaging and increased relevance. It moved from being an underperforming and unfocused organization to becoming a powerhouse of single-mindedness. With this focus, the US Fund for UNICEF in 2010 saw its annual revenue increase by 74 per cent from 2003 and a reduction in childhood deaths from 26,000 in 2008 to 18,000 in 2013.

'We spent two years defining the meaning of our brand and focus on childhood survival. We used the new focus as an energy force, as a guide to everything we do,' explained Caryl M Stern, president and CEO, US Fund for UNICEF. 'It is clear and people internally and externally have embraced it and rallied around a common belief, shared hope and commitment to believe in ZERO.' That is the power of a breakthrough brand.

The growing force of non-profits

The successes of the US Fund for UNICEF in both advancing real social change and galvanizing support for its cause is a testament to the enormous power of non-profits to solve societal problems and to engage citizens in building stronger, healthier communities. Throughout the past 30 years as government has further stepped out of its traditional role of providing public services much of the responsibility for ensuring the common good has been driven down to the community level. In response, non-profits have risen in remarkable numbers to address critical unmet needs.

While social service and humanitarian organizations used to dominate the landscape, the variety of groups and causes is growing. Some are dedicated to improving literacy, feeding the hungry, keeping children in school or advancing environmental stewardship. The scope and diversity appears almost limitless. So does the potential for impact – provided financial donations, membership support and volunteer human resource support are secured.

The world now boasts more than 2 million non-profits, fuelled by a 35 per cent increase in the number of organizations in North America in the past decade alone. As non-profits have grown in numbers and importance, the charitable marketplace has become more competitive.

In this crowded and growingly complicated philanthropic marketplace, people are overwhelmed by a deluge of overlapping messages from a vast array of organizations – many of which are often difficult to distinguish.

Donors and volunteers are also becoming more selective and discriminating. Individuals, corporations, foundations and government are basing decisions on more sophisticated criteria including values alignment, shared passion and commitment and the level of trust they have in the organization's ability to deliver tangible results. They are asking tougher questions and looking for outcomes commensurate with the time and dollars they commit. Non-profits of every size must continuously illustrate the ways support is making a difference and increase their relevance through meaningful opportunities for engagement. Effective branding is the key.

The new non-profit imperative: A competitive advantage

How does a non-profit organization stand out among this growing list of choices? How does it maintain and strengthen a vibrant community of supporters through unpredictable political and economic ups and downs? How does it stand out as a charity of choice? The answer lies in building a breakthrough non-profit brand.

In *Good to Great and the Social Sector*, Jim Collins argues that brand is more critical in the non-profit sector than in the for-profit world. In the business sector, customers give financial resources in return for a tangible product or service. In the non-profit sector, supporters provide financial resources based on the knowledge that their money will be used to achieve important but often intangible social goals, and they do not necessarily receive something concrete in return. Therefore, reputation and a sense of purpose and connection become critical differentiators.

A strong brand is more often than not a non-profit's most valuable asset. It can carry an organization through good times and bad as well as predispose people towards a personal and emotional connection to the organization. Built on tangible results and an emotional bond, brand reputation encourages potential supporters to understand and believe in a charitable mission and in a group's ability to deliver on that mission. It helps people decide which appeal to answer, given a growing list of choices. A breakthrough brand is an enduring competitive advantage.

From traditional to breakthrough

Every non-profit has a brand – regardless of whether it is a priority or not. As more non-profits try to set themselves apart, branding is an increasingly hot topic. A growing number of non-profits want to build a breakthrough brand, but many are not quite sure what this means, how to do it, or how to ensure that the resources invested will benefit their organization.

Traditional thinking is that a brand is more or less just an organization's logo or suite of communications materials. Some non-profits develop brand usage guidelines that prescribe fonts, colour palettes, and design parameters. More sophisticated traditional branding exercises get closer to the heart of the brand by providing a clear statement of values and a unified set of messages that express the organization's identity. Important as these aspects may be to support the brand, they do not provide the overriding idea that drives strategy and infuses every decision, activity and communication with a deeper and distinctive purpose.

Defining a breakthrough non-profit brand

A breakthrough non-profit brand (BNB) articulates what an organization stands for – the compelling, focused idea that sets it apart and is meaningful to its supporters. An organization that cultivates a BNB puts its constituents at the heart of its identity. It makes the brand personally and emotionally relevant and creates a sense of community around unifying values, commitments and concerns. A breakthrough non-profit brand has a three-dimensional value proposition:

- *Convinces the head:* people respond to an organization's need for support only after they understand what it stands for and see how it can be relevant and meaningful to them. Effective non-profits rationally articulate a unique and differentiated idea and purpose that explains what their organization does better than others. Then, they go further and demonstrate how this core concept is relevant to their supporters.

- *Touches the heart:* a BNB goes beyond institutional survival to serve a higher purpose. It puts a larger cause and the outcomes they seek ahead of organizational needs. While this approach may seem risky, it can act as a magnet for those who are passionate about the issue at the core of a non-profit's mission.

- *Engages the hands:* people believe what they are told only if their experience is consistent with that message. Stakeholders want the chance to get involved with the entire organization.

When reaching out to supporters, offer a variety of ways to engage them. Knowing that people like to be around other people who share the same beliefs and care about similar issues, a BNB creates a sense of community, both inside and outside the organization. It unites groups of strangers in an experience of kinship by fostering shared experiences and commitments.

Making the leap from a traditional brand to a breakthrough non-profit brand requires new thinking and new ways of doing things. Table 10.1 provides a checklist for transitioning from traditional practices to living the principles of breakthrough non-profit brands.

The non-profit brand journey

Brand building is not a haphazard process. A BNB is strategically focused and thoughtfully built. A high-performing non-profit carefully defines its brand and what it means to constituents. It uses the brand to prioritize and make decisions about its operations. It then brings the brand to life by aligning mission-based programmes, development activities, and communications outreach around it.

With the backing of the CEO and senior leadership, brand building can become the catalyst for continual self-assessment and innovation. It is a must-do for creating a unique organizational identity that is infused with passion and trust. Forward-looking senior leaders ensure that this brand-centric philosophy is embraced by the whole organization. They leverage the brand to strengthen donor loyalty, recruit top executives, rally staff members, meaningfully engage volunteers and partners, drive diversified funding streams, and, ultimately, make a greater social impact.

Breakthrough non-profits know that their brand identity must outlive individual management teams and economic fluctuations. A BNB becomes an enduring embodiment of the organization's essence. This requires a profound shift in philosophy, as well as a sophisticated approach to ensuring that what an organization stands for is communicated and lived through every action and stakeholder interaction.

More than simply a cosmetic makeover, at the base level, branding is about identifying what your organization stands for – the unique,

TABLE 10.1 Traditional versus breakthrough branding terminology and thinking

Traditional	Breakthrough
Organization	Cause and community
Transaction	Relationship
External	Internal and External
Users	Owners
Supporters	Community
Monologue	Dialogue
Messages	Conversations
Information	Stories
Static	Dynamic
Look and Feel	Experience
Simple	Complex
Own	Share
Direct	Quarterback
Command and Control	Empower
Status Quo	Risk Taking
Reach	Engage
Return on Investment	Return on Involvement
Marketing at	Connecting with

differentiated idea that sets it apart. Building your brand requires forging an emotional and personal connection with your core stakeholders. Your brand must stand for a cause – something bigger than organizational activities, something that your constituents care about and believe in. Yet, in order to truly breakthrough, you must rally a community around your brand's purpose that inspires action and builds champions.

Discover your authentic brand purpose

Identifying the brand's true purpose is the first step in building a breakthrough non-profit brand. Brand purpose answers the question 'What do you stand for?' It goes beyond a static identity and describes the singular overarching idea that conveys why the organization exists and its reason for being.

By discovering your authentic and differentiated purpose – what you do better than anyone else and how you deliver value and impact – you define your unique leadership position and set out your promise. This is transformational. An organization's unique brand purpose acts as its compass and driving force. Purpose drives passion – making staff, management, volunteers, board members and other stakeholders think bigger, reach higher and achieve stronger results.

'Brand purpose bridges a non-profit's organizational strategies and its identity in the marketplace. It provides deep rationale for those who serve and support the organization and its mission that will deepen relationships, foster loyalty, build sustainable organizations and achieve positive social change.

Three steps to success

A breakthrough non-profit doesn't assume its brand is resonating with key audiences. It is willing to take a brave and honest look at the current perceptions of the organization and ask, 'What is breaking through? What do we do better than any other organization? Where are we falling down? How can we align our strengths and engagement strategies to become a life-changing force in the world?' By candidly answering these questions, a non-profit can begin to discover, communicate and align with its authentic brand purpose. A breakthrough non-profit brand uses three steps to guide its work.

Discovery research: reveal current meaning

The branding journey begins with internal and external research to analyse and determine current attitudes and perceptions of the organization and positioning vis-à-vis other organizations. This will inform the process of discovering the singular, overriding idea that conveys what the brand stands for.

- *Internal evaluation* – What do you currently do best? What can you do best in the future?
- *External evaluation* – How are you different from other organizations? What distinctive space can you own?
- *Core constituent understanding* – What do your key audiences and stakeholders value?

Define: focus desired brand meaning

Defining the desired brand is the second step in discovering a brand's authentic purpose. Focus is critical. To be truly effective, non-profits cannot be everything to everyone. A BNB identifies the unique meaning of its brand – the singular, overriding idea that conveys what the organization stands for – in ways that are particularly relevant and meaningful to core constituents. At this stage, organizations must take the deep research from the preceding steps and hone in on the most important revelations to identify the authentic brand meaning. BNBs incorporate three critical dimensions within brand meaning – head, heart and hands. (See 'Defining a breakthrough non-profit brand' on pages 211–12.)

Refine: articulate brand purpose

Now that all the work has been done to research and define the brand meaning, it must be expressed in succinct words. It is critical to refine and articulate brand meaning simply and clearly and then repeat it through communications and actions. A BNB translates its brand meaning into appropriate internal and external messages. Doing so will help ensure consistency and also provide a summary for deeper market testing or future tweaking.

- *Develop* – a concise statement or message that articulates the brand purpose and is communicated regularly and consistently. Brand meaning is often articulated through a tagline, goal statement, or simply a primary word or phrase owned by an organization.

- *Establish* – the attributes that align with your brand purpose and showcase your brand's personality through words and actions. Your brand's attributes will dictate the tone of voice for all communications and activities, ensuring consistent and predictable messages that reinforce the brand and what makes your organization unique.

- *Communicate* – a promise or benefit to constituents who engage with your brand. Clarify what a person should expect when he or she interacts with the organization. Communications should describe the benefits of engaging with your organization and help to drive the brand meaning. While a call to action is critical to convey primarily, the promise or benefit should not be forgotten secondarily.

UNICEF's breakthrough brand journey

Having helped saved more children's lives than any other humanitarian organization, UNICEF articulates this leadership in child survival through its brand purpose and supporting tagline: *Believe in ZERO* (see the advert example on page 229). Brilliantly executed, the brand issues a call to action – *Believe in ZERO* – rallying supporters to help UNICEF reduce child mortality from 18,000 (2013 figures) preventable deaths each day to ZERO.

'Literally, there is a daily holocaust that goes largely unrecognized,' said Lisa Szarkowski, current vice president, marketing and communications. 'We're asking our supporters to join in and believe in a day when the number of children dying from preventable causes is ZERO. That's the heart and soul of the US Fund for UNICEF.'

'Our focused brand organized what we do in a highly memorable way,' added Jay Aldous. What follows is the story of how the US

TABLE 10.2 Articulating authentic brand purpose: from base to breakthrough continuum

	Base (organization)	Build (cause)	Breakthrough (community movement)
How:	Conduct basic research to discover the rational portion of brand purpose: Convince supporters' 'heads'.	Additional research to discover emotional portion of brand purpose: Touch supporters' 'hearts'.	Engage with 'hands' of supporters: seek their participation to refine brand purpose.
What	Construct position statement or message to succinctly articulate brand purpose.	Identify organization attributes to articulate brand purpose across words and actions.	Establish brand promise, communicate it, and fulfil it for those who engage with organization.
Why	Ensures constituents understand rational description of organization leadership position.	Connects constituents to emotional social cause that they believe in.	Call to action or invitation for constituents to be part of a community.

Fund for UNICEF discovered the true meaning and purpose of its brand.

UNICEF connects with the head via research to find authentic brand purpose

The initial focus group clearly demonstrated a lack of clarity around what UNICEF stood for. Further research showed that top-of-mind awareness among the general public was low. While the US Fund for UNICEF had grown its fundraising, other similar organizations were achieving higher growth and greater impact. They knew change was needed to stay relevant and continue to deliver extraordinary results.

Finding the unique purpose of the UNICEF brand involved significant introspection and external research. The organization analysed others doing similar work to pinpoint differences. UNICEF discovered its unique and authentic brand purpose was leadership in saving children's lives. UNICEF has helped save more children's lives than any other humanitarian organization.

Other organizations provided similar interventions, such as basic survival aids like water, medicine, and vaccinations. Yet, UNICEF's approach made it unique. It married its unsurpassed global reach and expertise with access, innovation, influence, efficiency, and resolve to truly do whatever it takes to save the life of a child.

UNICEF's connection to the United Nations provided additional credibility and influence in its work. The organization had brokered ceasefires to immunize children, it had reached remote locations to provide supplies essential for survival, and it had extraordinary supply systems that ensured efficient, broad-reaching delivery. Again and again, the organization proved its ability to overcome obstacles such as politics, ideology, war and poverty to give children the best hope for survival. The final piece of brand work involved additional research into the organization's core and prospective supporters. The team wanted to better understand supporters' interests, values and concerns, and how UNICEF's work could address them. This was a new way of thinking for the US Fund for UNICEF and required additional expertise.

Profiling donors

One major advantage for non-profit organizations is their ability to access highly skilled volunteers and professional services at greatly reduced cost. Through the knowledge and experience of an advisory group of industry thought leaders, advice, mentoring and connections were provided to the US Fund for UNICEF.

Before the advisory group got involved, the US Fund for UNICEF had conducted research with its own donors, garnering useful information. Yet, it didn't understand prospective supporters and what would motivate their commitment to UNICEF. To resolve this issue, the team analysed current and prospective supporters from psychographic and demographic perspectives. The process used to segment and understand donor motivations was identical to the one used to determine target market motivations at the sophisticated businesses represented by the members of the advisory group.

There is often scepticism in non-profit organizations when new research is started. People ask, 'Don't we already know this? How is this going to help? Can we afford to spend the money?' But once the process identified significant new insights, the US Fund for UNICEF staff was reenergized.

The research identified a core supporter community that was named 'empathetic globals'. These are individuals who care about the developing world and feel very strongly that people and the government should do much more to help those in need. When empathetic globals were asked which attribute of a charitable organization was most important to them in deciding to donate, 'providing basic and essential survival needs' was number one. UNICEF, among all of the other international aid groups, was identified as the organization most associated with this attribute.

Joining the 'empathetic globals' was a secondary group called 'free spirits'. Free spirits are younger, secular givers who listed international causes among their top concerns. This group was also committed to supporting an organization that provided basic and essential survival needs – work that UNICEF was uniquely providing.

With this research, the US Fund for UNICEF developed a profile of an empathetic global named Jackie and a free spirit named Paul to help the organization better understand who they were, what motivated their support, how to reach them, and with what messages. The US Fund for UNICEF has combined these segments into a group known as 'compassionate global givers'.

UNICEF: segmenting donors for greater impact

Meet Jackie, an empathetic globally focused giver (key characteristics of hypothetical donor):

- Jackie is a 48-year-old ad executive with a husband and two teenage children; they live in Connecticut.

- She has a liberal philosophy and feels society has a responsibility to address the ills of the developing world.
- She cares about children and makes them her top priority to help others.
- Spirituality plays a strong role in her life.
- Having achieved financial flexibility, she feels she can afford to give back.
- A concerned global citizen who wants to save children's lives, she has a number of international organizations on her radar, including UNICEF.
- She reads *The New York Times* and *Real Simple*, listens to NPR, and watches CNN, PBS, Bravo, and old films on Turner Classic Movies.

Meet Paul, a free-spirited secular giver:

- Paul is a 35-year-old, unmarried computer programmer living in Seattle.
- A free spirit, he feels there is no right or wrong way to live.
- He has extremely liberal views and believes it is society's responsibility to help others in need.
- International causes are among his top concerns, but he also cares about the environment and animal rights.
- Paul reads the news on CNN.com and enjoys blogging. He reads *National Geographic*, watches HBO and Animal Planet, and listens to alternative rock.
- He wants to pay off his debts but will still do whatever he can to help address issues affecting the developing world, and UNICEF is on his radar.

This constituent segmentation was critical in helping to hone the organization's brand, voice and message. These two groups represented 34 per cent of UNICEF donors. 'Trigger givers', those motivated to support international aid work in emergency or crisis situations, added 28 per cent, giving the organization a possible donor universe of 62 per cent of the US giving public.

With the research in hand, the next job was to build an internal case for the need to focus. Advisory group member, Jennifer Dorian, a senior marketing executive from Turner Broadcast Network (TBN), emphasized: 'The same is true in the corporate sector. To have the biggest impact, we can't be all things to all people. We had to concede certain groups and focus the organization's brand, messaging, and efforts on our best prospects.'

UNICEF touches the heart by communicating its cause

Sometimes the simplest things have the most dramatic impact. In early 2008, the US Fund for UNICEF invited advisory group member Jennifer Dorian to join its senior leadership retreat. She took a risk and wore a T-shirt from a small non-profit. It featured two siblings from Darfur and the word *hope*. Jennifer challenged retreat participants to build the same level of emotion into the messaging they were developing. 'If we're serious about ending needless child deaths, it can't be about us,' explained Jennifer. 'We needed to build a bigger tent, act as a catalyst working with others on the ground to achieve the greatest impact.'

The US Fund for UNICEF had built the rational story, but to effectively compete, it needed to add emotional, personal elements. The organization wanted to move beyond just the head and infuse the heart. The senior leadership team, led by president and CEO Caryl M Stern, recognized the power of the cause – ending the preventable deaths of thousands of children daily – and its rallying cry, *Believe in ZERO*.

'For me, it was about the privilege of saving children's lives, not the job of saving lives,' Caryl noted. 'We needed to inspire others to join us to make this happen.' Caryl presented the Believe in ZERO concept in the summer of 2008 at a meeting with the organization's volunteers, key individual donors, and corporate supporters. Caryl's speech was electrifying, and when she said, Believe in ZERO – join us,' the room exploded with energy. The concept galvanized the group around the compelling goal at the heart of the brand. 'We had 300 people chanting, "I believe in zero." The US Fund for UNICEF had never spoken with one voice and one message. It felt like a revival meeting, not an annual nonprofit conference,' Stern recalled.

'It helped all of us to think on a scale and at a level we never thought of,' said Jay Aldous. 'It's not "what" but "why and how" we do it now.'

'Believe in ZERO is why we do what we do. It is our purpose, the reason we get out of bed every day,' stated Lisa Szarkowski, vice president, marketing and communications:

> UNICEF entered the worlds' stage with a profound mandate: to save and protect vulnerable children. Nearly seven decades later, it has reduced child mortality, increased education rates and helped to eliminate or eradicate diseases. Along the way, there have been critics and doubters who ridiculed its goals as 'impossible' or improbable. Yet its staff, partners, volunteers and donors collectively believed that reaching 50 percent, even 75 percent of children is not enough. For us, every child is not a catchphrase: it's the reason for our existence. ZERO is the life force of UNICEF because every child on this planet is entitled to the same human rights without exception.

UNICEF's redefined brand was infused throughout the organization – from its operating structure to its financial dealings, and from its physical environment to its programmes. Subsequently, the mission, vision and values were updated to reflect the brand meaning. The US Fund for UNICEF developed a full complement of guidelines, communications tools, training programmes, and stories to provide the visual and verbal identity for the refreshed brand. Thanks to the US Fund's generosity in sharing its story with others, its brand communications framework is provided in the box (Table 10.3).

UNICEF engages the hands by encouraging participation

The US Fund for UNICEF began its transformation from a predominantly transactional megaphone approach, 'send us a donation because it's the end of the year and you can get a tax deduction', to an engagement model inviting supporters to 'help us do whatever it takes to put an end to the preventable deaths of children'. The

TABLE 10.3   Brand platform: US fund for UNICEF

Brand purpose: UNICEF is the authority on child survival.
At the US Fund for UNICEF, we believe the number of children dying from preventable causes should be ZERO.
Believe in ZERO.

Brand position statement: For those Compassionate Global Givers who care about the plight of the world's children, UNICEF does whatever it takes to help all children realize their full potential, and has helped saved more young lives than any other organization in the world. Only UNICEF has the influence, perspective, momentum, and reach to tackle the whole range of interrelated issues that are causing children to die.

UNICEF personality and voice: Wisdom, dignity, ingenuity, optimism and determination, leadership and collaboration.

Brand promise statement: Because Compassionate Global Givers (CGG) are looking to build a better world, they are committed to the survival and well-being of the world's children. When CGGs join with UNICEF, they feel confident in the knowledge that UNICEF offers the best hope for reaching that goal.

Mission: Our mission is to work toward the day when ZERO children die from preventable causes by doing whatever it takes to give them the basics for a healthy childhood. **How:** The US Fund for UNICEF saves and protects the lives of children by supporting UNICEF's work through fund-raising, advocacy, and education in the United States.

Vision: Mobilize the US Fund constituency of individuals, corporations, volunteers, campus groups, civic leaders, legislators, celebrities, and the media to actively work on behalf of children worldwide by providing financial resources for services, raising awareness for UNICEF's cause, and advocating for the survival and well-being of every child.

Values: UNICEF's reach, expertise, access and influence, innovation, efficiency, and resolve mandate – we fight for the survival and development of every child.

SOURCE US Fund for UNICEF

organization determined that it would create a brand purpose based on its strengths and then build a community around it. This mantra was a clear demonstration of UNICEF's single-minded focus on children's services and volunteerism.

'This required a complete shift in mind-set. It wasn't just about coming up with clearer messaging; it was going to take a totally different approach to branding. We needed to move from whatever it takes to get a donation to whatever it takes to save a child; from giving to joining; from donors to members; from an emotional reaction to shared values,' Lisa Szarkowski explained with conviction. Its brand platform helped shift its orientation from a monologue with UNICEF at the centre to a dialogue around a higher purpose.

Moving from a transactional to an engagement model has been core to the UNICEF brand. 'We're widening the banks of the river,' Lisa stated:

> In the past, the river was very narrow and the banks very high, meaning we totally controlled our brand and interactions with others. Our reality is making much more room for participation, driven by and for our community of supporters. We let people join on their own terms and support the issue in creative ways that we might not have come up with on our own.

There are a growing number of tangible examples of this change in action. The UNICEF Tap Project, founded in 2007 in New York City, is a dynamic consumer engagement effort created by adman David Droga. It involved a simple concept: Restaurants ask their patrons to donate $1 or more for the tap water they usually enjoy free. All funds

FIGURE 10.1   UNICEF Tap Project

SOURCE Courtesy of US Fund for UNICEF

raised support UNICEF's efforts to bring clean and accessible water to millions of children around the world. In 2013, to encourage even greater reach, the UNICEF Tap Project evolved from the physical world to the digital world, connecting virtual communities to create widespread online conversation and support for the world water crisis (see Figure 10.1).

Letting others utilize UNICEF's brand in a highly decentralized way was unheard of. Yet the power of the brand permitted experimentation and new ideas, especially from others outside the organization. Tap (www.UNICEFTapProject.org) embodied a change in the way UNICEF engaged, communicated, and raised funds.

Brand drives innovation – in the United States and beyond

UNICEF's brand was designed as a foundation that would differentiate the organization from others in the space. As Lisa Szarkowski stated, 'Helping kids' wasn't enough to break us out of the sea of sameness and the clutter of children's/humanitarian charities. *Believe in ZERO* was a rallying cry that helped us establish our identity and create an emotional connection with our target audience that was sorely missing. By presenting our brand in a way that inspires people to join us – to make the impossible, possible and believe in ZERO.'

Today, UNICEF's brand remains the driver of its organizational strategy. The brand facilitates innovation that continues to strengthen UNICEF's work, deepen engagement with current supporters and draw in new ones. In September 2012, the US Fund for UNICEF launched a revitalized 'Believe in ZERO' ad campaign.

One of the challenges of using 'Believe in ZERO' was that its emphasis was limited to child survival. UNICEF knew it needed to be able to use ZERO to talk about UNICEF's development work. They sought a creative execution to broaden its child survival focus to encompass the breadth of UNICEF's work in child development.

With a clearly defined target audience, a compelling, deep brand strategy, and powerful brand story, new creative resources were developed to represent the brand inside and outside of the organization. Resources and training for USF staff and regional offices were provided as well.

In addition, an integrated organization-wide effort was undertaken to ensure that the 'Believe in ZERO' efforts would broaden the reach and deliver the greatest value outside of the organization. This included:

- the volunteer and community partnerships team activating their 40,000+ volunteer community to take action and spread the Believe in ZERO message;
- teach UNICEF developing a ZERO-inspired lesson plan ('What's Your ZERO?'), which was deployed to more than 8,000 educators across the country;
- direct response and integrated monthly giving aligning their communications at launch as well;
- the IT and admin departments updating resources to reflect the ZERO message, from e-mail signatures and desktop screensavers to building signage and branded-merchandise; and
- human resources committed to emphasizing Believe in ZERO training as part of hire orientation.

The launch of the ad campaign was planned to coincide with UNICEF's announcement of global child mortality rates in September 2012. The challenge was to create an advertising campaign that cut through the charity clutter.

'We were determined that there would be no guilt-ridden pleas to help save a child and donate; rather we wanted to present a campaign in line with our brand position (relentlessly fighting for the survival and development of every child) and personality traits (optimistic, determined, etc),' explained Desma Deitz, deputy director of marketing. 'We also provided resources and training for USF staff and regional offices to become effective brand stewards – an important component of an effective and sustainable brand refresh.'

Since the original 'Believe in ZERO' launched in 2008, 11 UNICEF National Committees have adopted the campaign in their home countries – a testament to the power of work and the depth of their brand.

'When we launched our brand platform, 26,000 children died every day from preventable causes,' explained Lisa Szarkowski with pride and conviction. 'Today, 18,000 children die from causes we know how to prevent with a simple vaccine, clean water and nutrition. Our progress is proof that we can get to ZERO in our lifetime.' That is the power of a breakthrough brand.

The way forward

The approach presented does not entail making simple additions to traditional views of branding; rather it reflects the emergence and acknowledgement of an entirely new way of thinking about non-profit branding, how it works, what is possible and the implications for the third sector.

To breakthrough, non-profit brands need to think, act and operate differently. You can tell that an organization's brand is breaking through by the way it walks and talks. Breakthrough non-profits see brand:

- *As a strategic commitment.* In the traditional view, branding equals a new look, logo, or language and is often expressed in conjunction with an annual campaign. To build a breakthrough brand, a non-profit must align its brand purpose – and every brand expression – with an aspirational idea and higher cause. That bigger purpose is used to tell an enduring story that helps unify the organization's actions from year to year.
- *As a way to communicate benefits.* There is an old saying that 'activities tell and benefits sell'. Rather than just reporting on activities, a BNB focuses its communications on the benefits and outcomes that deliver value and address values.
- *As a way to build relationships and a community of owners.* Being better known does not equate to being better understood or valued. Mass awareness is helpful, but it does not necessarily lead to support and, even less so, long-term commitment. A BNB appreciates the importance of awareness and fundraising but spends just as much time engaging internal and external communities around the cause. Rather than experiencing themselves as mere names on a list, supporters feel pride and

ownership, and view the organization as an extension of themselves and a means to achieve goals they value.

- *As a way to ensure the organization maintains focus.* Leading a non-profit organization can feel like mission impossible: so many social and community needs, so many conflicting interests, so many different directions to pursue. Being a leader is about focusing mental energies and channelling it in the right direction, and BNB leaders understand there is no tool better than a brand to unite employees and rally stakeholders inside and outside of an organization.

- *As owned by the whole organization.* In traditional settings, the marketing or communications team is singularly responsible for branding. Although marketing is critical in shaping and presenting a brand, brand building and marketing are not the same. A high-performance non-profit uses brand as the force behind everything that the organization does, making it the central management preoccupation for the CEO, board, executive team, and all staff and volunteers. Brand is at the heart of governance, operations, and mission achievement. Because a BNB views its brand as synonymous with the organization itself, care for the brand belongs to everyone.

- *As the key innovation driver.* Doing things the way they have always been done does not position an organization for the future. A BNB asks the hard questions, does the research, and takes calculated risks in embracing big, bold ideas and innovation. It makes strategic investments and hard trade-offs, cutting legacy programmes that no longer fit to free resources needed for achieving audacious goals. To ensure harmony with the organization's core identity, all potential actions are assessed according to how well those initiatives reflect the brand. Then, the organization dares to live its brand purpose in ways that are innovative and different, creating a new definition of leadership in its field.

- *As the filter to facilitate the right partnerships.* The traditional non-profit brand strategy is generally to become the biggest, richest or furthest-reaching organization possible. Although

FIGURE 10.2 An advert from the Believe in ZERO campaign

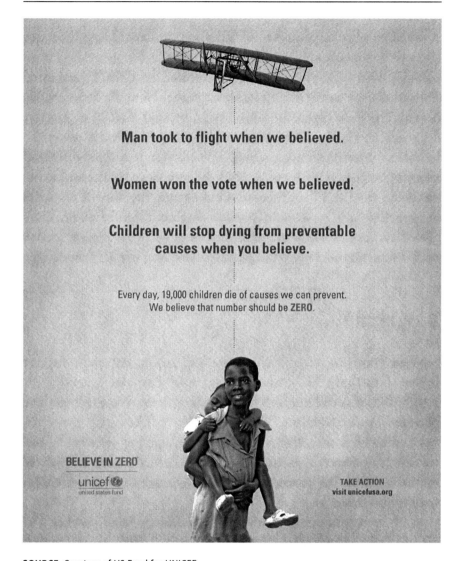

SOURCE Courtesy of US Fund for UNICEF

all non-profits must carve out a meaningful and differentiated niche, a BNB uses its brand to find the right aligned partners and to grow its mission and results through strategic alliances.

- *As a strategic investment.* While some non-profits may view brand building as too expensive and best suited to large organizations with ample resources, BNBs of all sizes know that it is one of the most cost-effective, sustainable ways to strengthen and sustain any organization.

A steadily growing number of visionary non-profits are breaking through by intentionally building, and carefully managing, their most valuable asset – their brand. Like the US Fund for UNICEF, organizations as diverse as the American Heart Association, Big Brothers, Big Sisters, The Food Bank for New York City, and YMCA of America are realizing that branding is not just for corporations. A non-profit brand can create a strategic sustainable advantage and provide focus to an organization's efforts. A BNB delivers clear results and maximizes the trust and loyalty required to sustain the flow of resources necessary to fulfil its mission. Breakthrough non-profits ensure disciplined and consistent brand execution to achieve the biggest returns on investment and deliver the greatest value and impact for society.

Biography

Jocelyne Daw is a recognized pioneer and leading expert in the evolution of authentic business and community partnerships and in the integration of social purpose branding, community engagement and partnership development. Throughout her professional career she has embraced a steadfast commitment to building substantive and sustainable partnerships and has developed countless innovative and mutually beneficial partnerships that have delivered solutions for society and business.

Jocelyne is an internationally published author and speaker. Her books *Cause Marketing: Partner for purpose, passion and profits* and *Breakthrough Nonprofit Branding: Seven principles to power extraordinary results* have been Amazon best-sellers.

Currently Jocelyne is CEO of JS Daw & Associates, a boutique consulting firm that guides leading organizations in designing innovative social purpose brands that engage and inspire today's increasingly active citizen and employee. They specialize in developing brand strategies and experiences that help clients stand out, build relationships, inspire action and power significant social impact.

A brand/story conceptual framework
for understanding mass fashion

11

JOSEPH H HANCOCK, II PhD

For many of us, our choice of clothing is one way we choose to visually express our identity. But what makes some styles and fashions more prominent than others? Our relationship with a particular garment is special. Through strategic methods, a retailer, manufacturer or designer label must create an emotional response in us as a consumer to elicit a response, so that we will purchase a particular item and incorporate it into our wardrobe. This process is done through fashion branding.

For instance, I have explicitly grown attached to Ralph Lauren, and most specifically his division Double RL Company along with its design of garments and methods used to merchandise them. Not surprisingly, my most recent clothing purchase was a pair of this company's cargo pants from their Winter 2013 Collection. But what made me want to pay US$390 for these pants? The Double RL Company enforces a strong presence of historicism based in Americana and is enriched with the clothing that was historically worn by men who represent an outdoorsy and rugged demeanour. Most of this clothing line utilizes styles from the military, blue-collar workers, and the American cowboy – icons of US popular culture that are prominent in men's sportswear. One mimetic, the cowboy is such a prominent recurring theme of this fashion brand it has been blatantly featured in the windows of the Double RL Company Stores (Figure 11.1). This simple mimetic communicates a lot about the brand, even conjures up a story in my mind as it is supposed to.

As a consumer, it is my own personal understanding of what is being communicated to me and how the particular division of Ralph Lauren inspires my own needs to buy. But what draws my wanting to purchase from this line is more than individual components of the ideology behind this brand that include: the marketing of the brand; the clothing; sales assistants; and the actual store space; it is these parts combined and more...

The collaboration of each part of a brand's context generates an understanding in a customer to purchase the goods and services of a particular retailer or designer if that individual understands what is being communicated. For me, the relationship to Ralph Lauren's Double RL Company is a cultural and personal tie to the brand – perhaps because I grew up in the Midwestern part of the United States

FIGURE 11.1 Ralph Lauren Double RL Company store in New York's Nolita area (Note the various icons associated with the Western and the blatant use of the cowboy as a marker of acceptable men's fashion.)

in Kansas, where cowboy culture is historically prominent and a part of my own personal internalization processes; there is an enjoyment of this historicism and a romanticized lifestyle enjoyment that I receive from this type of storytelling by Ralph Lauren. But before we go too far, let's start from the beginning by defining some basics about fashion, style and branding.

Style, fashion and branding

In order to move forward and understand how the fashion industry works, it is important to understand the differences between a fad, style and fashion.

A *fad* is a garment or accessory item that becomes popular for a moment in time, but then quickly vanishes. A great example of a fad is the recent Nike produced *Livestrong* Lance Armstrong yellow rubber wristbands that everyone was wearing for the Lance Armstrong Livestrong Cancer Foundation. While Armstrong was in the media's good graces everyone could be seen wearing the yellow rubber wristbands, however they soon vanished after it was found out that Armstrong had been accused of doping to win his cycling races.

A *style* is a particular or distinctive manner or appearance particularly found in a method of designing a garment or how a garment is perhaps presented or worn. In the retailing industry, each retailer presents a particular style of a garment in the hope that theirs will become the fashion. Those styles that become the prevailing style of a particular time period become accepted as *fashion*. And while many may assume fashion moves quickly, it actually evolves slowly with few changes occurring so that consumers are not scared away. Think about it: many of us wear the same clothes we purchased last year or even two years ago, but we are still somewhat in fashion. Fashions are the garments that are popular during a period of time, not just one day.

One example of a garment's style turning into a major mass fashion that is now a classic item is denim blue jeans. While jeans were not considered fashion when Levi Strauss developed them in the late 19th century, jeans became very popular in US culture during the revolts and rebel youth movement of the 1950s and 1960s. Stars such as Marlon Brando in his 1953 film *The Wild One*, and James Dean in his iconic role *Rebel Without A Cause* (1955) made the pants popular. Then, throughout the 1960s, jeans became the staple garments of the radical hippie and punk movements. During the 1970s, jeans were seen being worn everywhere in the streets of New York and Los Angeles with top brands such as Levis, Lee and Wrangler dominating the market. New York designers saw an opportunity to gain the market dollars of these denim consumers and began to develop their own versions of high-end luxury jeans.

By the early 1980s the fashion market was flooded with designer jeans brands in the hope of becoming the most fashionable. Some of the top brands during this time, such as Calvin Klein, Jordache, Gloria Vanderbilt and Bugle Boy, dominated the jean fashion market with their stylistic branding techniques. Klein's sexualized 1980 advertising campaign featuring a 15-year-old Brooke Shields stole the show. Long before the risqué advertising of today's retailers it was Shields' words of *'Want to know what comes between me and my Calvins? Nothing.'* that stole the consumer markets' craving for denim blue jeans through Klein's ingenious strategies (Hancock, 2009: 28–9). Additionally, the denim brand Jordache used the 1970s Disco dance craze as a major theme in their denim ads to create the *'Jordache Look'*, while Gloria Vanderbilt promoted her jeans using the iconic Debbie Harry from music band Blondie. In a similar musical themed promotion the Bugle Boy brand had The Go-Go's to do a television advertisement to promote their line (Bugle Boy, 1991). Each of these top designer jean companies chose a specific target market building a successful coherent fashion branding message in order sell their jeans. Whereas couture garments rely on craftsmanship to sell, mass-produced products from premium to low-end depend on fashion branding to make them appear unique among their benchmark competitors. The ingenious techniques of Calvin Klein, Jordache, Gloria Vanderbilt and Bugle Boy allowed their mass-produced jeans to become exciting fashion commodities sold in a wide range of markets.

Fashion branding is unique because it 'separates' otherwise understated styles by building a context around them so that they become uniquely distinguishable collections from a particular designer, retailer or manufacturer (Matthews, Hancock and Gu, 2013: 40). As competition among mass-fashion retailers grows, branding becomes an essential constituent in the retailing strategy (Hameide, 2011: 178). As the mass fashion retail industry provides transnational similar garments and styles such as T-shirts, denim jeans, skirts, sweatshirts, khaki pants, baseball caps and shoes, hence making it necessary for these garments to have a clear differentiated identity in the global market. This is where fashion branding comes into play.

'Fashion branding is the process whereby those who work in the apparel industry such as clothing designers, manufacturers, wholesalers, merchandisers, buyers, strategists, creative directors, retailers and those responsible for selling fashion an image for giving a garment a unique identity' (Hancock, 2009: 6).

It is exclusive because it defines the cumulative image of a style that consumers quickly associate with a particular brand or clothing item. This is done through promotions and display using either print marketing or live models including sales associates in retail stores and even through various selling means such as online, catalogue or television (Hancock, 2009). It offers an overall experience that is unique, different, special and identifiable (Kim, Sullivan and Forney, 2007: 327).

'Fashion branding is also a competitive strategy that contextualizes clothing products with advertising, and promotion around a coherent message as a way to encourage the purchase and repurchase of products from the same company' (Brannon, 2005: 406). It allows the retailer to create an image that is based upon functional as well as emotional characteristics that identify a garment to a specific market (Brannon, 2005: 405). As stated, this is achieved through cohesive business strategies such as creating thematic retail space, in-store marketing, atmospherics, and hiring sales people who reflect the image of the company (Shultz and Hatch, 2006: 15–22).

In the 21st century, successful fashion branding strategies are no longer just perceived to be the quantitative-like mass demographic sales data and public-at-large studies of the past (Holt, 2004: 299–302). Instead a more micro-marketed and tailored-to-individual understanding is accepted and notions that each person is unique is taken into account as consumer meaning and interpretation are viewed as crucial to successful brands (McCracken, 2005: 162).

By examining each person's psychographics (lifestyle preferences, descriptors, individual's attitudes, values and interests), a fashion merchant can compose and evolve the styles alongside changes in culture. Branding adopted narratives in the fashion industry, and those companies with the ability to communicate appealing narratives seem to be the most successful (Hancock, 2009; Manlow, 2011).

Individual interpretive branding through the concepts of visual storytelling allows the consumer to feel that the brand is concerned specifically with them and their needs as an individual (Vincent, 2002: 15). Fashion companies aim at producing images that reflect people, narratives or myths in popular culture (Hancock, 2009).

Cultural fashion branding is about reflecting the cultural context, *spirit of the times* referred to as the *zeitgeist*. Cultural activists and individuals who understand popular culture develop successful brands through good storytelling that consumers understand. For example, Calvin Klein's ability to brand their basic clothing using few words and great photography is genius. Since the early 1980s Calvin Klein ads both in print and on television have become iconic with his use of terrifically airbrushed models in contemporary settings. He has made models such as Brooke Shields and Kate Moss famous in his simple, yet bold ads. His famous ad for Obsession cologne and denim jeans feature models in various poses and use very little words, but the viewer understands the brand/story just by the photo.

Problems that lead to failure with some fashion brands are their ignorance with regard to art, history, popular culture and trends. As a fashion company develops, the successful designer, merchant or retailer will listen to and understand the consumer, producing the product that they desire. A successful brand manager will understand the historic equities of products and position them according to a strategic marketing rank toward the most advantageous customers.

Brands that become iconic brands develop a reputation for revealing an appropriate narrative (Holt, 2004: 219). New brands earn higher profits when they are woven into social institutions and political awareness (Holt, 2004: 300). For example, Nike's political support for gay marriage (Huffington Post, 2013), and the controversy surrounding proposition 8 in the United States; Nike's acceptance of this lifestyle provided customers with what Holt's called 'real

informational, interactional, and symbolic benefits (Holt, 2004: 300)'.
In a quote:

> NIKE, Inc., has long supported the recognition of same-sex civil
> marriage, domestic partnerships and workplace non-discrimination,
> and we are pleased the Supreme Court has ruled in favor of marriage
> equality. NIKE, Inc., endorsed and signed the business coalition
> amicus brief opposing the Defense of Marriage Act because we are a
> company committed to diversity and inclusion, and we believe all of our
> employees should be treated equally. (Huffington Post, 2013)

Conventional branding and brand/story

As stated, the main function of fashion branding is to provide a structure that uses images and language to impart meaning in retail products. While an advertiser's main goal is to sell the products, good
advertising requires the marketers' ability to take into account the
inherent qualities of products as well as generate a specific meaning for the consumer. Advertisements should be more than consumer
goods in ads, there should be connections between the consumer and
the products; these connections generate associations of identity and
status in consumer culture (Williamson, 2002: 12). For example,
Ralph Lauren's ability to elevate a garment, such as his polo shirt
to an ideology of an upper-class luxury is done through high-end
sporting activities such as showing the model wearing it while riding a horse during a polo match, or when playing cricket, driving a
speed boat or racing in an expensive car. This allows the consumer to
see an actual use for the garment. While not all of us ride horses or
race expensive cars, we do physical activities that may be strenuous
so we can see how this polo shirt may hold up in a diversified range
of activities, but Ralph Lauren takes it to the luxury level.

Conventional fashion brand development is actually more 'physical' in the actual creation of the garment in order to differentiate
between the product's style and its relationship to the designer, retailer
or manufacturer's brand assortment. This is usually done by managing each step of actual design and production processes to create the

right silhouette, style, fit and most importantly a pleasing aesthetic to the customer. Also each garment must be 'brand right' to the culture of the retail establishment. Successful styles are then incorporated into the specific retailer's fashion assortment and selling season.

But importantly, mass fashion and sportswear garments are created for *established* selling seasons. The fashion industry works on an Autumn, Holiday, Spring and Summer quarterly calendar with each season with little variations each year. With the largest seasons for most retailers being Autumn and Holiday, because of back-to-school for youth and the celebrations that occur during November and December such as Christmas and Hanukkah. Spring and Summer are usually defined by such themes as Resort and Family Vacation. These types of annual patterns can be seen in all garment types from everything from suits to swimwear.

With the fashion system working on an annual cycle that has little change, the role of manufacturers and sometimes merchandisers are to micro-manage each step in the production process and facilitate the physical branding processes such as creating the proper finishes, features, tags, hang tags, and in-store marketing for the garment that make it unique from the previous year. Additionally, ensuring that price points are in perfect alignment to the retailer's brand image and target market is very important so that consumers will want to buy it. More importantly, this new produced garment must meet upper management's specifications for a proper brand presentation on the selling floor.

For example, when you shop in a retailer such as The Gap, there is an aesthetic and type of garment that you expect to find at that particular store. If you suddenly walked into The Gap and the assortment did not fit the image of the retailer, you might stop shopping there. It is the branded garments along with the store image, marketing and sales associates that generates the non-traditional emotional part of shopping – storytelling.

For fashion branding, the storytelling process relies on a fashion company's ability to make an emotional connection through their brand to build target markets. A retailer, manufacturer or designer reaches their full potential when an emotional attachment to consumers is attained; when the consumer and employees of the brand are able to understand the company's values and messages (remember the example from Figure 11.1). Storytelling is the vehicle that communicates these values in a process that is easy for consumers to understand (Fog, Dudtz and Yaka, 2005: 13–25). Globally most individuals understand the processes of storytelling – advertisers, marketers and merchandising strategists use the basic concepts of storytelling for fashion branding. Even the simplest fashion advertising reflects the basic framework of a story that includes: a *message, conflict, characters* and *plot*. Fashion advertisers and merchandisers use this same formula and are able to pique consumer interest while building associations to their products and creating emotional meaning.

For example, over the last two years the brand Ralph Lauren Double RL Company has held a promotional motorcycling event to build associations to their clothing line. *RRL Riders* (www.rrlriders. com) allows them to build historical connotations to the activity of motorcycle riding as well as their brand Double RL Company. The genius of this co-branding of motorcycle riding is that it allows the clothing to be featured with another activity that most individuals can understand and enjoy. Motorcycle riding is one of the largest multinational activities and really appeals to a diverse range of target customers. Therefore, by combining both, Ralph Lauren is able to draw from his customers who enjoy his Double RL Company clothing and riding motorcycles.

The storyline for this particular co-branding scenario creates images of the well-dressed Ralph Lauren gentleman who also likes to ride motorcycles, with the *message* and *characters* being the ideas and images that are created in one's mind. If one visits the www.rrlriders. com website they are given some actual *conflict* and *plot* by photos of riders that are either going different places or perhaps just standing next to their motorcycles. The montage of images allows for stories to be created by the viewer and give them various ideas about what the Ralph Lauren Double RL Company is trying to portray as the particular brand message.

Another example of this type of brand building and storytelling can be seen in the product promotion of women's skinny black pants in September 2006 ad campaigns of the Gap. In the ads, the Gap featured the legendary actress Audrey Hepburn, bringing her 'back to life' through digital methods. The ad for the slim leg pants creates a narrative story that most women would relate to in their own lives with Hepburn dancing around the screen in pants that appear to be stylish, chic yet practical to wear. The iconic Audrey Hepburn, her movies, or just her 'total beatnik 1960s look' from the images used in the television commercial make these pants a must-have fashion item. Consumers unfamiliar with Audrey Hepburn might be interested enough to investigate further, young hipsters might connect to a bygone era. The music played in the ad is heavy metal band AC/DC's hit song *Back in Black* which gives the ad a contemporary vibe and allows the ad to stand out. The story becomes one of Audrey Hepburn dancing to a heavy metal song, thus creating a new selling story for skinny black pants.

Fashion scholar, Jean A Hamilton's article 'The Macro-Micro Interface in the Construction of Individual Fashion Forms and Meaning' addresses the transfer of individual fashion forms and their meanings from the *macro* (global) interface to the *micro* (individual) level. Her study delves into how culture and fashion arbiters globally influence consumers' interpretations of ideas associated with fashion goods and branding. Hamilton touches on issues of *how* and *why* merchandise is made and distributed. Hamilton's innovative argument focuses on the use of storytelling to create brand concept of continual consumption (Hamilton, 1997: 165–71). Hamilton's theoretical ideology suggests that through storytelling, a context is created to entice consumers to repurchase mass produced items.

Hamilton's work illustrates a model based on the notion that macro influencers effect the micro-level meanings that consumers associate with their personal products. Her theoretical framework illustrated the movement from (MICRO) negotiations with the self → to negotiations with others → to fashion system influencers → to cultural system influencers (MACRO) (Hamilton, 1997: 165). The following list includes the cultural system arbiters (macro) that underlie this process:

- Designers, product developers, and state planners in controlled economies.
- Fashion forms and ideas created by designers and product developers.

- The spontaneous, free-flowing interaction of components on the delivery side (supply side) of the fashion system; for example, designers, media, producers (including manufacturers), distribution (including retailers).
- The interaction of components that work in collaboration together in the fashion system; these range from major events/ phenomena in the cultural system that influence fashion system participants and institutions as well as individual consumers. Examples of these are war, national elections, political revolution, economic recession/depression.
- Trends in the cultural system (or in subcultural systems) that may influence all or some participants in the fashion system or some individual fashion consumers; for example, Eastern religions, avant-garde music, art, films, literature.
- Any or all of the above in combination with one another. (Hamilton, 1997: 167).

Hamilton recognizes the ambivalence of fashion in the consumerist society, but her article emphasizes the importance of decisions made by the cultural and fashion system influencers/intermediaries. These decisions serve as persuasive devices for consumers. Each garment carries only a certain amount of meaning and are signifiers of only the styles they represent. It is the arbiters who give them meaning through the selling context, merchandising and visual display. Moreover, the arbiters must be aware of what will appeal to a particular consumer or niche market for their styles to become fashion; failure to do so could result in a loss in sales.

As Hamilton notes, a great vehicle for demonstrating her theory are television networks designed to sell fashion to their viewers. International networks such as QVC (Quality, Value, Convenience) and HSN (Home Shopping Network) connect meaning to their fashion goods by displaying them and creating 'selling stories' about the products' function and aesthetics. The consumer listens to the story and begins to relate to the item. The item begins to have meaning associated with it, and the consumer feels the need to add it to his or her collection. This collection of goods serves to establish the individual's identity (Hamilton, 1997: 168).

One example of successful fashion system arbiters creating a contextual meaning for products is found in the Joan Rivers line of jewellery that is promoted on QVC. Joan Rivers (an international mega-star and icon, who died recently in September 2014) and QVC are fashion arbiters of her jewellery collection. QVC has a database of information about previous customers who have purchased Rivers' jewellery. The company also knows what previous scripted segments of its show sold the most jewellery. Therefore, when Rivers was on QVC discussing her jewellery line, she may have discussed the product referring to topics and the characteristics of her market niche. Also, when she was on the air, Rivers listened and talked to callers who had previously bought her jewellery. These callers told Rivers about their experiences with the jewellery and how to wear it. The viewer watching may relate to Rivers, her jewellery, or the stories, as well as discussions she had with the callers and other QVC employees on the air. The jewellery gains significance through the selling context that is created around it. Without the context, Rivers' name, or the television channel popularity, the jewellery is less enticing for consumption.

Another view on fashion brand storytelling comes from Matthew Debord's 'Texture and Taboo: The Tyranny of Texture and Ease in the JCrew Catalog'. Debord discusses the relevance of US mass retailer JCrew's reinvention of otherwise insignificant mass fashions through their catalogue. By creating retail catalogues that depict exotic and imaginative lifestyles JCrew purposefully entices consumers to purchase indeterminate styles that they probably already own. According to Debord, the catalogue is a work of art that creates visual spectacle and an aura of exclusiveness and allows consumers to shop from the privacy of their own homes (Debord, 1997: 263).

Since Debord's article was published, the JCrew company has continued to widely distribute their catalogue and open stores internationally. What is significant about Debord's contextual analysis is his ability to recognize a retailer's talent to create meaning and fantasy associated with mass apparel for selling to consumers. Debord takes an art critic's view when discussing JCrew's contextual marketing techniques. He has no qualms about expressing his frustration with JCrew's manipulation of what he believes are disappointing and insignificant fashions. He does not admire the company's ability to generate revenue by creating totally fantasy lifestyle advertising. Although overall Debord takes a negative view of JCrew's tactics, they do have redeeming qualities. The clothing marketed by JCrew's catalogue represents mass styles that are practical. Reasonable prices and the classic styling and versatility of the garments mean that they can be worn virtually until they wear out. And while JCrew continues to situate models in fantasy settings wearing clothes that never seem to move past the styles that Debord refers to from 1997, these fashions have remained the same over the years demonstrating the old adage that it's not so much what you sell, but how you merchandise and sell it.

Lifestyle merchandising

Teri Agins reveals in her book, *The End of Fashion*, that the survival of designers and retailers is dependent on their proficiency in branding their products. Fashion, according to Agins, is not about products, but rather about how they are marketed and sold as 'brand image' or what she calls *lifestyle merchandising*. Whereas garments such as mass fashion styles such as T-shirts, khaki trousers, and jeans are staples found in many people's closets, what makes them unique or special is the meaning given to them through branding campaigns (Agins, 1999: 14–15).

This phenomenon suggests that although clothing is an essential component of consumption, the actual garment itself is secondary to the branding techniques used to sell it. Mass global designers and retailers such as Gap, Nike, Tommy Hilfiger and Donna Karan utilize lifestyle merchandising. However, the most famous for this skill has been Ralph Lauren.

After attending a polo match and seeing the opulent lifestyles associated with the sport, Ralph Lauren put the cart in front of the horse, so to speak, and created the name of his product line – Polo – prior to the creation of any actual products. Then, in 1967, Beau Brummel, the Cincinnati-based tie firm, gave Ralph Lauren an opportunity to launch his own line of ties. By looking beyond the fashion trends at the time, Lauren's concept was to introduce a new style and sell wider ties with a larger knot at the top. During a time when ties were only 2 to 3 inches wide, his ties measured 4 inches across.

To Lauren, brand image was everything. Lauren also sold his ties at higher prices than the competition. To him, if the price was higher the client would perceive that the quality was better. *Playboy* magazine and the now defunct periodical *Daily News Record* featured articles about Ralph Lauren's new ties. The title of the article in the *Record* was 'The Big Knot' (Birrittella, 1967). This led to interest from buyers for Bloomingdale's and other high-end retailers. After his line of ties was established, from 1968 to 1969 Ralph Lauren expanded his Polo menswear line. Conceptualizing the perfect in-store presentation for his product, Lauren opened the first men's shop-within-a-shop for his collection at Bloomingdale's in New York City (McDowell, 2003: 29).

In 1971, Lauren established a line of tailored shirts for women, based on the cut of men's suits. That same year, he debuted the Ralph Lauren women's shop-within-a-shop at Bloomingdale's and introduced the iconic Polo player logo on his product lines. During that same year, Ralph Lauren opened his first store on Rodeo Drive in Beverly Hills, California. This was quite an accomplishment for the young merchant who had only been in the business for five years. The store is also significant because it marked the very first freestanding store for a US designer fashion brand. By 1980, there were seven more stores in the Ralph Lauren chain, in Fort Lauderdale, Atlanta, Houston, Detroit, Chicago, Palm Beach and Dallas (Lauren, 2007).

The branded Polo logo shirt was introduced in 24 colours in 1972 and continues to be one of the most recognizably worn fashion logos on a shirt internationally. The original marketing campaign stated, 'Every team has its color – Polo as 24' (McDowell, 2003: 202). In 1974, Ralph Lauren's design style was recognized around the world through the release of *The Great Gatsby* starring Robert Redford and Mia Farrow. Although most of the costumes for the movie were actually styled and constructed by costume designer Theoni V Aldredge, Lauren inspired the men's garments. Aldredge won the Oscar for the costumes and was even asked to sell her styles from the movie at the Bloomingdale's store in New York.

Today the Ralph Lauren Corporation produces clothing, accessories, footwear, fragrances and home décor. Its various divisions include for men: Polo Ralph Lauren, Black Label, Purple Label, Lauren Ralph Lauren, RLX (launched in 2008), Double RL, Denim & Supply; and there is also Big & Tall, Golf sportswear (launched in 1998) and Tennis sportswear.

For women, the company includes: Collection, Black Label, Blue Label (launched in 2002), RLX (launched in 2008), Lauren Ralph Lauren, Double RL, Denim & Supply; and there is also Golf and Tennis sportswear. There are also Ralph Lauren Children, Baby Ralph Lauren, and Ralph Lauren Home with his subsidiary fashion brands being Club Monaco, Chaps found at Kohl's Department Stores in the United States. The brand is sold globally in Austria, Belgium, France, the United Kingdom, Korea, China, Japan, the Netherlands, Luxembourg, Spain, Germany, Australia, Sweden and Russia, just to name a few.

Meaning management

Another approach to understanding storytelling is to focus on the meaning and relationships connected to fashion brands. Grant McCracken continually investigates clothing as an essential component of the cultural evolution of society. According to McCracken, meaning moves from the 'culturally constituted world' to the gatekeepers of fashion goods to the individual consumer; all three add meaning to a brand as it passes through their domains. McCracken's theoretical models suggest that through social interaction, individuals (and eventually society) assign status to fashion-branded garments (McCracken, 1988: 71–89).

In his most recent scholarship, McCracken's research connects meaning to brand management. He emphasizes the need for brands to be studied from a meaning-based model instead of the traditional information-based (conventional branding methods), because meaning-based models are more intricate allowing better nuanced understanding of what consumers want and desire. For the consumer market to evolve, meaning will become more effective in determining consumer patterns of consumption. Fashion marketing is one key to the creation and generation of future consumer consumption (McCracken, 2005: 162–70).

McCracken suggests that context creates meaning for fashion goods. He identifies nine different types of meanings that are usually targeted by clothing companies: gender, lifestyle, decade, age, class and status, occupation, time and place, value, and fad, fashion and trend. For McCracken, the company, its competitors and collaborators, customers, marketing segmentation, product and service positioning, marketing mix, and price of each consumer item determine meanings. He suggests that future fashion brands study the various types of meaning used to create context around fashion goods and view each as if they are their own cultures. By examining each aspect of a fashion business, an individual can see how the fashion brand story reflects the products and services specific to that retailer. Take, for instance, the brand Abercrombie & Fitch and their risqué and over the top form of creating a fashion brand around an otherwise insignificant and indeterminate set of clothes.

The David T Abercrombie Company was founded in 1892 as a retail outlet carrying high-quality camping, fishing and hunting gear. The early clientele consisted of avid sportsmen, including a New York lawyer name Ezra Fitch. Abercrombie & Fitch (A&F) became partners in 1904. The two men had different ideas about the store's image and Abercrombie left the company in 1907. In the 1920s, Ezra Fitch's 12-storey Madison Avenue store served affluent outdoorsmen, including US President Theodore Roosevelt and the famous American Amelia Earhart. The company struggled for a number of years and was eventually bought by The Limited Corporation in 1988 and they reinvented A&F to reflect a new contemporary image.

In 1998, A&F separated from The Limited to become an independent global retailer with store locations in the United States and four in Canada. In Europe it has stores in London, Dublin, Milan, Copenhagen, Paris, Madrid, Brussels and Amsterdam as well as three stores in Germany (Düsseldorf, Hamburg and Munich). Abercrombie & Fitch also operates stores in Asia located in Singapore, Tokyo and Hong Kong. The company's fashion assortment consists of basic items such as cargo shorts and pants, T-shirts, polo shirts, woven shirts, sweaters, denim jackets, jeans, sweatshirts, zip fleece tops, leather belts, flip-flops, underwear, cologne, baseball caps, men's and women's jewellery, bags, and various other types of active wear.

A&F takes basic garments and makes them 'brand right' by refitting garments such as Oxford shirts, T-shirts, and polo shirts with a more body-conscious silhouette, for example a T-shirt becomes a muscle-T, whereas traditional garments such as Oxford and polo shirts have the word *muscle* sewn into the label of the garment. A&F attaches traditional outdoor and rugged iconic patches on almost all of their clothes allowing the brand to gain strong recognition in the fashion market. The company has taken their style and grown it into a fashion style that is easily identifiable among competitors (Figure 11.2).

The company is surrounded by controversy over their use of marketing using young college aged men and women. Retail sales both domestically and internationally indicate that young consumers still

FIGURE 11.2 Interior space of the Abercrombie & Fitch store (The reader will note the distressed appearance of the product assortment, rugged patches, and the slim fit of the garments.)

continue to shop at A&F in spite of the criticism. The company per-
petuates its sex-driven image and continues to perpetuate eroticism
with every new advertising campaign. Even today, this youth-obsessed
marketing, which features predominantly masculine themes, is a key
to A&F's success in the retail market. It was during the late 1990s
that A&F's marketing strategy gained momentum with promotions
geared towards college coeds and other A&F enthusiasts. The Abercrombie *magalogue* (a lifestyle catalogue), as it was referred to in
The Wall Street Journal on 29 July 1997, was popular and became
more than a mail-order catalogue; it was a lifestyle guide for millions
of consumers (Bird, 1997). These photographic magalogues have
become collector's items and are sold on the US eBay site sometimes
for more than $100 each. But A&F did not stop there and the com-
pany brought this concept into their stores with the presence of a
shirtless greeter in all of their flagship stores across the world. The
A&F greeter stands in front of the store only wearing denim jeans
and flaps. Most shirtless greeters are accompanied by a fully clothed
female chaperone, who will take photos of the greeter with various
patrons in the store (Figure 11.3).

It is clear to understand that A&F has created a cultural brand
through the use of refining basic garments to fit their store image
and have reflected these ideals by featuring a shirtless *muscle* greeter
in their stores. By creating an exclusive product line and giving it a
real life model for customers to see, a narrative is created generating
feelings and emotions among their shoppers. Whether these feelings
are good or not does not matter, the company's branding and use of
live models triggers a strong response. Unlike brand Victoria's Secret
that uses women to define their brand, A&F creates a triple threat by
using male sex symbols for selling their clothes. It draws the male customers who want to look like the A&F guy, the woman who wants
to resemble an A&F woman or who wants her boyfriend to look like
the A&F man, and the over masculinized look of this shirtless greeter
gets the attention of gay men who feel the company is sympathetic
towards their lifestyle. Whatever narrative a customer receives, it is
clear that this retailer is challenging notions of fashion branding.

However, in keeping with global trends in retailing, A&F has created
an experiential retail setting where customers are entertained while

FIGURE 11.3 The live model greeter at A&F branch store in Westfield Mall, San Francisco, CA, 2008

buying their products. In order to compete with online shopping, brick and mortar retailers, such as A&F, are now focusing their attention to storytelling to reflect aspirational lifestyles and dreams. As we all know, 'sex sells' and it is no longer the products that draw a customer into a store, but also the retail space. Stores have become strategically branded destinations where customers are deluged by sensory experiences. A&F's use of a retail store as the place where the customer can see the product, hear music and smell the brand's *Fierce* cologne that the retailer sells, allows him or her to become part of an emotional shopping experience enveloping them into A&F's brand/story.

Like other retailers such as Gap and Ralph Lauren, A&F creates a cultural brand through merchandising generating feelings and emotions among consumers who visit their store. One can think of retailers creating brand/stories to be in line with a particular target market. While the A&F brand might not appeal to everyone, the retailer does not care. They do not want the customer who is insecure to shop in their stores or wear their product. Additionally, the company's *in your face* blatant marketing allows them to engage the types of consumers they want. The future of branding is not one where retailers try to get *every* customer, but ones who are brand loyal to them and can relate to their brand/stories (Hancock, 2009).

So, if you're still not convinced over the whole idea of storytelling as a means for fashion brands to build their names for mass consumption, then let's take a step out of fashion and look at Coca-Cola. This company reaches a global market and has created an iconic image with their red-and-white label that people know as Coke. However, did you know that Coca-Cola is responsible for creating the familiar American Santa Claus in the red-and-white suit? In 1931, Coca-Cola introduced the character and, by including him over the years in various poses, with elves, and in different scenarios, Coca-Cola not only generated stories about the American Santa Claus, they actually co-branded him with their product and spread him all over the world making him an international icon. How's that for a great brand/story?!

The next time you go shopping for a fashion item, remember that fashion branding is not a trend, it will continue to communicate through methods of storytelling – print media, in-store environments, the internet, mobile devices, and even through sales associates and their own customers. Fashion brands will continue to create exclusive notions about their mass-produced products through strategies such as limited production, unique design and other methods of product development. Fashion branding will continue to create experiences that have to be physically experienced by consumers for their essence to be understood. It cannot be experienced virtually, but through participant observation and ethnographic methods. *Go outside!*

And finally, fashion branding will always give customers the feeling that they are not part of a group, but individuals and that they should feel special. That's the most important part about good storytelling in fashion brand practices.

Biography

Joseph H Hancock, II, PhD, teaches, publishes and conducts scholarly activities at Drexel University in the Department of Fashion, Product Design and Merchandising. He has a 20-year retailing background having worked for the Gap Corporation, the Limited Inc and the Target Corporation and continues to do publishing and merchandising consulting work on an international level. He has published numerous articles in such journals as the *Journal of Popular Culture*, *Journal of American Culture, Fashion Practice* and the *Australasian Journal of Popular Culture.* He is the author of the book *Brand/Story: Ralph, Vera, Johnny, Billy and Other Adventures in Fashion Branding* (Fairchild/Bloomsbury, 2009). His most recent edited book *Fashion in Popular Culture* (Intellect, 2013) was the inspiration for his new journal *Fashion, Style and Popular Culture* (Intellect, 2013).

Contact: joseph.hancockii@gmail.com

References

Agins, T (1999) *The End of Fashion*, HarperCollins, New York

Birrittella, B (19 December 1967) The Big Knot, *The Daily News Record*

Brannon, E (2005) *Fashion Forecasting: Research, analysis, and presentation*, Fairchild Books, New York

Bird, L (1997) Beyond Mail Order: Catalogs Now Selling Image Advice, *Wall Street Journal*, July, 29, section B1

Bugle Boy (1991) 'We Got The Beat – Bugle Boy', www.youtube.com/watch?v=cw3XzC0x8Ng (accessed 3 January 2014).

Debord, M (1997) Texture and taboo: the tyranny of texture and ease in JCrew Catalog, *Fashion Theory*, 1 (3), pp 26–178

Fog, K, Dudtz, C and Yaka, B (2005) *Storytelling Branding in Practice*, Springer, Denmark

Hameide, M K (2011) *Fashion Branding Unraveled*, Fairchild Publications, New York

Hamilton, J (1997) The macro-micro interface in the construction of individual fashion forms and meaning, *The Clothing and Textiles Research Journal*, **15** (3), pp 165–71

Hancock, J (2009) *Brand Story: Ralph, Vera, Johnny, Billy & Other Adventures in Fashion Branding*, Fairchild Publications, New York

Holt, D (2004) *How Brands Become Icons: The principles of cultural branding*, Harvard Business School Press, Boston, MA

Huffington Post (2013) *27 Companies That Aren't Afraid to Support The Supreme Court's Gay Marriage Rulings*, www.huffingtonpost. com/2013/06/26/companies-support-gay-marriage_n_3503981.html (accessed 30 October 2013)

Kim, Y K, Sullivan, P and Forney, J C (2007) *Experiential Retailing*, Fairchild Publications, New York

Lauren, R (2007) *Ralph Lauren*, Rizzoli, New York

Manlow, V (2011) Creating American Mythology: A Comparison of Branding Strategies in Three Fashion Firms, *Fashion Practice*, **3** (1), pp 85–110

Matthews, K, Hancock, J and Gu, Z (2013) Rebranding American men's heritage fashion through the use of visual merchandising symbolic props and masculine iconic memes historically found in popular culture, *Critical Studies in Men's Fashion*, **1**(1), pp 39–58

McCracken, G (1988) *Culture and Consumption*, Indiana University Press, Bloomington, IN

McCracken, G (2005) *Culture and Consumption II*, Indiana University Press, Bloomington, IN

McDowell, C (2003) *Ralph Lauren: The Man, the Vision, the Style*, Rizzoli, New York

Schultz, M and Hatch, M J (2006) A Cultural Perspective on Corporate Branding: The Case of Lego Group, In *Brand Culture* (eds) J E Schroeder and Salzer-Morling, M, pp 15–33, Routledge, London

Vincent, L (2002) *Legendary Brands: Unleashing the power of storytelling to create winning market strategy*, Dearborn Trade Publishing, Chicago, IL

Williamson, J (2002), *Decoding Advertisements: Ideology and meaning in advertising*, Marion Boyars Publishing, New York

Research advances in the building of hotel brands

12

PROFESSOR JOHN O'NEILL

Branding has emerged as a key component of strategic processes in the hotel industry (O'Neill and Mattila, 2010). To maximize brand equity, most hotel mega-companies have developed multiple brands to serve multiple markets (Jiang, Dev and Rao, 2002; O'Neill and Mattila, 2004). The value of a brand is based on the awareness of the brand, its quality perception and overall customer satisfaction (Aaker, 1996; O'Neill and Mattila, 2004). Lodging operators have turned their attention to branding because brand name operates as a 'shorthand' for quality by giving the guest important information about the product/service, sight unseen (Brucks, Zeithaml and Naylor, 2000; Jacoby, Szybillo and Busato-Schach, 1977; O'Neill and Mattila, 2004).

A recent annual brand report in *Hotels* magazine listed 285 lodging brands worldwide (Hotels, 2005 July; O'Neill and Xiao, 2006). Some companies, such as Marriott International, include the corporate name in most of their brands, while others, such as Wyndham, employ a house-of-brands strategy, ie individual brand names for each segment (O'Neill and Mattila, 2006).

Branding is particularly critical in service industries such as the hotel business (Onkvisit and Shaw, 1989). The recognized goal of hotel branding is to provide added value to both guests and hotel companies by building brand loyalty (Cai and Hobson, 2004; O'Neill and Xiao, 2006). From a corporate strategy viewpoint, well-managed hotel brands tend to gain increasing market share (O'Neill and Mattila, 2004). However, a unique challenge of hotel branding is the perishability of the guest room inventory, ie a room night that is not sold tonight may never again be sold. Thus, it is vital that hotel brands are continuously top-of-mind. A further challenge is that hotels are a combination of both an operating business and real estate with different parties being involved in the different aspects of the business at an increasing rate as international hotel conglomerates have evolved away from being hotel owners and are increasingly brand management organizations.

As a hotel brand represents the company itself, it should always be very consistent in the market. Though there are cases when hotel companies change their positioning or strategies, corporate colours, and even their logos and typeface, very few hotel companies ever change their brand names (Vaid, 2003). A hotel brand now must communicate with customers in real time through technological advances by delivering four basic qualities: offering and communicating a clear customer promise; building trust by delivering on the promise; continuously improving on the promise; and innovating beyond the familiar (Barwise and Meehan, 2010).

Hotel brands relate to consumer emotions. Gobé (2001) explains that the biggest misconception in branding strategies is people tend to believe branding is about market share, but it is really about mind and emotion share. Emotion share arises, in part, from the promise that hotel brands make to their customers (O'Neill and Mattila, 2010). Of course, superficial aspects of branding are ubiquity, visibility and function, but the major significance is to remain in the mind as something that is emotionally relatable, by creating a personality for an otherwise intangible entity (Kim and Kim, 2004).

There are several reasons why people become emotionally connected to a hotel brand. Brands are supposed to be intense and vibrant, and to connect on multiple levels of the senses. Hotel brands too are unique and should be admirable because they signify a promise to consumers. For example, all Hilton brands offer a 100 per cent satisfaction guarantee; if guests are not satisfied with their experiences with the brands, they may receive a refund of up to 100 per cent of the guest room rate. Hotel brands consistently interact with consumers and should not disappoint them by breaking the promise in any way. A brand is something for consumers to feel attached to and good about (Vaid, 2003). Starwood, for example, has instituted unique, pleasant aromas in each of its hotel brands, literally connecting with guests on a sensory level.

In sum, a hotel brand is a relationship with people. Developing this relationship is the real purpose of hotel branding as brands provide value to guests and build brand loyalty. The promise to the consumer and the products and services should be unique to the identity of the hotel brand, and should be strong in people's minds. As O'Neill and Mattila (2010) suggest regarding hotel brands, 'ultimately, the brand represents the consumer's experience with its organization'.

How to measure value of a hotel brand

Among other things, hotel brands are marketing organizations that attempt to maximize the occupancy and average daily rate (ADR) of their hotel properties. Recent research evaluated the effects of hotel brands on the real estate value (ie market value) of brand affiliated hotels. Earlier research revealed that a number of factors were shown to be correlated with a hotel property's market value. Net operating income (NOI), ADR, occupancy rate, and number of guest rooms were proven to be significant predictors of a hotel's value (O'Neill and Lloyd-Jones, 2001; O'Neill, 2004; O'Neill and Carlback, 2011). Some brands consistently have stronger bottom lines, ie net operating incomes, or NOIs, than do others (O'Neill and Mattila, 2006), although ADR (an indicator of a hotel's 'top line') is a better predictor of a hotel's market value than its NOI (an indicator of a hotel's 'bottom line') (O'Neill and Mattila, 2006), and some brands have consistently stronger ADRs than others. Research also has shown that hotel brand affects hotel market value, and it does so above and beyond the effect of NOI, ADR, occupancy rate, and number of guest rooms (O'Neill and Xiao, 2006).

Brand affiliation is an important factor affecting hotel revenue. Branding literature has demonstrated that consumers use hotel brand name as an important quality cue. The quality associated with a company's characteristics of the brand portfolio (number of brands owned, number of segments in which they are marketed, degree to which the brands in the portfolio compete with each other, and perceptions of the quality and price of the brands) is associated with the firm's marketing and financial performance (Morgan and Rego, 2009).

More specifically in a hotel context, consumers are typically willing to pay a price premium for brands they view as high in quality (O'Neill and Mattila, 2006). Marriott hotel brands, for example, have a long history of achieving such premiums in both price and quality. Brand affiliation, name recognition and reputation for high-quality service together can contribute as much as 20 to 25 per cent of the value of a successfully operating hotel (Kinnard, Worzala and Swango, 2001).

Hotel brand as a value creator

Brand equity results in the potential to expand the brand in a variety of markets (Mahajan, Rao and Srivastava, 1994). One example of a hotel brand creating value and leveraging its equity was the Borgata hotel opening in Atlantic City, which attracted 'Atlantic City rejecters', ie people who rejected Atlantic City in favour of travelling to Las Vegas. The Borgata capitalized on the Las Vegas trend of trading-up (guests choosing increasingly higher quality hotel accommodations over time) and became, 'everything Las Vegas is like' and now captures one out of five dollars spent in Atlantic City casinos (Parry, 2013).

The level of brand equity is positively related to a hotel company's financial performance, eg revenue per available room (Kim, Kim and An, 2003; Kim and Kim, 2005; O'Neill and Xiao, 2006). Realizing that a hotel brand's strength ultimately drives stock price and shareholder value, the lodging industry has been recognized as a 'brand-equity business' (Morgan Stanley Report, 1997; O'Neill and Xiao, 2006). Additionally, brand equity measures have been related to the stock price and value of a firm (Keller and Lehmann, 2006).

Well-established hotel brands create financial value due to their ability to generate cash flows via relatively higher margins (Aaker and Jacobson, 1994; O'Neill and Mattila, 2006). In general, major contributors of generating cash flows and high margins for hotel brands are customer loyalty, brand extension including licensing opportunities (such as using the hotel brand's name to sell bedding products), and enhanced marketing efficiency (Keller and Lehmann 2003; Rao, Agarwal and Dahlhoff, 2004).

Hotel executives recognize brand quality as an important intangible company asset and as a potential source of strategic advantage (Damonte *et al*, 1997; O'Neill and Mattila, 2004; O'Neill and Mattila, 2010). Patents, trademarks, and franchises are examples of intangible assets as well as brand equity (Simon and Sullivan, 1993). Westin Hotel's 'Heavenly Bed' is an example of an intangible asset boosting the power of a tangible asset. The Heavenly Bed includes a thicker than normal mattress, extra pillows, a duvet cover that is cleaned after each check-out, and all white linens so guests feel like they are sleeping on a cloud.

Hotel guests rely on brand names to reduce the risks associated with staying at an otherwise unknown property (Bharadwaj, Varadarajan and Fahy, 1993; O'Neill and Xiao, 2006). In that regard, strong brands enable hotel chains to be part of and to differentiate themselves in the minds of customers (Prasad and Dev, 2000; O'Neill and Xiao, 2006). Branded hotels (as opposed to independent properties) have a higher NOI in recessionary times and a comparable NOI to independent hotels during periods of economic expansion. The higher NOI for branded hotels during recessionary times has been attributed to the intangible asset value of hotel brands (O'Neill and Carlback, 2011). Westin, for example, has maintained relatively high market share during recessionary periods due to its unique Heavenly Bed.

Hotel brands first create value for consumers by helping to assure them of a uniform level of quality (Keller and Lehmann, 2003; O'Neill and Xiao, 2006). After hotel patrons become loyal to a brand, the brand owner can capitalize on the brand's value through price premiums, decreased price elasticity, increased market share, and more rapid brand expansion. Finally, lodging companies with successful brands benefit in the financial marketplace by improving shareholders' value (Ambler *et al*, 2002; O'Neill and Xiao, 2006).

Although it is important for hotel owners to be able to recognize the effects of a brand on hotel market value, other benefits associated with a brand, such as guest satisfaction and loyalty, should be considered to fully assess the brand's total value (O'Neill and Xiao, 2006). Ritz-Carlton, for example, has built fierce guest loyalty because of its focus on guest satisfaction. Ritz employees are empowered to spend hundreds, and in some case thousands, of dollars to satisfy disgruntled or inconvenienced guests. Ritz is the only hotel brand to have received the Malcolm Baldridge award for quality.

Hotel brand and satisfaction

Due to increased attention to a customer focus, hotel brand managers use satisfaction as a measure of operational success of their overall branding strategies (Shocker, Srivastava and Ruekert, 1994; O'Neill and Mattila, 2004; Aaker, 2011).

The strategic management of satisfaction is of utmost importance in today's crowded marketplace, where customers are overwhelmed with lodging choices (O'Neill and Mattila, 2004). Guest satisfaction is believed to lead to repeat purchases (Oh, 1999; Mattila and O'Neill, 2003; Aaker, 2011), favourable word-of-mouth behaviour (Gunderson, Heide and Olsson, 1996; Mattila and O'Neill, 2003; Kim, Kim and Kim, 2009), and loyalty (Dube and Renaghan, 2000; Jaiswal and Niraj, 2011), as evidenced by the Ritz-Carlton brand, for example.

Satisfaction in the lodging industry is composed of several factors, including guest room cleanliness, hotel maintenance, employee friendliness and knowledgeable employees (Oh, 1999; Mattila and O'Neill, 2003), as well as the hotel's physical environment (Mattila, 1999; Mattila and O'Neill, 2003). In early 2013, guest satisfaction in hotels hit a seven-year low according to J D Power and Associates, and hotel executives identified three areas that the lodging industry could improve to drive global guest satisfaction while making smart investments. The three areas identified were: (1) capital investments, such as upgrading in-room amenities such as televisions; (2) services, such as introducing free Wi-Fi into hotels; and (3) staffing levels and training programmes, such as establishing the number of employees determined by specific business levels while spending the appropriate time to train members of the staff (Wehe, 2013). Hotel organizational culture and values are a huge part of employee training programmes. For example, in their employee training, Ritz-Carlton employees are indoctrinated regarding their being in the service business, but are not considered subservient. The Ritz credo is that they are 'ladies and gentlemen serving ladies and gentlemen'. Also, Ritz employees have numerous opportunities to stay in Ritz hotels to experience the guest environment for themselves, often for free or at steeply discounted rates. In general, hotel brands with higher levels of guest satisfaction achieve not only higher average daily rates, but these brands achieve significantly greater percentage increases in their average daily rates over time, as well (O'Neill and Mattila, 2004).

Rebranding can have a positive effect on hotels even when the property does not change its flag, but when the brand itself goes through a rebranding process like Holiday Inn did in 2007. In a rebranding of a Holiday Inn in Singapore, the Holiday Inn Park View changed to the Holiday Inn Singapore Orchard City Center as part of Holiday Inn's global rebranding in concert with InterContinental Hotel's worldwide initiative. The rebranding coincided with new signage, renovations and a new service promise: the new Holiday Inn 'Real Stay'. Overall guest satisfaction increased after the rebranding and the hotel achieved higher average daily rates, revenues per available room, and even net operating profit (Huang, 2010).

Hotel brand extension

In many industries, including the hotel business, marketing new products and services as extensions of the original brand name has been a popular strategy for many reasons (Lane and Jacobson, 1995). Hilton, Hyatt, InterContinental, Marriott, Starwood and Wyndham have all grown through brand extensions. One major reason why consumers depend on trusted brands is to economize on time and search costs (Zeithaml, 1988; Lane and Jacobson, 1995). Consumers immediately conceive brands' extensions' attributes and benefits through established brand names. According to Keller (1993), favourable, strong and unique brand associations are stored in memory when the consumer possesses familiarity with a brand (Keller, 1993; Lane and Jacobson, 1995; Benedicktus *et al*, 2010). Holiday Inn's development of Holiday Inn Express is such an example.

Consideration sets are 'a set of alternatives that the consumer evaluates in making a decision' (Peter and Olson, 2005). Consumers choose products and services that are familiar to them more often than those with which they are unfamiliar. Therefore, the extensions of familiar brand names are in consideration sets, and are highly likely to be chosen by consumers using peripheral cues (Lane and Jacobson, 1995). This situation happens more in cases when consumers are without specific product knowledge in the purchase situation, and serves as a heuristic to guide product choice (Hoyer and Brown 1990; Lane and Jacobson, 1995). In competitive settings such as the hotel market, competitor brand familiarity mediates the relationship between the consumer and the subject brand's assessment of fit with the potential guest (Milberg, Sinn and Goodstein, 2010).

The advantages of hotel brand extension provide firms with not only higher revenues, but with savings in marketing expenditures as well (Tauber 1981; Lane and Jacobson, 1995). In addition, more highly familiar brands tend to generate greater future revenues because of opportunities in expanding markets (Park, Jaworski, and MacInnis, 1986; Lane and Jacobson, 1995). Brand extensions such as co-branding may allow companies to reach a better fit with consumers, which should increase purchase intention (Lin, 2013). An example of co-branding in the hotel business would be operating a Starbucks' branded coffee shop operating in a hotel lobby.

Despite the advantages of hotel brand extensions, there are negative points to be noted, as well. First, a brand that possesses a rather unfavourable image may negatively affect consumer choice. If a brand is familiar but not preferred by consumers, it could suffer in its brand extensions relative to brands that are more preferred (Nedungadi, 1990; Lane and Jacobson, 1995). Holiday Inn executives appear to have discovered such a situation when they rolled out the Holiday Inn Crowne Plaza upscale hotel brand, which they later rebranded as simply Crowne Plaza. Second, if the brand extension is viewed negatively, it can adversely affect the perceptions of the parent brand (Sood and Keller, 2012).

Even if a firm has maintained a positive image, dilution or confusion about the brand image can happen via inconsistent brand extensions (Loken and John, 1993; Lane and Jacobson, 1995). One area where a brand extension was viewed negatively was with Trump Casinos and Resorts extension into Atlantic City with the Trump World's Fair Casino. The Trump World's Fair was a casino that was an extension of the Trump Plaza Casino; unfortunately the World's Fair was not well received by the market gaining the dubious distinction of being the first Atlantic City casino to go into bankruptcy and close, costing the organization significantly (Curran, 2000).

Third, dilution of the core image of the original brand can be possible when the brand loses consumer conception of exclusivity or status (Park, Jaworski and MacInnis, 1986; Lane and Jacobson, 1995), and can lead to reduction of demand for the original product or service (Lane and Jacobson, 1995). This effect appears to have happened to the Clarion Hotel brand after it was acquired by Choice Hotels International, a company historically focused on limited service hotel brands.

Fourth, brand extensions have a greater risk of cannibalizing the firm's other products than actual new brands (Buday, 1989; Lane and Jacobson, 1995; Aaker, 2012).

One example of a brand cannibalizing another brand from the parent company, is that of Conrad Hotels opening inside the same building as the Waldorf Astoria in New York (King, 2012); the Conrad actually took physical rooms away from the Waldorf Astoria when opening. Conrad, which has little traction in the United States, was expanding in other markets around the world, and the Waldorf Astoria brand was just beginning to grow outside of the United States. These two luxury brands of Hilton Hotels are now beginning to open in gateway cities around the world, such as Dubai (Morningstar, 2013). In this regard, hotel brand extensions can create but also destroy a firm's stock market equity by increasing or decreasing future economic earnings (Lane and Jacobson, 1995). Therefore, when a firm is to launch a new product or service connected to its original brand, the strategic decisions are critical regarding the types of branding strategies it adopts (Rao, Agarwal and Dahlhoff, 2004).

Hotel branding and franchising

Protecting reputation for guest satisfaction has become a key issue for hotel brands, both in terms of consumer perceptions and franchisee willingness to sign and/or stay with a particular hotel brand (Prasad and Dev, 2000; O'Neill and Mattila, 2004). Since today's hotel franchisees are quick to change their brand loyalty, it may be more important than ever for hotel brand executives to maintain consistent brand quality (O'Neill and Mattila, 2004). One reason franchisees may be quick to change their brand is that hotel rebranding for franchisees has been shown to have a long term-term positive effect on hotel financial performance (Hanson *et al*, 2009).

Since chain affiliation is incorporated in lenders' tight underwriting formulas, obtaining financing for an independent hotel is generally more difficult than for a branded one (O'Neill and Xiao, 2006). Potential franchisees need to examine the parent firm's brand portfolio because hotel companies differ in their choice of branding strategies (O'Neill and Mattila, 2006, 2010). Different hotel brands deliver different levels of profitability. Hotel owners have figured out this situation based on their prior brand relationships and they have become less hesitant to seek brands that are in closer conformance to their financial goals (O'Neill and Mattila, 2006).

For hotel owners, whose goal is to maximize the market value of their assets, recognizing the role of brand name in hotel market value is beneficial for positioning and flagging decisions. The strategies that hotel owners employ influence their properties' financial performance, specifically their expertise in determining the optimal brand for a specific hotel in question (Xiao, O'Neill and Mattila, 2012). For hotel companies' brand management teams, effectively assessing brands' effects on hotel market values can strengthen the overall value of the brands and possibly improve the brands' franchise sales. Such rational analysis can signal weaknesses and assist with the development of re-imaging, retrenchment or remedial brand strategies, when necessary. Furthermore, such analysis can assist corporate brand managers in evaluating whether their intended brand strategies are being achieved (O'Neill and Xiao, 2006).

Hotel brand growth via franchising might have an adverse effect on quality (Michael, 2000; O'Neill and Mattila, 2004). The percentage of franchised units within a hotel brand has been shown to be negatively correlated with both guest satisfaction and occupancy percentage (O'Neill and Mattila, 2004).

As hotel brand executives continue to focus their growth strategies to a greater extent on franchising and brand management rather than actual property management and ownership, the issue of guest satisfaction could become an increasingly important factor in determining the ultimate revenue success of hotel brands (O'Neill and Mattila, 2004). One study longitudinally investigated 26 hotel brands between 2000 and 2003 (O'Neill, Mattila and Xiao, 2006). It is interesting to note that 23 out of 26 brands studied achieved guest satisfaction improvements while at the same time many of them were experiencing average daily rate and occupancy decreases. In fact, 18 brands suffered from average daily rate decreases during the recessionary study period. Apparently, average daily rate may serve different strategic goals for brands in different market environments. After 11 September 2001, it is more likely that some hotel operators and brand managers voluntarily chose to reduce their average daily rates to maintain or enhance the level of guest satisfaction. It is possible that lower prices might have increased customers' value perceptions, thus having a positive effect on satisfaction. For example, Marriott and Wyndham were among the brands that experienced the most dramatic drops in average daily rate (–14.0 per cent and –13.7 per cent, respectively); on the other hand, they also significantly improved their guest satisfaction during the same period of time (2.5 per cent and 4.0 per cent, respectively) (O'Neill, Mattila and Xiao, 2006).

Among the brands studied by O'Neill, Mattila and Xiao (2006), several specific cases further clarify the possible effect of franchising on guest satisfaction. For instance, La Quinta Inn & Suites was virtually a franchise-free brand in 2000, but by 2003, 25.8 per cent of its hotels were franchised. Unfortunately, such a growth strategy correlated with a decrease in guest satisfaction at La Quinta (–2.6 per cent) during the course of the study period. As another example, Hampton Inn & Suites increased its room inventory by 16.1 per cent during the study period, with 99.3 per cent of its properties being franchised in 2003. Despite this rapid growth, Hampton Inn & Suites experienced improvements in occupancy (3.7 per cent), average daily rate (6.6 per cent), and guest satisfaction (2.5 per cent) during the same period. Such overall success suggests a healthy balance among Hampton Inn's branding, franchising, and service and quality strategies. Westin increased its percentage of franchised properties (9.6 per cent increase) with minimal decreases in average daily rate (–0.5 per cent change) and occupancy rate (–4.4 per cent change). Its widely touted Heavenly Bed programme, which it implemented during the course of the study period, may have contributed to enhanced guest satisfaction (up by 6.4 per cent between 2000 and 2003), which in turn probably acted as a buffer to downward average daily rate and occupancy pressure (O'Neill, Mattila and Xiao, 2006).

Concluding remarks

Ultimately, by focusing on intense, vibrant and consistent employee training; clear, direct and sharp brand promises and guest service satisfaction standards; and consideration of unique, experiential features such as bedding or aromas every single day, hotel brands have an opportunity for competitive advantage in a crowded marketplace. Coupled with an organizational culture that supports these platitudes at the property level, and holds franchisees accountable for maintaining high standards of employee orientation and training, as well as hotel physical plant standards, hotel brands have an opportunity to be strong and successful in the years to come.

Biography

(Dr John W O'Neill, MAI, CHE, PhD, Director, School of Hospitality Management, The Pennsylvania State University)

Dr O'Neill has taught and conducted research in the area of real estate, branding and strategy in the lodging industry at The Pennsylvania State University School of Hospitality Management in

University Park, PA, since 2001. In 2011, he was also named Director of the School. Prior to his professorship at Penn State, he was Professor in the International Hotel School at Johnson & Wales University in Providence, RI. Previously, he was Senior Associate in the Hospitality Industry Consulting Group at the international accounting and consulting firm of Coopers & Lybrand in New York, Director of Market Planning for Holiday Inn Worldwide in Boston, and held unit-, regional-, and corporate-level management positions with Hyatt and Marriott in Chicago, Kansas City and Washington, DC.

O'Neill is also a licensed real estate appraiser, holds the MAI (Designated Member) designation from the Appraisal Institute and the CHE (Certified Hospitality Educator) designation from the American Hotel & Lodging Association, and is a member of the International Society of Hospitality Consultants (ISHC). He has served as consultant to numerous public, quasi-public, and private organizations, and has been admitted as an expert witness pertaining to lodging cases.

Dr O'Neill is frequently quoted on a variety of topics related to the hotel industry in *USA Today*, *Business Week*, *Business Travel News*, *Lodging* and *New York Times*. In addition, he has written articles for the *Appraisal Journal*, *Cornell Hospitality Quarterly*, *Journal of Hospitality & Tourism Research*, *International Journal of Hospitality Management* and *Lodging* magazine.

O'Neill holds a BS in Hotel Administration from Cornell University, an MS in Real Estate from New York University, and a PhD in Business Administration from the University of Rhode Island.

References

Aaker, D (1991) *Managing Brand Equity: Capitalizing on the value of a brand name*, Free Press, New York

Aaker, D (1996) *Building Strong Brands*, Free Press, New York

Aaker, D A (2011) *Building strong brands*, Simon and Schuster

Aaker, D A (2012) Brand extensions: the good, the bad and the ugly, *Sloan Management Review*.

Aaker, D and Jacobson, R (1994) The financial information content of perceived quality, *Journal of Marketing*, 58, pp 191–201

Ambler, T, Bhattacharya, C B, Edell, J, Keller, K L, Lemon, K N and Mittal, V (2002) Relating brand and customer perspectives on marketing management, *Journal of Service Research*, 5(1), pp 13–25

Barwise, P and Meehan, S (2010) The one thing you must get right when building a brand, *The Harvard Business Review*, 88(12), pp 80–84

Benedicktus, R L, Brady, M K, Darke, P R and Voorhees, C M (2010) Conveying trustworthiness to online consumers: reactions to consensus, physical store presence, brand familiarity, and generalized suspicion, *Journal of Retailing*, 86(4), pp 322–335

Bharadwaj, S G, Varadarajan, R P and Fahy, J (1993) Sustainable competitive advantage in service industries: A conceptual model and research propositions, *Journal of Marketing*, 57, pp 83–99

Brucks, M, Zeithaml, V and Naylor, G (2000) Price and brand name as indicators of quality dimensions for consumer durables, *Journal of the Academy of Marketing Science*, 28(3), pp 359–374

Buday, T (1989) Capitalizing on brand extensions, *Journal of Consumer Marketing*, 6(4), 27–30

Cai, L A and Hobson, J S P (2004) Making hotel brands work in a competitive environment, *Journal of Vacation Marketing*, 10(3), pp 197–208

Curran, J (2000, 2 May) In A C Trump World's Fair still in trouble, even after closing. *The Las Vegas Sun*. Retrieved from www.lasvegassun.com/news/2000/may/02/in-ac-trump-worlds-fair-still-in-trouble-even-afte/

Damonte, T, Rompf, P, Bahl, R and Domke, D (1997) Brand affiliation and property size effects on measures of performance in lodging properties, *Journal of Hospitality Research*, 20(3), pp 1–16.

Dube, L and Renaghan, L (2000) Creating visible customer value: How customers view best-practice champions, *The Cornell Hotel and Restaurant Administration Quarterly*, 41(1), pp 62–72

Gobé, M (2001) *Emotional Branding: The new paradigm for connecting brands to people*, Allworth Press, New York

Gundersen, M, Heide, M and Olsson, U (1996) Hotel guest satisfaction among business travellers, *Cornell Hotel & Restaurant Administration Quarterly*, 37(2), pp 72–81

Hanson, B, Mattila, A S, O'Neill, J W and Kim, Y (2009) Hotel Rebranding and Rescaling Effects on Financial Performance, *Cornell Hospitality Quarterly*, 50(3), pp 360–370

Hotels, 'The Largest Hotel Brands', July 2005, pp 50–50

Hoyer, W D and Brown, S P (1990) Effects of brand awareness on choice for a common, repeat-purchase product, *Journal of Consumer Research*, 141–148

Huang, P (2010) *The impact of rebranding on guest satisfaction and financial performance: A case study of Holiday Inn Singapore Orchard City Centre*, Unpublished master's thesis, The University of Nevada Las Vegas, Las Vegas, Nevada

Jacoby, J, Szybillo, G and Busato-Schach, J (1977) Information acquisition behavior in brand choice situations, *Journal of Consumer Research*, 3, pp 209–215

Jaiswal, A K and Niraj, R (2011) Examining mediating role of attitudinal loyalty and nonlinear effects in satisfaction–behavioral intentions relationship, *Journal of Services Marketing*, 25(3), pp 165–175

Jiang, W, Dev, C and Rao, V (2002) Brand extension and customer loyalty: Evidence from the lodging industry, *The Cornell Hotel and Restaurant Administration Quarterly*, 43(4), pp 5–16

Keller, K L (1993) Conceptualizing, measuring, and managing customer-based brand equity, *Journal of Marketing*, 57(1), pp 1–22

Keller, K L and Lehmann, D R (2003) How do brands create value? *Marketing Management*, 12(3), pp 26–40

Keller, K L and Lehmann, D R (2006) Brands and branding: Research findings and future priorities, *Marketing Science*, 25(6), pp 740–759

Kim, H B and Kim, W G (2005) The relationship between brand equity and firms' performance in luxury hotels and chain restaurants, *Tourism Management*, 26(4), pp 549–560

Kim, H B, Kim, W G and An, J A (2003) The effect of consumer-based brand equity on firms' financial performance, *Journal of Consumer Marketing*, 20(4), pp 335–351

Kim, W G and Kim, H B (2004) Measuring customer-based restaurant brand equity: Investigating the relationship between brand equity and firms' performance, *Cornell Hotel and Restaurant Administration Quarterly*, 45(2), pp 115–131

Kim, T T, Kim, W G and Kim, H B (2009) The effects of perceived justice on recovery satisfaction, trust, word-of-mouth, and revisit intention in upscale hotels, *Tourism Management*, 30(1), pp 51–62

King, D (2012, 30 May) Where's Waldorf? *Travel Weekly*. Retrieved from www.travelweekly.com/travel-news/hotel-news/where-is-waldorf/

Kinnard, W N, Worzala, E M and Swango, D L (2001) Intangible assets in an operating first-class downtown hotel. *Appraisal Journal*, 69(1), pp 68–83.

Konecnik, M and William, C G (2007) Customer-based brand equity for a destination, *Annals of Tourism Research*, 34(2), pp 400–421

Lane, V and Jacobson, R (1995) Stock market reactions to brand extension announcements, *Journal of Marketing*, 59, pp 63–77

Lin, Y C (2013) Evaluation of co-branded hotels in the Taiwanese market: the role of brand familiarity and brand fit, *International Journal of Contemporary Hospitality Management*, 25(3), pp 346–364

Loken, B and John, D R (1993) Diluting brand beliefs: when do brand extensions have a negative impact? *The Journal of Marketing*, 57(July), pp 71–84

Mahajan, V V, Rao, V R and Srivastava, R (1994) An approach to assess the importance of brand equity in acquisition decisions, *Journal of Product Innovation Management*, 11, pp 221–235

Mattila, A S (1999) Consumers' value judgments, *Cornell Hotel & Restaurant Administration Quarterly*, 40(1), pp 40–46

Mattila, A S and O'Neill, J W (2003) Relationships between hotel room pricing, occupancy, and guest satisfaction: A longitudinal case of a midscale hotel in the United States, *Journal of Hospitality & Tourism Research*, 27(3), pp 328–341

Michael, S (2000) The effect of organizational form on quality: The case of franchising, *Journal of Economic Behavior & Organization*, 43(3), 295–318

Milberg, S J, Sinn, F and Goodstein, R C (2010) Consumer reactions to brand extensions in a competitive context: does fit still matter? *Journal of Consumer Research*, 37(3), pp 543–553

Morgan, N A and Rego, L L (2009) Brand portfolio strategy and firm performance, *Journal of Marketing*, 73(1), pp 59–74

Morgan Stanley, 'Globalization: The next phase in lodging' (Morgan Stanley Report, 5 May 1997), as cited in Jiang, W, Chekitan, D S and Rao, V R, Brand extension and customer loyalty: Evidence from the lodging industry, *Cornell Hotel and Restaurant Administration Quarterly* 43, 5 (2002): 5.

Morningstar (2013, September, 18) Conrad Hotels & Resorts debuts in United Arab Emirates with opening of Conrad Dubai. Retrieved from www.morningstar.com/advisor/t/80960108/conrad-hotels-resorts-debuts-in-united-arab-emirates-with-opening-of-conrad-dubai.htm

Nedungadi, P (1990) Recall and consumer consideration sets: Influencing choice without altering brand evaluations, *Journal of Consumer Research*, pp 263–276

Oh, H (1999) Service quality, customer satisfaction, and customer value: A holistic perspective, *International Journal of Hospitality Management*, 18, pp 67–82

Onkvisit, S and Shaw, J J (1989) Service marketing: Image, branding, and competition, *Business Horizons*, 32, pp 13–18

O'Neill, J W (2004) An automated valuation model for hotels, *Cornell Hotel and Restaurant Administration Quarterly*, 45(3), pp 260–268

O'Neill, J W and Carlback, M (2011) Do brands matter? A comparison of branded and indepdent hotels' performance during a full economic cycle, *International Journal of Hospitality Management*, 30(3), pp 515–521

O'Neill, J W and Lloyd-Jones, A R (2001) Hotel values in the aftermath of September 11, 2001, *Cornell Hotel and Restaurant Administration Quarterly*, 42(6), pp 10–21.

O'Neill, J W and Mattila, A S (2004) Hotel branding strategy: Its relationship to guest satisfaction and room revenue, *Journal of Hospitality & Tourism Research*, 28(2), pp 156–165

O'Neill, J W and Mattila, A S (2006) Strategic hotel development and positioning: The effect of revenue drivers on profitability, *Cornell Hotel and Restaurant Administration Quarterly*, 47(2), pp 146–154

O'Neill, J W and Mattila, A S (2010) Hotel brand strategy, *Cornell Hospitality Quarterly*, 51(1), pp 27–34

O'Neill, J W and Xiao, Q (2006) The role of brand affiliation in hotel market value, *Cornell Hotel and Restaurant Administration Quarterly*, 47(3), pp 210–223

O'Neill, J W, Mattila, A S and Xiao, Q (2006) Hotel guest satisfaction and brand performance: The effect of franchising strategy, *Journal of Quality Assurance in Hospitality & Tourism*, 7(3), pp 25–39

Park, C W, Jaworski, B J and MacInnis, D J (1986) Strategic brand concept-image management, *The Journal of Marketing*, 50(October), pp 135–145

Parry, W (2013, 1 July) Borgata, Atlantic City casino, celebrates 10 years. *The Huffington Post*, Retrieved from www.huffingtonpost.com/2013/07/01/borgata-atlantic-city_n_3529186.html

Peter, J P and Olson, J C (2005) *Consumer Behavior & Marketing Strategy*, McGraw-Hill/Irwin, New York

Prasad, K and Dev, C (2000) Measuring hotel brand equity: A customer-centric framework for assessing performance, *Cornell Hotel and Restaurant Administration Quarterly*, 41(3), pp 22–31

Rao, V R, Agarwal, M and Dahlhoff, D (2004) How is manifested branding strategy related to the intangible value of a corporation? *Journal of Marketing*, 68, pp 126–141

Shocker, S, Srivastava, R and Ruekert, R (1994) Challenges and opportunities facing brand management: An introduction to the special issue, *Journal of Marketing Research*, 31, pp 149–158

Simon, C and Sullivan, M (1993) The measurement and determinants of brand equity: A financial approach, *Marketing Science*, 12, pp 28–52

Sood, S and Keller, K L (2012) The effects of brand name structure on brand extension evaluations and parent brand dilution, *Journal of Marketing Research*, 49(3), pp 373–382

Tauber, E M (1981) Brand franchise extension: new product benefits from existing brand names, *Business Horizons*, 24(2), pp 36–41

Vaid, H (2003) *Branding: Brand strategy, design, and implementation of corporate and product identity*, Watson-Guptill, New York

Wehe, M (February, 2013). Improving guest satisfaction scores. *Lodging Magazine*, Retrieved from www.lodgingmagazine.com/PastIssues/PastIssues/Improving-Guest-Satisfaction-Scores-2705.aspx

Xiao, Q, O'Neill, J W and Mattila, A S (2012) The role of hotel owners: the influence of corporate strategies on hotel performance, *International Journal of Contemporary Hospitality Management*, 24(1), pp 122–139

Zeithaml, V A (1988) Consumer perceptions of price, quality, and value: a means–end model and synthesis of evidence, *The Journal of Marketing*, 52(July), pp 2–22

The city as a brand

13

JEREMY HILDRETH AND JT SINGH

How many cities can you name? How many cities mean something to you? And the cities you recognize, are your associations mental or visceral? Do they include certain sights or smells? Do you have a sense of the people in a particular city, and what their lives are like there? Do you know anyone there? Or maybe you've been there yourself – are your impressions imagined, or are they first-hand recollections?

What does (or might) it feel like to *be in* one of these cities you're aware of? What landmarks catch your attention? What does it feel like to be there? What moods and emotions would the city subject you to? Tranquillity? Overstimulation? Boredom? Frustration? Elation?

Of cities you don't know well, how much have you heard or read about them? Were these snippets intriguing, or off-putting to you? Foreign-seeming, or familiar? How much do you *respect* these cities? Which ones would you like to visit, to live in, to be sent to for work, or – because cities can be objects of fantasy – run away to for a while? Why do you feel one way about City A and another way entirely about City B?

The realm explored by questions like these: *that's the realm of city brands*, or what we usually prefer to call urban identity.

Before we explore this realm, let's define two central terms: city brand and city branding.

Significantly, when we say Rome has a stronger *city brand* than Rangoon, Rochester or Riga, all we are saying is that Rome *means more to more people* around the world (the city's outsiders; we'll discuss the relevance of outsiders and insiders shortly). Simply put, a city with a stronger urban identity is more evocative and conjures more associations – and more positive, generally (but not always), and more specific ones – in people's hearts and minds.

As an active verb, *city branding* is the craft of shaping the meanings and associations people have with cities for the purposes of increasing quality of life or fostering economic development.

Cities don't go out of business

'Brand' and 'branding' are words that come from commerce. People are most used to using them in that context. So it is worthwhile spending a minute comparing the ways in which these concepts are different in the context of urbanism.

To begin with, compared to corporations or products, cities can sustain very mixed and complex brand images. Corporations, if their reputations become too tarnished, may go out of business or be chopped up and sold off in parts.

But cities can and do persist for decades with tremendous black marks on their reputations and serious dysfunctions in certain areas. Cities, more than corporations, can be well-regarded and prosperous in one aspect while being condemned or poorly regarded in others; Rio de Janeiro is an almost exaggerated example of this kind of reputational dichotomy, being, in modern times, nearly as widely known for its flaws as for its strengths.

And unlike commercial businesses, cities never entirely lose their 'customer base': even when they go bankrupt, like Detroit, they do not just fall off the map; people may move away from a place (or resist moving to it), but hardly ever does a city's population disappear entirely.

When it comes to brand and reputation management, cities and companies are utterly distinct beasts. Try as it might, a city can't decide, in the way that a firm does, to focus on one line of business, or to position itself neatly according to market research. Any big gestalt idea that *does* circulate about a city – Paris and romance, for example – emerges over a long period of time; such seemingly simplistic 'positionings' really cannot, for practical reasons, be arti-ficially constructed or shamelessly promoted (and for moral reasons should not be, anyway).

At the heart of the matter is the fact that the ability to alter corporate identity is concentrated in the hands of the company's management. By contrast, the power to influence urban identity is distributed among many actors: mayors and city councils, urban planners, architects, property developers, transportation authorities, neighbourhood asso-ciations, airport administrators, tourism and investment promoters, major employers and exporters, universities … and individual citizens.

To us, the distributed responsibility for urban identity is exciting. The fact that any number of actors, working in concert or indepen-dently, can choose to grapple with the issues of urban identity *without asking anyone else for permission* means that good ideas and trans-formative initiatives can come from many sources, and that these activities can be as grand and ambitious as the actor can manage.

A paramount example: Las Vegas, Nevada is home to a corpora-tion that is currently rising to the occasion in grabbing the mantle of shaping urban identity. The Downtown Project is a $350 million pro-gramme led (and chiefly funded) by Tony Hsieh, CEO of Zappos, an outrageously successful US mail order shoe company. In 2011, Hsieh was looking to move his growing company away from its founda-tions in Las Vegas, to somewhere where Hsieh could create a self-contained compound for employees like the ones made famous by Facebook, Apple and Google.

Daringly, however, Hsieh decided he preferred to try to create the benefits of these campuses within an existing urban environment. He purchased blocks and blocks of real estate at the downtrodden end of the Las Vegas strip, and got to work, heavily influenced by Harvard urbanist Edward Glaeser's ideas about the value of density and com-munity. Hsieh believes:

> If you bring entrepreneurial and creative people from diverse
> backgrounds and networks together into a community that has a bias to
> share and collaborate, the magic will happen on its own… [and] rather
> than maximizing short-term return on investment, we maximize long-
> term return on community.

We applaud Hsieh's efforts, and hasten to add that any city actor who wishes to take effective deliberate action to develop a city's urban identity or 'brand' must take cognizance of a few realities intrinsic to cities.

Cities are massively influenced by pre-existing macro factors

Cities do not wholly determine their own brands; the game for cities on the hunt for better brands is to masterfully play whatever cards they've been dealt.

Above all, geography tends to be destiny. There isn't a city on Earth that isn't substantially the way it is because of *where* it is. How's the climate? Is there an ocean nearby? A desert? Enormous mountains?

Nationality, too, matters a great deal. The biggest difference between Helsinki and Stockholm is that one is Finnish and the other is Swedish. The differences created by that fact alone – laws, culture, history, etc – dwarf any local urban differences, although there are plenty of those also.

As you'd expect, cities tend to take on the attributes of their wider society. Sometimes this is a hindrance to urban identity; sometimes it works out extremely well for the city. Toronto's enormous strength as a cosmopolitan metropolis is entirely dependent on Canada's immigration laws, which favour openness to the world.

Likewise, cities vary enormously in their power and fame in any given moment, era or epoch. Right now, surprisingly, a mere 100 cities collectively account for 30 per cent of global GDP. Indeed, as sociologist Saskia Sassen points out, 'The organizational side of today's global economy [ie, the enterprises and people that pull the strings and wield the lion's share of economic power worldwide] is located in what has become a network of about 40 major and lesser global cities.'

Indeed, some cities are what academics call 'world cities', whereas others, no matter how much land area they cover or how packed with people they may be, are not of great intrinsic consequence to outsiders. World cities are defined by their higher degree of *connectedness* to the international network of cities, and this registers in their economies if not their population sizes: nations that do not have at least one world city in them account for only about 13 per cent of global GDP.

Mind you, we are not attempting to reduce everything to economics. That would be folly, and tantamount to saying that a city doesn't matter, even if it's home to 20 million people, if it is not prosperous. What we *are* saying is that when it comes to *doing* city branding, serious account must be taken of a city's prominence, relevance and clout, and of its existing degree of fame or notoriety. Just as good branding practice for a mega-company like Nestlé is different from what makes good branding practice for a domestic-only Indonesian candy company, when it comes to city branding what works for Mexico City won't work for Macao (and vice versa).

Smallness can be advantageous, though: were one single video to go viral about Lviv, Ukraine (for instance), it could put that city on the map in hundreds of thousands of people's minds, whereas a wildly popular video set in New York City will probably have zero net effect on people's views about New York; there's simply too much we already know about the Big Apple for new information to 'move the needle' on how we recognize that city.

Cities have an eclectic mix of audiences and 'consumers'

Normal commercial brands generally are created by one set of people (managers and employees) and 'sold' outwardly to a vastly larger set of people (customers).

City brands work in almost the opposite way.

Firstly, the 'external audiences' of a city – namely, business people and tourists, students and temporary residents, and corporations (who have their own inhuman ways of reasoning) – desire a greater array of things from a city than a company's customers want from a company.

And secondly, the 'internal audiences' – citizens – are arguably the primary beneficiaries of urban identity (they are sometimes causal agents as well, contributing to a city's brand. Consider the way the immigrant striving of New York City has driven that city's personality, or how the reputation Parisians have for being sniffy toward non-Parisians affects outsiders' opinion of Paris).

We must also recognize that the way citizens perceive their own city is not always the same as the way outsiders see it. This is actually one of the greatest obstacles to effectively marketing cities and 'doing city branding', especially when a local actor (a mayor, for example) hires a foreign agency to assist in promoting a city to outsiders.

What happens is that a foreigners' evaluation of what is interesting to outsiders about a city and how that should be portrayed almost never jibes neatly with locals' self-perception. Compromises are then made, and the result is often dull marketing campaigns that bore outsiders and irritate insiders – the worst of all outcomes.

But the truth is, and has always been, that some of the best aspects of a city, the most endearing idiosyncrasies that make outsiders fall in love with it, are indeed 'not featured in the prim official tourist handbooks', as Ian Fleming put it bluntly in his 1964 travelogue *Thrilling Cities*. Cities, unlike commercial products and brands, absolutely resist being neatly packaged – and thank God for that.

Cities are the ultimate word-of-mouth product

Remarkability is the literal capacity for something to be remarked upon. Remarkability is the force that summons the power of word-of-mouth. The term was coined by Seth Godin, and in his book *Purple Cow* he provides an example of remarkability as it pertains to place identity:

> The leaning Tower of Pisa sees millions of visitors every year. It's exactly as advertised. It's a leaning tower. There's nothing to complicate the message. There's no 'also,' 'and,' or 'plus.' It's just the leaning tower. Put a picture on a T-shirt, and the message is easily sent and received. The purity of the message makes it even more remarkable. It's easy to tell someone about the leaning tower. Much harder to tell them about the Pantheon in Rome. So, even though the Pantheon is beautiful,

breathtaking, and important, it sees one percent of the crowds that the harder-to-get-to tower in Pisa does.

Word-of-mouth, amplified by social media, is a key success driver at every stage of the so-called marketing funnel, from 'awareness' to 'purchase' (or, in the case of a city, some other kind of action equivalent to purchase, eg taking a holiday there, or choosing to enrol in university there).

In *Conversational Capital*, Bertrand Cesvet, one of the geniuses behind the identity and marketing of Cirque du Soleil, explains: 'Your reputation is the result of the relative proximity of who you are, who you say you are, and who people say you are. The closer these three are to one another – the more continuous and integrated – the more likely you are to enjoy great word-of-mouth.'

Cities aren't particularly susceptible to being advertised. At least, advertising is a very weak tool for city branding. Which is why nearly all of our recommended city branding techniques revolve around creating *remarkability* in the context of urban identity.

Levers for branding the city

In this section, we present our favoured branding levers as though they were separate functional categories from one another; in reality, they are building blocks that can be handled individually or in combination, but should always be understood to be interconnected. A fictional exchange between Marco Polo and Kublai Khan in *Invisible Cities* by Italo Calvino poetically explains the phenomenon:

> Marco Polo describes a bridge, stone by stone.
> 'But which is the stone that supports the bridge?' Kublai Khan asks.
> 'The bridge is not supported by one stone or another,' Marco answers,
> 'but by the line of the arch that they form.'
> Kublai Khan remains silent, reflecting. Then he adds: 'Why do you speak to me of the stones? It is only the arch that matters to me.'
> Polo answers: 'Without stones there is no arch.'

What follows are the stones of the arch of urban identity most worth paying attention to and most susceptible to being shaped.

The built environment

In *Design of Cities*, Edmund Bacon (famous for his work as head of Philadelphia's City Planning Commission in the 1950s and 1960s), explains the fundamental interaction effect between people and the built urban environment:

> One of the prime purposes of architecture is to heighten the drama of living. Therefore, architecture must provide differentiated spaces for different activities, that must articulate them in such a way that the emotional content of the particular act of living which takes place in them is reinforced . . . This is architecture, not to look at, *but to be in* [italics ours] . . . The designer's problem is not to create facades or architectural mass but to create an all-encompassing experience, to engender involvement . . . Through the cumulative effect of various kinds of association with different part of the city, its citizens may build up loyalty to it . . . Much of Greek architecture was designed to infuse spaces with spirit.

And from spirit flows pride: architect Frank Gehry told the *Financial Times* recently: 'If you live in Greece, you are proud of the Parthenon, if you live in New York you are proud of the Chrysler Building. Here in L.A. we have the "Hollywood" sign.'

The sense of place, and the spiritual uplift, that the built environment can provide has been understood for ages. Unfortunately, this knowledge of the power – or even the moral requirement – for the city's built environment to have *soulfulness* is too often suppressed in the name of pragmatism, rapid development, or, sometimes, honest differences of opinion about what type of architecture looks and feels good. Global fads and standardisation have, in our view, resulted in a cancer of architectural sameness. (This is all the more true now that achieving higher density is a high-order urban development goal.)

As well as answering to their own subjective intuition, architects should attend carefully to local identity. In that way their work will tend to advance the identity and even improve upon it and take it to new heights and into new directions, and avoid inadvertent homogeneity and sameness.

In China, on a regular basis, a lot of unique residential architecture from the past is destroyed. In many cases, it should be, because the old homes can't accommodate sewage pipes or power cables or other features people need today. However, that doesn't mean that the *essence* of these structures must be destroyed, too. Elements of the original architecture can be kept, such as the façade, and decorative techniques can be adapted to the modern context. Every site is different and by responding to the locality, a city can create a natural diversity and appropriateness – and a richer urban identity.

We're convinced that the built environment is the greatest lever that can be pulled to make a city look and work better for insiders – and be better recognized by outsiders. For that reason, people whose sole role it is to be the champion or lobbyist for urban identity should be involved in all major projects; they should have a seat at the table when architectural and planning decisions are being made and executed.

Lighting and the night-time city

The night is half of the day, and it is one of the real opportunities a city has to strengthen its identity. Frankly, the reason to be in a city, it sometimes seems, is to be there at night. A complete transformation occurs to cityscapes as they become illuminated: from the external lighting of the streets, squares and parks, to the glow emanating from residences and businesses. Many great cities have great night-time environments where light and crowds merge to create a night culture, and a night economy.

Conventionally, city lighting has been regarded as a purely functional or technical feature. However, lately urban development and regeneration programmes have begun actively to incorporate lighting in order to humanize the built environment by making more engaging and aesthetically pleasing spaces. Doing so greatly improves urban life, and influences, consciously or unconsciously, whether we use and visit places after dark and how much we enjoy them.

Also, since lighting can be 'superimposed' on already existing constructions, it can be an extremely feasible way of breathing new life and identity value into older buildings or neighbourhoods.

The East is generally ahead of the West when it comes to lighting. The Grand Canal in Hangzhou, China is a great example of where lighting has been hugely responsible for enhancing a city's local identity.

Hangzhou has long been a water-orientated city, with a canal, and also the Tang Qian River and the West Lake, which is a big deal in China – it is on the back of the 1 Yuan banknote. However, Hangzhou is only a 40-minute high-speed rail ride from Shanghai, a city known for its spectacular urban environment. Therefore to differentiate Hangzhou, instead of grand spectacles, which would be more appropriate in nearby Shanghai, subtlety and softer touches were harmoniously embedded into the nightscape around the canal and lake. Great consideration was taken of local cultures and rituals in implementing this. Spring and summer is very warm in Hangzhou, so people wait until it is night and then they come out and gather on the banks of the bodies of water – they dance, practise tai chi, sing and stroll. Therefore people-centred design was embraced and the Grand Canal's lighting was engineered to elegantly illuminate civic life with a soft touch that can be perceived and experienced by anyone, whether insider or outsider. 'Our unapologetic aim was to bring life by light to the Grand Canal of Hangzhou throughout the hours of darkness and at the same time unlock the distinctive identity of the city,' said Julie Tao, marketing director of Zhongtai Lighting, the company that spearheaded the project.

Streetscapes and street-level leitmotivs

Kidnap someone and take him to London. Remove the blindfold, and within five seconds he knows he's in London. The same is true for New York. But very few other cities have this degree of pervasive recognizability at street level.

Many cities do of course have widely known features of some sort, which may or may not be unique. For example, Taipei, Taiwan is a city that teems with motorbikes, and that's an authentic – and extremely visible – element of the city's urban identity; however, a number of other Asian cities also have this hallmark.

But astonishingly few cities seem to lift a finger to create a low-amplitude, unmistakeable, one-of-a-kind, only-here sense of place on the ground. To our way of thinking, this is a missed opportunity, for a city's streets are, along with the built environment, the most visible canvas for the expression of urban identity.

'If we think of ourselves in Rome,' writes Charles Landry, author of *The Creative City*, 'we see ourselves in the Via Condotti – we don't envision the abstract entity of "Rome." If we think of ourselves in Sydney, we remember the view of the Opera House as we walked along George Street, the central artery that winds through the Rocks. The street provides the central building block of our place memory, reconciling a larger entity with the scale of human perception.'

Granted, many of the cities that have ubiquitous street-level recognizability have been very lucky or very clever: either they baked the recognizability in from the beginning, as in the layout of Washington, DC, or were given distinctiveness by divine providence, like the hills of San Francisco, or practical necessity, like the canals of Amsterdam.

Nevertheless, most of these cities do a good job of accentuating their distinctive, can't-miss features, and trying hard not to lose them to entropy: DC's strict building codes insist that façades run parallel to the street (even at intersections, resulting in triangular and semi-circular building fronts), San Francisco's cable cars and wooden Victorian houses are meticulously protected amidst the inconvenience of the steep hills, and Amsterdam's canals require constant and intense maintenance. Retaining a valuable urban identity can require both labour and vigilance.

There are many low-cost and 'after-market' approaches to creating streetscapes and recognizable urban leitmotivs. Street art has the potential to bring an enormous amount of character to a city, especially if well curated; it is an enhancement through which city brands can express themselves without high budgets. Or, why doesn't Ulaanbaatar, Mongolia – the capital of a country whose chief deity is the great blue sky – paint all of its buses Pantone 292 sky blue? There can be a role for light-heartedness, myth and narrative in the construction of urban identity.

Vibrancy and vibe

AA Gill, a restaurant and culture critic for *The Times* of London, has strong views about the relative importance of vibrancy as compared with comfort. In his inimitable style, he comes out very much on the side of vibrancy:

> Urban is noisy. It smells. It's full of people who want to drink your claret, enter your wallet and stuff your daughter. Restaurants are more important to cities than you are, any of you. Having Tom's Place down the road is an amenity that improves the neighbourhood. Next door, it makes the curtains smell, and takes £10K off the asking [price]. Well, tough. I know where this leads. The creeping countrification of the city; an infection of niceness . . . I've seen it in Manhattan; now, the city that doesn't sleep pops a Xanax at 10pm and leaves at the weekend . . . everything that was exciting, entertaining and important and had a life, rather than a lifestyle, has been poisoned and pulled up.

Exaggerated? Definitely. But in his caustic, cautionary tones, Gill makes a valid and accurate point: while high levels of organization and decorum are valuable to a city, it's possible to go too far with *niceness*. Some of the world's greatest cities, and some of the best parts of the lesser cities, are noisy, smelly and adversarial. And that's *why* they're wonderful, or at least it is part and parcel of their wonderfulness, and their productivity (see Figure 13.1, p 290). 'Living in Greenwich Village [New York] is almost as exciting as war service,' Jonathan Raban wrote of his home turf in *Soft City*. For cities, niceness is an altar upon which it is possible to sacrifice too much.

Landmarks and legibility

Landmarkability is a term we use to refer to buildings, structures and spaces which create distinct visual orientation points that provide a sense of location. They can be created by a significant natural feature or by an architectural form that is highly distinctive relative to its surrounding environment.

So much the better if the landmark is also a social object or social space that encourages people to take a picture in front of it. The giant mirrored bean in Chicago had a price tag of $23 million. But to purchase publicity, affection and recognition equal to that with advertising – an impossibility anyway – how much would that cost?

We believe monuments and landmarks can be devised with the express purpose of enhancing urban identity. That said, there is irony in the fact that some (if not actually most) of the world's most famous urban landmarks were not deliberately intended to manipulate a city's brand. Nor were many of them rousing successes from the get-go. The Eiffel Tower, for instance, which was built for the first World's Fair in 1889, was initially widely disliked by Parisians. One critic called it, in print, 'a truly tragic streetlamp.' Another described it as an 'iron gymnasium apparatus, incomplete, confused and deformed'. A third dismissed it as 'a half-built factory pipe... a hole-riddled suppository'. Petitions against the tower were circulated, and signed by celebrities of the day (including Alexandre Dumas, author of *The Count of Monte Cristo*).

Monuments can be valuable not only as physical landmarks or urban reference points, but also by helping provide the city with what scholar Kevin Lynch called 'temporal legibility' – a metaphorical signpost about where the city has come from, and where it's headed:

> Cities need a sense of history also. Legibility... [ought to] show how what is here now relates to the past, even if this means exposing the scars of history... It took Bristol [England] many years to acknowledge publicly its past as a slave trading port. Only recently have public monuments been commissioned and placed. Pero's Bridge – a new pedestrian bridge crossing the historic harbour – is named after a slave boy who lived in the city. Though painful, this is an essential part of legibility and a symbol of future intentions.

Bottom line: you can't fall in love with a city you don't understand. So, helping people find their way around town, and absorb a sense of place, is crucial. (Indeed, 'branding' a city via its signage and way-finding system is a subject unto itself.)

Arrivals and first impressions

Jonathan Raban writes of the 'mythology of initiation to the city' and asserts the value of demonstrating to people that they have entered the city, that they have 'crossed a frontier into a new world':

> The architects of the city in the 19th century instinctively grasped [the] importance [of arrival]. They filled the outskirts areas of great cities with grandiloquent gestures and promises, signs, notices, and monuments, whose extravagant tone was in keeping with the heightened, self-mythologising emotional state of the newcomer. . . . [London] turned the Victorian railway termini into technological wonderlands [of] science and engineering. Until 1964, when it was knocked down in a typical act of official vandalism, you left Euston station under a massive, triumphal Doric arch. The city lay before you like an anticipated victory, celebrated before it had been won.

Contrast this with the banality and frustration that attends one's arrival at most – but not all – international airports today. (No surprise that the arrivals experience is something we help client cities improve.)

First impressions matter. They seem to stay with us longer than secondary impressions. And they shade our later impressions by priming us to see more of what we think we've already glimpsed.

Public policy and problem solving

There are a lot of problems in the world and a lot of urban problems, particularly. If a city can solve one or two, in an original way, it redounds to the city's brand.

Problem-solving cities gain recognition. Cartagena, Colombia first got famous for having a crime problem. Then it got famous for resolving its crime problem – and task forces from other Latin American cities now flock to Cartagena to learn how they did it.

Amsterdam is another great example: with its well-honed bicycle riding habits, it is influencing other cities' cycle riding cultures and infrastructures. Importantly, the city is constantly strengthening its leadership, lately with an initiative to build heated bike paths which would extend the safe cycling season into the inclement winter months.

Far from being mundane, simply being highly functional can be a brand feature for a city. As Edward Glaeser writes, 'Much of the world suffers under awful government, and that provides an edge for those cities that are administered well.' Good governance is always good branding. Simply (although there's rarely anything simple about it) solving the problems of being a city, and modelling those solutions to others, can work wonders for a city's standing in the minds of insiders and outsiders.

People, culture and cuisine

A major job of city branding is to accentuate and enliven the things that are different about a place. As such, in our work we are always obsessed with identifying those differences. Unsurprisingly some of the biggest differences between cities arise from people and culture. City life is not remotely homogeneous, and what people are like in one city can be nothing like what people are like somewhere else.

Prominent citizens or organizations may be well utilized as ambassadors for a city. Have you got a famous artist or composer among your ranks? Send him or her on tour. More than a handful of cities have an international awareness fuelled largely or even entirely by sports teams. How many Asians would even know about Manchester, England were it not for the famous football club?

Food and beverage are highly tangible forms of culture: you've got to try the Shanghai dumplings when you're in that city; and how could you not have a lobster while passing through Portland, Maine, or fail to drink a daiquiri in Havana, Cuba? The panoply of culture-identity cuisine includes Singapore noodles, California roll sushi, Hyderabad's biryani, Hangzhou's loose-leaf green tea, New Orleans's gumbo and Chongqing's spicy hot pot.

In fact, Chongqing hot pot is a great case story of a local dish that was actively developed as a conscious branding manoeuvre. Although the dish originally appeared at the time of the Qing dynasty (1644–1911), it was only quite recently popularized by a female entrepreneur called Heyongzhi. She started with one restaurant, and grew it into a national chain. Here's where it gets interesting: around 15 years ago, the city of Chongqing realized that the neighbouring city of Chengdu was also promoting a version of the spicy hot pot dish, and that this was distracting attention from Chongqing hot pot. In a very enlightened move to protect its brand equity in hot pot, Chongqing city government got Heyongzhi to form the Chongqing Hotpot Association to train and certify restaurateurs all over China – for little or no fee – in how to prepare authentic Chongqing hotpot and, furthermore, how to manage their restaurants. The result: the promotion of Chongqing and the nationwide triumph of that city's dish over Chengdu's rival version.

Rituals and experiences

One of the ways that commercial brands (or product categories) get under our skin is by associating themselves with rituals or occasions: the insertion of the lime wedge into the bottle of Corona beer, for example, or the use of champagne as *the* go-to beverage for celebration (why should it be?).

Often by accident of history, similar rituals or activities can become inextricably linked with cities, such that people can be heard to say: 'Oh, you *really* haven't been to X until you've done Y!' And not only heard to say it, but made to feel it! There is at least a portion of foreign visitors to London, we can guarantee, who would not feel their visit were complete without seeing the changing of the guard at Buckingham Palace… or riding a double-decker bus… or posing for a photo in a red phone box… for these, according to legend, are the rituals that mark one as having been to London.

Rituals typically arise more or less organically. But they can also be concocted deliberately, and if that's done cleverly, they can create a vector for authentically communicating and amplifying something of the soul of a place. The city of Key West, Florida, for example, throws a bit of a party down at the waterfront every evening in honour of the sunset; street performers and food sellers come out, and it's become a well-known ritual. People go there just for that.

Not every ritual or routine will become world famous, but that doesn't mean its not worth doing. You'd be astonished at how many 'timeless traditions' were actually begun a few decades ago! The main trick, as we say, is to be artful, authentic and identity-centric in designing it. The ritual should connect powerfully to the place.

Identity-embodying special events

A near cousin to rituals and experiences is special events. The best special events for branding purposes are designed from the beginning to have a strong urban identity component: they are created in such a way that they couldn't really happen anywhere but in the host city. In actual fact, though, what mostly happens is a city starts out hosting an event and then over time – sometimes quite a long time – becomes closely associated with that event (the festival of San Femin, also known as the running of the bulls, in Pamplona, Spain, for instance, has been going for more than 150 years; SXSW [South-by-Southwest] in Austin, Texas started in 1987).

Sometimes it's a little of both – an event isn't held at a location in order to project that city a certain way, but it arrives there because the place is well-suited to that kind of event. In such cases, the event *does* have the effect of fortifying identity. An example of this is the 'TT' motorcycle races. These are held annually on the Isle of Man, a self-governing British Crown Dependency in the Irish Sea between Great Britain and Ireland. The island is semi-independent; it's parliament, the Tynwald, is the oldest continuously existing ruling body in the world and was established by the Vikings; it is not part of the EU and is low-tax regime friendly to offshore banking; its spirit is fiercely independent, and the island has its own spoken dialect.

Meanwhile the TT Races are famously dangerous, with riders going at extreme speeds on winding roads past stone buildings and cliffs. Since 1907, some 240 riders have died on the course (contrast with 'only' 15 deaths since 1910 at Pamplona's running of the bulls). Such a race could only happen in a place like the Isle of Man – whose sense of freedom and *laissez faire*, and whose politically independent government, would permit it; any 'normal' place would forbid such an event – which makes it a strong and honest reinforcement of the island's identity.

Branded consumer goods and city exports

Provenance (aka, MADE IN _____), or the place of origin effect – that is, the preference that consumers attach to where products are made – was identified a long time ago as a factor in marketing and branding. It's mostly been countries, however, that brands have chosen to align themselves with: French perfume, Japanese technology, Italian fashion, and so on. Occasionally a region pops up; Apple products have been emblazoned on the back for a while now: 'Designed in California by Apple.'

When place of origin is invoked, a product purchased becomes a souvenir from a locale you've never physically been to. It can help build an affinity between product and purchaser.

Another factor supporting development of city of origin brands is that countries are too big now as units of mental accounting. Okay, we don't really mean *countries* – we mean China particularly, where more things are made than anywhere else. But 'MADE IN CHINA', although that label is gaining reputability, is a long way off from being a mark of prestige. We predict that luxury brands like Shang Xia, which is backed by Hermès and has recently opened a shop in Paris, will be thought of not as originating in the abstraction of 'China', but rather in the world city of Shanghai – a city with genuine sex appeal. Equally, we expect Chinese provinces to emerge from their present occlusion and begin to gain recognition for certain types of products, and for particular brands.

As commercial brands search for new ways to distinguish themselves, associating themselves with particular cities will quickly become a highly attractive option. Western consumers already are used to seeing LONDON – BRUSSELS – ROME – DUBAI – BEVERLY

HILLS on awnings in fancy shopping districts. In 20 years, it will be a different set of cities listed on those awnings. We have already had a hand in one shop proclaiming, in the French-speaking part of Switzerland: ULAN BATOR – GENEVE.

Where is the explosion of city of origin brands? It's coming. The rise of cities as the dominant 'meta landscape' of global geography in the 21st century practically guarantees it.

Conclusion and call to arms

How do we know how we're doing as humans? We look at our cities.

Cities are the great human stage, playing host to a cast of characters, starting with you, us, and – at extrapolated growth rates – 75 per cent of the world's population within a few decades.

And cities are *themselves* a cast of characters: fully fledged personae with lightness and darkness, opportunity and banality, tragedy and joy.

Cities are all flawed geniuses, driven by visible and invisible hands through individual historical arcs, fulfilling or failing to fulfil their own respective destinies.

Undoubtedly – and excitingly – the destiny of some cities will be to foster the next transformation in human civilization. The futurist Daniel Pinchbeck, in *Notes from the Edge Times*, writes:

> Reality is becoming more improvisational and up-tempo… [meanwhile] it appears that successive transformations of human civilisation have happened at exponentially faster rates of linear time: while the agricultural revolution took thousands of years, the industrial age took under 200 years, and the Knowledge or Information Age required only a few decades. By this model… the next revolution in human society could happen in [a duration of] two or three years. This would be a revolution of wisdom, of consciousness.

Cities everywhere and at all stages of economic and social development have the opportunity to participate, in their own ways, in this great-wave transmogrification of human society.

FIGURE 13.1   The messiness of cities can be made captivating, even beautiful

SOURCE   Photo by Rob Whitworth. Used with permission.

FIGURE 13.2   The airport in Vilnius, Lithuania delivers fresh fruit alongside arriving suitcases

SOURCE   Copyright *Thrilling Cities*. Used with permission.

Realizing a city's urban identity, and leveraging it and shaping it to serve the city's well-being and greatness, is the prerogative of every civic leader and the opportunity of every city dweller.

The remarkable expression and relevant amplification of authentic elements of a city's identity is the crux of most effective urban branding techniques. However, the form of that expression always varies. For instance, the mesmerizing short film *This is Shanghai* portrays the Chinese metropolis as the world's new New York; meanwhile, in the northern European city of Vilnius, Lithuania, a simple box of fresh fruit, routinely placed onto the baggage carousel among the luggage, introduces every arriving passenger to the city's light-hearted, bohemian spirit (see Figure 13.2).

Biographies

For more than a decade, **Jeremy Hildreth** has been carving his singular niche as a thinker and a practitioner at the nexus of place-making and brand identity, with his output characterized by its value creation and sheer diversity. With an Ivy League degree in economics and an MBA from Oxford University, Hildreth has performed unconventional work for 'conventional' branding clients (including legends like Nike and Louis Vuitton), and has perennially pushed the envelope in place branding, developing promotional strategies for former trouble spots like East Timor and Northern Ireland, and spending six months in Outer Mongolia to devise the country's first-ever national cashmere export platform. Described as 'lively and original', and 'nuanced', Hildreth's thought leadership includes the book *Brand America* (with Simon Anholt, 2010). In the media, Hildreth writes about landmarks and icons of culture for *The Wall Street Journal*, and regularly hosts Monocle 24 radio's 'Place Branding Roundup'.

Living by the credo 'Evolve immediately', **JT Singh** refuses to be categorized as his bohemian approach to place branding intermingles many disciplines, from design, economics, art, and storytelling, to sustainability, public policy and much, much more. Singh's clients range from numerous downtowns, creative districts, commercial centres and industrial zones to entire cities (big and small) such as Toronto, Shanghai, Beijing, Tianjin and Vilnius. Renowned for his talent for urban exploration, Singh's insightful reconnaissance of hundreds of emerging cities offers a lens on 'where things are headed' on all aspects of the urban world. When time permits, he speaks and lectures on urban identity and sustainability (find his TEDx Seoul talk on YouTube), and pontificates on his two favourite subjects: urban life and good design. Singh is currently engaged with a pioneering urban regeneration development project with the Shanghai Expo district and several feature film projects related to city branding.

References

Aspden, Peter. Interview: Frank Gehry, by Peter Aspden, FT, 22 November 2013, www.ft.com/cms/s/2/1c87963c-51cb-11e3-8c42-00144feabdc0.html#axzz2m9zuHcNx

Bacon, Edmund N (1967) *Design of Cities*, Viking Press, New York

Calvino, Italo (1974) *Invisible Cities*, Secker & Warburg, London

Cesvet, Bertrand (2009) *Conversational Capital*, FT Press, New Jersey

Dalrymple, William. Home truths on abroad, *The Guardian*, 19 September 2009, www.theguardian.com/books/2009/sep/19/travel-writing-writers-future

Fleming, Ian (1964) *Thrilling Cities*, New American Library, New York

Glaeser, Edward (2011) *Triumph of the City*, Macmillan, London

Kay, John (2010) *Obliquity: Why our goals are best achieved indirectly*, Profile Books, London

Kelly, Andrew (2001) *Building Legible Cities*, The Bristol Cultural Development Partnership, Bristol

Pinchbeck, Daniel (2010) *Notes from the Edge Times*, Tarcher/Penguin, New York

Raban, Jonathan (1997) *Soft City*, Picador, London

Shattuck, Aaaron. *Scientific American*, 26 August 2011. 'Cities in Fact and Fiction: An Interview with William Gibson,' www.scientificamerican.com/article.cfm?id=gibson-interview-cities-in-fact-and-fiction

Technology branding
Building long-term value in a system-update world

14

HOWARD BREINDEL, JONATHAN PAISNER AND SETH MARGOLIS

A brand is a brand is a brand. And then there are technology brands. To create a powerful technology brand you need to think different, to crib Apple's famous advertising campaign that went directly to the heart of IBM's long-time 'Think' brand.

Of course, the pace of change in every corner of technology makes branding in this segment an often perilous pursuit. Other industries merely face new competitors. Technology companies face disruptors – a product or company or even just an idea that completely alters the competitive landscape and threatens the very survival of legacy players. And these disruptors have a habit of coming at us more and more frequently. Can any brand withstand a disruptor? Do technology brands have staying power, or must they evolve – or be completely reinvented – as fast as the companies and products they stand for are updated or replaced? In a category ever abuzz about the latest and the greatest, is branding – which by definition builds long-term equity – even important? In an environment where many think you are only as good as your latest release, it might be argued that brand is even more important for companies looking to truly break through into long-term success. Brand can separate today's flash-in-the-pan hit from tomorrow's market leader. Brand can drive a constant promise or experience across a product or service line, even as a company continually introduces new features and functionality or even reinvents itself. Technology companies that embrace their brand as an articulation of the promise that they deliver through their people, their products and their services will elevate their value in the market and will better position themselves for long-term success.

Before we dig in, it's worth noting that the very definition of 'technology' is evolving, with major implications for branding. Not long ago, the industry was defined by hardware and software – IBM and Microsoft and everything in between. Today, old definitions don't cut it. Is IBM a technology brand or a professional services brand? Is Netflix a technology company or a media company? Is Amazon an online juggernaut or a web-enabled catalogue retailer? While we prefer an expansive (and porous) definition of technology amid an industry of shifting boundaries, we will focus our discussion in this chapter on companies who generate the bulk of their business directly through the sale of technology products and services.

In fact, adopting too narrow a definition can be dangerous. The *Wall Street Journal* never thought of itself as a technology company, nor did it see itself as competing with technology companies. Then along came Bloomberg LP, which understood that it stood at the intersection of technology and financial information. The *Journal* (and its parent, Dow Jones) was sold to News Corp for $5 billion in 2007; in 2008, Bloomberg LP was valued at $25 billion. (And in 2009, News Corp wrote down the value of Dow Jones by $2.8 billion.) The *Journal* had – and continues to have – a venerable brand. But that brand was stuck in a world in which media and technology were oil and water. Failure to understand what constituted a 'technology' company may have cost Dow Jones shareholders billions of dollars.

Despite shifting definitions, and amid all this change and uncertainty, there are several principles that underlie successful technology branding:

- Understand ROI vs ROE.
- Keep up with the ever-changing technology buyer.
- Know your place on the brand spectrum.
- Brand confidence.
- Simplify ... but don't dumb down.

Understand ROI vs ROE

In any category, branding always begins with understanding your audience. In consumer products, audience segmentation typically encompasses demographic and psychographic segmentation. These are important in technology brands, but they're really not the whole story. Technology markets are usually either business or consumer, although some companies – for example Apple and HP – straddle both. B2B technology products must deliver a return on investment (ROI), and it is the job of technology brands to convey confidence that the promised ROI will be delivered: for a significant new investment in an ERP system or data centre, what can I expect by way of results. A brand can support the expectation of positive returns. In B2B sales, these expected returns can be communicated in dollar terms or some measure of operating efficiency. But instilling assurance that these financial and operational results will materialize is the job of a brand. In fact, as technology becomes more and more complex, and technology solutions more and more interconnected, a brand has to work even harder to instil confidence in the promised ROI.

A recent client, a national energy conservation firm, went to market with a message that was built on a simple proposition: its technology-driven process would deliver savings that were guaranteed to exceed its fees. But research showed that customers didn't understand or even trust how the savings were calculated. In light of this scepticism, what good was the guarantee? Despite the company's deep reliance on technology in the delivery of their consulting services, they had built their business around the notion of behavioural change, typically failing to communicate their wealth of technology-driven capabilities. Massive energy conservation could be achieved, the story went, simply by altering habits of building operations and management. By downplaying – or even avoiding – the technological prowess of the company, potential customers failed to appreciate the value of this ROI promise. Highlighting the behavioural change, rather than the technology tools and resources that supported this change, was leading potential clients to believe that they could easily achieve the results themselves. DIY energy cost savings. The value proposition had been based on technology-enabled, guaranteed savings; but the brand didn't inspire the trust needed to make that value proposition credible. With a new value proposition – reflecting a go-to-market story that repositioned the firm as the technology company they truly are – the firm was able to communicate a powerful and relevant story that converted technology and data from features into powerful support for the company's ROI promise.

In contrast to B2B, B2C brands must deliver a return on emotion (ROE). Increasingly, consumers feel a strong personal bond with their technology products: smartphones, tablets, PCs. More than most consumer products, technology products influence how we conduct our lives. It used to be said that 'clothes make the man'. But we would argue that today, technology defines the person far more than apparel. Your choice of smartphone, the case you carry it in, the apps you download and the games you play on it say more about you than almost anything not directly linked to your genetic code. For the consumer, the tech buying decision is about identity and personal expression as much as it's about features and functionality. Within a year of Apple introducing a new tablet or smartphone, its competitors inevitably come out with their own models that often outpace the original, if reviews and blogs are to be believed. Yet there remains an enormous customer base that won't consider anything but an Apple product. Apple makes the technology 'clothing' these consumers want to wear. It delivers unique ROE. Interestingly, Samsung, which outsells Apple in the mobile category, markets its Galaxy S4 smartphone as a 'life companion', a clear play to ROE.

ROE isn't irrelevant in B2B technology branding, although we would argue that ROI takes precedence. Recently, a Swiss-based company was looking to break into the US market with its tablet-based presentation platform for global pharmaceutical and financial services companies. The company's legacy brand was all about what the product did, and their communications tended towards the jargon of the B2B technology world. Yet research showed that a core reason senior sales and marketing executives purchased the platform was that it enhanced their own brands and inspired confidence in their sales force. Yes, the dazzling tablet-enabled graphics were great, and they loved the analytics the platform provided – the all-important ROI. But what clinched the sale was the *emotional* connection between the product and the people who would be using it – ROE. The company ultimately came to market with a strategy driven by 'impact with insight', reflecting the dual nature of the company's value proposition: dazzling presentations, real-time sales and marketing intelligence. The offering empowered customer sales teams like nothing else in the market – and while the nuts and bolts (the ROI) told a nice story, it was the passion it engendered among the users (ROE) that has enabled this company to expand well beyond its roots to a global client base across a range of industries.

Understanding the role of ROI and ROE in B2B and B2C technology branding is crucial to developing brands that will really resonate. ROI and ROE are important in many categories, but they are deeply embedded in the very heart of technology.

Keep up with the ever-changing technology buyer

Understanding buyer behaviour is, of course, critical to brand building. In technology branding, understanding buyer behaviour requires ongoing vigilance, because the nature of the technology buyer is always evolving, with profound significance for branding.

On both the consumer and B2B sides, this change is a result of technology becoming more integral to the way we live our lives and conduct business. Remember the very earliest days of the PC, dominated by brands such as Tandy, Radio Shack and Compaq? With no internet, no portable memory, and with digital photography 20 years off in the future, these companies struggled to find a value proposition that would impel someone to shell out thousands of dollars for a big, clunky piece of electronics. Organize your recipes! Consult an encyclopaedia! Teach yourself chess! The reality was, in the absence of truly practical applications, tech products were for tech junkies, the 'early adopters' who star in every intro marketing textbook. On the business side, technology decisions were the exclusive province of IT specialists – after all, they were most likely to be the only ones who would actually use the stuff.

Fast forward to the present. The internet, digital photography, mobility, social media, word processing and myriad other applications have transformed technology from a nice-to-have to a must-have. And consumer technology brands have evolved with this change. Ironically, as consumers have become more sophisticated, the brands have become less 'techie'. Where they used to focus on how a product works, they now focus on what a product can do for you. Think of Apple, whose brand has become increasingly pared down as its products have become more powerful and ubiquitous. In a sense, technology branding became more like CPG branding. Think about it: does P&G talk about the various chemicals that make up Tide detergent? Do Crest toothpaste ads dwell on the baking soda you scrub on your teeth? Of course not. It's all about making your clothes and your teeth whiter and brighter. Does Microsoft market the code behind Word or PowerPoint or its new operating system? Of course not. It's all about the power these programs and systems put at your fingertips. It was not too long ago that Intel-powered messages in the PC market focused on technical specs (chip speed, capacity) as the defining criteria in the purchase experience. As computers moved to more day-to-day usage – and as the technology specs soared to a point where even 'good enough' was well beyond the needs of 95 per cent of users – manufacturers increasingly differentiated on the intangibles: design, experience, brand.

On the B2B side, the big change has been the decentralization of the buying decision. As with consumers, this change has been driven by the ubiquity of technology throughout the organization. Buying power is shifting away from the CIO. As the importance of technology has grown, so has the overall cost to the business; not surprisingly, the CFO is more involved than ever before in the purchase decision. A 2012 report by Gartner (a leading information technology research and advisory company) and the Financial Executive Research Foundation suggests that over 40 per cent of companies anticipate that their CFOs will have a significantly larger role in IT buying. Furthermore, IT services research and consulting firm Everest Group conducted a survey in 2012 that found that IT professionals initiated only 25 per cent of IT initiatives within companies. In other words, three-quarters of IT initiatives began with the users of technology.

Chief marketing officers are also getting in the game. The rise of 'Big Data' brings a virtual infinity of information at the marketer's fingertips. Tools such as SalesForce and various marketing dashboards put technology to work identifying and tracking customers and their behaviour. In another 2013 report, Gartner predicted in an oft-quoted study that CMOs will spend more on IT than CIOs by the year 2017. Today, marketers have the ability to track purchasing behaviour online and, with the rise of mobile networks and GPS, out in the 'real' world. Little wonder marketing executives are getting intimately involved in technology decision-making. In fact, nearly every functional area of the modern enterprise has a role in major B2B technology decisions, including human resources, operations, supply chain, manufacturing and product development.

What does all this mean for branding? It means that a B2B tech brand must have a value proposition that appeals to very different audiences. The CIO will want reassurance that the product or service will integrate smoothly with legacy systems. The CFO will want an appropriate return on investment. The department head – Chief Talent Officer, for example, or CMO – will demand the right functionality above all else. Because there's no feasible way to create distinct, siloed brands for a single offering, the B2B technology brand must resonate strongly with each of these audiences.

Consider a brand like Cisco. The Cisco brand is driven by an underlying promise of 'Changing the way we live, work, play and learn'. Technology is more suggested than stated, more implicit than explicit in illustrating *how* they can drive this level of change. This is a powerful, visionary message that needs to translate more tangibly across a range of key stakeholder audiences – from business decision makers to technology decision makers to policy-makers to investors, and many others. How Cisco has gone to market behind this promise has evolved, but this central idea has been foundational to the Cisco brand. For the technology decision makers, Cisco delivers on this promise with size, scale, leadership and security. For business decision makers, the message is more about what Cisco enables from a business standpoint: collaboration, richer communication, global connectivity. Several years ago this led to a change from talking about connecting machines and powering the internet to the bigger idea of connecting people: The Human Network. Cisco needs to continually instil confidence among the IT buyer, but it also needs to project the bigger promise that creates relevance for the business decision maker.

And therein lies the challenge: identifying the pillars of a brand that support a complex, multidimensional value proposition. How can you create a brand that's relevant to a broad group of decision makers while making it resonate powerfully – and specifically – with each individual?

As with most branding challenges, the solution begins with research. It is vital to determine who the buyers are, who influences decision making, and what their criteria are. Simply talking to the person who signs the purchase order will not work; in today's technology landscape, that person probably wields little if any purchasing power.

As information has become more readily available to buyers, more and more decision makers are becoming involved in the buying process. And because technology companies are putting out reams (or terabytes) of content to drive buyers to engage, everyone that the buyer comes in contact with must be just as knowledgeable about the products as the marketing department. The pitfall for many technology companies is that they rely on techno-speak, forgetting that the business decision maker – the CMO or CFO, for example – may be confused or even turned off by a stew of jargon and acronyms.

Research is invaluable in understanding the language, pain points and triggers across each of the decision makers and influencers. In the B2B space, a technology purchase is a considered decision. With multiple voices driving and influencing a purchase decision, the sales cycle can take months, sometimes even years, as products are evaluated and tested, contracts vetted and negotiated. Consumer purchases are generally faster, sometimes even impulsive, and typically involve only one individual who is both the technology buyer *and* user. Market research in the consumer space to understand the differing demographic and psychographic profiles of your audiences is standard fare for major consumer product brands. Online tracking tools – such as retargeting, A/B testing and customer journey tracking, particularly in those products that are purchased online – further enhances marketers' knowledge of consumer behaviours and perceptions. But the

B2B process is more complex: more voices at the table, longer sales cycles, and rarely a straight-line experience that can track end-to-end customer journey through to purchase.

In an increasingly interconnected world, a technology decision does not happen in a vacuum. Compatibility, interoperability, availability of product or applications, network issues, etc are all factors that will lead to a more considered purchase. Influencers can play a crucial role – peers, family members, product reviews and bloggers. In both B2B and B2C technology products and services, the temptation is strong to create a brand that speaks to one feature, or appeals to the buyer alone and not to the ecosystem of influencers and decision makers. This temptation is strong because it is easy – both from a marketing perspective and operationally. But it is not a long-term strategy. Features are quickly copied or have a limited shelf-life. (Remember the 'push to talk' feature from Nextel? It was a singular application that resonated with a niche audience. Today it's extinct.) Standalone products are quickly usurped by multipurpose tools – think point-and-shoot video cameras or GPS devices.

Considered decisions require brands that can withstand multiple layers of scrutiny. This means that creating a technology brand is more complex than finding a catchphrase or tagline. The brand must attract attention at a high level but stand up to deeper and deeper levels of evaluation. Often, this means that the brand must be supported by messages that are carefully 'mapped' to different audiences: the user, the influencer, the partner, and so on. What's more, the technology brand must address different levels of investigation, from the superficial (Is this a quality offering?) to the deep (Is this interoperable?). Consider Cisco, again. Product specs and detailed performance indicators will read as technobabble for many key influencers – but this information remains a vital part of the communications journey for the user. By the same token, IT decision makers may see high concept Cisco TV ads connecting elementary school students across the globe and find them, well, elementary. Yet the high concept stuff couldn't fly with the IT guys without the 'goods' to back it up. And IT may never even be engaged in the discussion if the business leaders don't see the big idea benefit that the technology presents to the business. These are messages, of course, and not brands, but they must foot back to a brand that can carry all of them to the right audiences at the right time in the purchasing decision-making process.

Know where you stand on the brand spectrum

The diversity and shifting dynamics of the technology buyer and the complexity of the purchase decision are further exacerbated by the rapid evolution of most technology products and technology companies. All successful companies travel along a spectrum, from start-up to established leader. In technology, this journey occurs in what can seem like nanoseconds. Where a technology company or product happens to be on the spectrum has profound implications for how it brands itself.

Recently we worked on a global rebranding initiative with a leading provider of payments technology. For many years, the company was the dominant player in the payments space, their products playing a role in trillions of dollars in payment transactions per year. The company was squarely on the left side of the brand spectrum, illustrated in Figure 14.1. It was the clear leader in a relatively new market. Companies on this side of the brand spectrum tend to brand around features and functionality, and for an obvious reason: as an early mover in a new market, they often possess the breakthrough features that the market wants and no one else can provide.

But as the market matured – and in technology, markets mature faster than bananas – more players entered, so simply branding around features and functionality no longer worked. A product upgrade was quickly matched – or surpassed – by competitors. Branding around features and functionality proved to be a loser's game. Which isn't to say that the products and their capabilities aren't important. But, as this market leader has seen, 'mine is better than yours' is not in itself the recipe for a sustainable brand.

Being an established leader in a mature market allowed this company to survive with a brand mired in the land of features-and-functionality, even as new competitors emerged and potential disrupters (including eBay and Google) were challenging its very existence. The

FIGURE 14.1 The Brand Spectrum

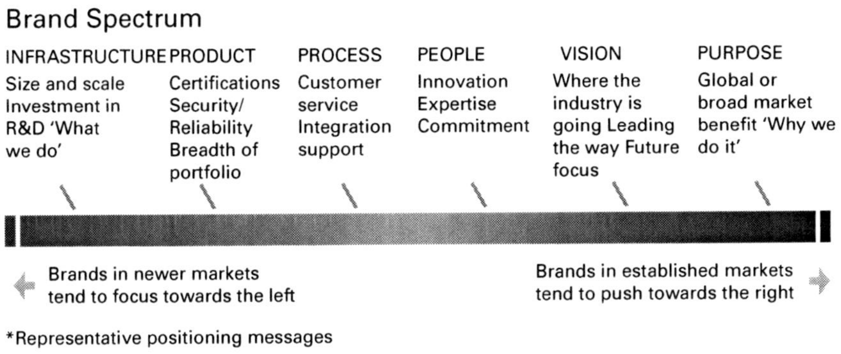

Brand Spectrum

INFRASTRUCTURE	PRODUCT	PROCESS	PEOPLE	VISION	PURPOSE
Size and scale Investment in R&D 'What we do'	Certifications Security/ Reliability Breadth of portfolio	Customer service Integration support	Innovation Expertise Commitment	Where the industry is going Leading the way Future focus	Global or broad market benefit 'Why we do it'

⬅ Brands in newer markets tend to focus towards the left

Brands in established markets tend to push towards the right ➡

*Representative positioning messages

SOURCE © 2014 DeSantis Breindel

brand needed to refocus on the qualities that underpinned the products, not the products themselves. On the brand spectrum, this suggests a position more towards the right building upon qualities of the company's people, its character and its ultimate purpose.

A technology brand based on the company's people offered an opportunity to focus on the more inimitable qualities of the firm, how and where great products are created, not the products themselves. In the B2B space, some companies use a case study approach to brand around their people and the people they serve. SAP and Xerox do a good job of building their respective brands not on the products and services they sell, but rather by focusing on what they have enabled for their clients. With Xerox, for example, the 'Ready for Real Business' line drove some memorable case study advertising initiatives with Ducati and Michelin, among others, highlighting their outsourcing capabilities that enable their clients to focus on their own core strengths.

Back to the payments technology company. Research among the company's customers, prospects and employees revealed that while its products were generally given high marks, they weren't seen as differentiated from those of competitors. What did stand out was the reputation of its people, particularly the engineers, product specialists and customer relations professionals responsible for large-scale implementation. The company needed to change the conversation. A game of leapfrog around features and functionality was missing the point. The brand needed to be recast around the business challenges they solved – and the people who solved them. In a highly depersonalized technology category focused on baud rates and model numbers, a people-based brand offers an opportunity to highlight the real points of difference – and to speak in ways that resonate as powerfully with business decision makers as they do with the technology buyers.

The position on the spectrum farthest to the right is 'purpose'. This refers not to the customer benefit – this needs to be baked into any brand at every position on the spectrum. 'Purpose' refers to the company's reason for being ... a higher purpose, if you will. Companies that brand around purpose are generally very well established in mature markets and have maintained leadership over multiple product cycles, and can thus project a spirit of confidence and even altruism without risk of being seen as grandiose. IBM certainly falls into this category. Though the company has endured some well-publicized rough patches, it successfully transitioned from a pure hardware play to a hardware and services powerhouse. 'Big Blue' is bigger than ever, and its brand reflects this stature: 'Smarter Planet.' That's a brand as far right on the spectrum as you can get ... until someone comes along claiming to edify the universe or the galaxy! And yet it works. It connects and elevates everything IBM does into one stunning and differentiated value proposition: we're making the world smarter. Smarter Planet is a territory that not many brands other than IBM could have claimed. Considering the heritage and deep technology reputation of IBM, their expertise is not questioned. And when they tell a story of bringing technology-driven insight to make mass transit systems run more efficiently or to facilitate load balancing in a power plant, you get it. IBM has the credibility to tell a big global story to the point where they can inject their technology brand into almost any large-scale challenge in a relevant way.

Google is an example of a technology brand that has effectively straddled the 'character' and 'purpose' territories. The company's mission is clear: 'to organize the world's information and make it universally accessible and useful.' This simple line goes to the heart of its brand. But there's a light-heartedness to Google's brand that speaks to its character. Think of the way it is constantly playing with its logo – how many companies have the confidence to do that? Humour and confidence are very much part of the Google brand – and they're classic 'character' traits.

Cisco's brand evolution demonstrates how a technology company moves along the spectrum – and quickly. Twenty years ago, Cisco's brand was built around 'Empowering the Internet Generation'. It was a bold idea but also rather specific: the company's products were a key driver of the burgeoning world wide web. As the company matured – along with the market for networking hardware – Cisco adapted its brand. 'This is the Network. Now' voiced more confidence, and replacing 'internet' with 'network' spoke to broader ambitions. This in turn was replaced by a brand built around 'The Human Network' – which both reflected the talents of its people and humanized the enormous complexity of its networking products. But in 2012, Cisco determined that it wanted to be more than the largest computer networking equipment manufacturer. It wanted to be a sort of pathfinder in the global information ecosystem, moving further along the brand spectrum to a 'purpose' brand. This new aspiration is summed up in Cisco's new brand – 'Tomorrow Starts Here'. As the company's core router market continued to mature and evolve, the brand (and the business strategy) of this global leader evolved right along with it.

Thinking of branding in terms of a spectrum is a particularly useful tool for technology companies as a highly innovative market will quickly push companies to speak in terms of their benefit – what they enable or what they make possible – once the basic tenets of *what* they do is well understood by customers and mimicked by fast followers. The key is knowing where on the spectrum you have the relevance and credibility today – and where you see yourself moving towards in the future.

Brand confidence

Like all brands, technology brands need to convey a differentiated value proposition that supports a set of clear and compelling buyer benefits. Yet technology brands bear an additional burden: they need to communicate reliability and, often, compatibility or interoperability.

Think about it. When you buy a jar of peanut butter, you need not worry about what type of bread you will be eating it on or what brand of jelly you'll be pairing it with. Ditto most products, whether

B2C or B2B. But technology has become so pervasive in our personal and professional lives that it seems as if none of our gadgets operate in a vacuum. In the consumer space, this can be a nuisance and make a considered technology decision that much more so. In the B2B world, these stakes are much higher. Commitment to a technology brand is a long-term play. How will it play with the rest of our systems? Will this product integrate with my CRM or my billing software? Will this company be able to support the software upgrades of my other vendors? Will this company remain a viable entity for the expected life of this product (for which I may need ongoing support or upgrades)? These questions get well beyond our typical definition of brand – but they are often integral buying criteria in the B2B space and, thus, play a role in how a brand communicates to the market.

At its most basic, in both B2B and B2C, compatibility and interoperability is communicated through co-branding – often a seemingly endless string of logos on sell sheets or packaging or, in the case of many flat screen TVs, right on the product itself. These co-brands are a way for companies to try to calm the nerves around interoperability – though the sheer abundance of these logos can often be more confusing than reassuring. Apple over the years has striven to simplify this concern by building and supporting a closed product ecosystem. For the user, all they need to see is the Apple logo. Though, as Apple has grown and the product line has expanded across computers, tablets and handsets with upgrading operating systems, this decision point is not nearly as simple as it once was. Still, the Apple brand suggests a certain commitment to the experience that gives consumers the reassurance they need. Apple further supports this notion with the Genius Bar in the Apple Stores. While many large-scale technology companies are hesitant to even let you reach them by phone, Apple makes it relatively easy for you to walk into a store for some troubleshooting and advice. As brand experiences go, this is a home run.

Simplify . . . but don't dumb down

Technology is complicated. Technology brands cannot be. Simplification is almost always a core component of a successful technology brand. For Apple, this is exemplified by its products, its advertising, its interfaces. Think of Google's homepage. Even as the company has expanded well beyond its basic search function, this still remains at the heart of what they do – and the simplicity of the Google homepage reflects this. But reducing a technology brand to its simplest form isn't always the best approach. Sometimes a bit of techno-speak can be useful in creating differentiation or building credibility. The leading mobile service providers all advertise some variation on 'the fastest 4G network'. How many consumers know that 4G stands for fourth generation, let alone what makes the fourth generation faster than the third? Yet that '4G' suggests that there are a lot of moving pieces, and smart minds, behind every mobile call.

Often in technology branding, the key is to make it easy for the buyer to understand how complex a product really is. Intel implicitly does this with its long-standing 'Intel Inside' brand. It's a thoroughly simple concept that strongly suggests the ability to execute highly complex but unseen processes. The technology-powered energy conservation company detailed earlier had a brand that made its technology and data-fuelled processes seem very simple – so simple, in fact, that a lot of its prospects felt they could achieve results without the company's help. Adding jargon and showing the market the true complexity of comprehensive energy saving solutions helped decision makers understand the value this firm brought to market. In technology, there is a subtle but critical difference between simplifying and dumbing down.

More often than not, technology brands almost always need to simplify and clarify. And it's the rare brand, such as Apple or Google, that can completely obscure, from a brand perspective, the vast layers of complexity its offering represents. Finding the balance – between simplicity and complexity – for a given product or company is vitally important to developing a winning technology brand.

In technology, the pace of change, buyer dynamics and the multiple levels of complexity demand a unique approach to brand development. Outside of technology, brands can endure for decades – think 'Friendly Skies' or 'See the USA in a Chevrolet', both enjoying a renaissance as we write this chapter. But it's the rare technology brand that can withstand the almost constant change affecting buyers, influencers, channels and, of course, the products and services themselves. Among the most celebrated of these changes might be the likes of Apple Computer becoming the technology and digital media juggernaut we now know as Apple; and the Big Blue of old, the dominant mainframe/PC manufacturer, evolving into the thought-leading global technology services company we know today. Yet in both of these cases, there is a core story that runs through even these massive evolutions in business model. For Apple, a simplicity of purpose and an ideal that technology should be subservient to man has carried them through into a wide range of applications where technology is the means rather than the entire story. For IBM, the intelligence and the deep industry knowledge and exposure that their scale allowed became a pathway to the 'Smarter Planet'.

A great brand is built on core principles that carry well beyond the product experience to define the people, the culture and the approach. For technology companies this is no different. Yet as one day's technology company is tomorrow's media company or professional services company, it is imperative that technology brands truly understand what it is that makes them special and ensure that they look to these tenets to define how they continue to evolve their offerings and their customer relationships into the future.

Biographies

Howard Breindel (Co-CEO, DeSantis Breindel) has a long-standing track record of building businesses that draw on his expertise in marketing and leveraging technology. He began his marketing career at Grey Global Group, as the co-founder of an innovative computer graphics subsidiary. Howard led the firm's rapid growth among Fortune 500 companies, establishing them as an internationally recognized leader in C-Suite corporate and investor communications. Later, Howard pioneered interactive multimedia and internet communications for many of the largest global financial services, healthcare and media companies and built the firm into one of Grey's most profitable subsidiaries. Howard was also a co-founder of Directors Desk, a revolutionary digital communications platform for boards of directors of public corporations, which was purchased by NAS-DAQ in 2007. Today, as partner and co-founder of DeSantis Breindel, Howard leads branding and marketing strategy engagements for companies in financial services, technology, professional services, life sciences, real estate and energy. He has worked with clients such as VeriFone, Interactive Data, Honeywell, Deutsche Bank, CIT, Guggenheim and Pfizer.

Jonathan Paisner (Managing Director, DeSantis Breindel) leads the brand strategy practice at DeSantis Breindel, working with companies across a variety of industries to harness the power in their brands as a vehicle to drive business growth. Throughout his career, Jonathan has helped clients like Cisco Systems, AT&T, VeriFone, Adobe, Allstate, Tektronix and The Arc address a host of strategic brand challenges including positioning, messaging, naming, brand architecture, co-branding and internal communications. After earning his MBA at Columbia Business School, Jonathan created and ran the licensing division of A&E Television Networks, overseeing the development of dozens of brand partnerships to extend the A&E family of brands into a broad range of media products and experiences.

Seth Margolis (Strategy Director, DeSantis Breindel) has over 20 years of experience in brand strategy and marketing communications. After receiving an MBA from New York University's Stern School of Business, Seth served as an Advertising Director at McGraw-Hill and a Marketing Director at KPMG. At DeSantis Breindel, Seth has extensive experience working with organizations to distil and communicate their brand position. With a perspective grounded in research, Seth works with a variety of financial services, professional services, not-for-profit, healthcare and technology organizations to clarify their key messages and deliver them through a range of strategic outputs. Clients include VeriFone, Interactive Data, Symyx, Logitech, The American Bankers Association, Pfizer, CIT and Deutsche Bank.

Football brands

15

SUE BRIDGEWATER

Football clubs *are* brands.

That statement alone will probably put up the hackles of many football fans, so this chapter begins by examining why this is and must be the case.

Sport often symbolizes for its fans higher ideals; achievement, victory, commitment, excellence, endurance. Attending a sporting event, often in leisure time after a hard working week, serves as a form of escapism and, hopefully, entertainment. Many of us play, or have played the same sports that we enjoy as fans. Maybe not to the same level, but sufficiently that we feel ourselves to be engaged and immersed in a sporting event, rather than as detached spectators or viewers. Fans can imagine themselves scoring that winning goal, or rugby try, or cricket run, and feel the thrill vicariously. Fans may feel that they are 'kicking every ball' or at least are straining with every fibre to will on their sporting favourites on track, pitch or court. Fans of a sports club, or sports star are often passionate in their support, uplifted and united in moments of triumph and hope; grown men exchanging hugs with strangers, or downcast, despondent and despairing in defeat.

This intense emotional appeal and engagement, is why sport has a value as an entertainment, and hence as a business. Sport also has something, which many other forms of entertainment do not; we do not know what will happen in a match between two opponents, even if these are the same opponents as in a match earlier in the season, or if finances suggest that one should be stronger than another. Sport is 'unscripted drama' and has what economist call 'uncertainty of outcome' (Kuper and Szymanski, 2012) and this adds immensely to its value and keeps us coming back week after week, year after year.

The value of this unscripted drama, or – in other words - of this 'uncertainty of outcome' has been recognized by businesses. So sport sponsorship has become a major field of commercial activity (Bridgewater, 2014), creating associations between sports stars or clubs whose massive emotional appeal garners attention and creates an emotional resonance with brands. Similarly, the market for broadcast of sports events has grown and with it, opportunities for sport as a means of market communication. Advertising slots in the Superbowl Final in American Football are the most widely viewed and most expensive in the world.

In football, the creation of the English Premier League in 1992, the entry of Sky Sports into live coverage of matches in England and before that the legacy of Berlusconi who established the link between clubs and TV rights in Italian football set football on a pathway towards greater commercialization. Attracting the best talent, signing players from different countries, became not just a case of putting together a winning football team, but a more complex mix of appealing to different target markets, such as China, or South Korea, or the United States. The teams in football had most certainly moved from amateur sporting clubs to professional businesses. The 'business of football' became a largely accepted term. Its customers are the fans who pay to attend matches or to watch them via broadcast media. In football, the broadcast rights for English Premier League rose to a massive £1 billion a year as of 2013–14 with the entry of BT Sport and the rights for live European Champions League coverage to £900 million in a deal announced on 9 November 2013 (*The Guardian*, 2013).

Football has been referred to by its fans as 'the beautiful game' but it is without doubt now also a global business, with fans in all parts of the Triad, to mega markets such as China and India, to Africa and its recent massive growth in the Middle East with the award of the 2022 World Cup to Qatar and with investment by Middle Eastern investors in some of football's biggest clubs.

The clubs who make up the major leagues in these countries have sporting aims, and many come from amateur roots, but they are also businesses which engage in marketing activities, they study and design promotional, price and other packages for fans to consume their services. Fans are intensely loyal to particular clubs (Tapp, 2004; Tapp and Clowes, 2002; Bridgewater, 2010; Mahony *et al*, 2000; Mahony *et al*, 2002, Madrigal, 1995).

Different clubs have different identities, they have logos, or crests, and are associated with different colours, shirts, stadia and geographies. These clubs have all the attributes of brands (Aaker, 1996; Keller, 2001) from Awareness, differing levels of Perceived Quality and Loyalty. They *are* brands, which attract sponsors and customers and co-branding deals; Chelsea and Samsung, Manchester City and Ethihad, Barcelona and Qatar Airways, Bayern München and Deutsche Telekom. Global brands are allying themselves with football's global brands.

It is, however, equally clear that many fans do not like them to be referred to as brands, seeing this as a reinforcement of the commercial development of sport. For these fans, viewing sport as a business interferes with the purity of sport as a heroic challenge, as a contest. Moreover, 'fans' point to their intense loyalty and passion for the sports stars and clubs that they support and contend that they are not 'just' paying customers. Accordingly, fan status is seen by some as being distinct from consumer or customer in the nature of its relationship with the sports' club or sports' star. Indeed, it does appear that while clubs and sports' stars might be viewed as brands, that these are distinct types of brand that have some unique characteristics which will be expanded upon in the remainder of this chapter.

What are the unique characteristics of football brands?

Football brands:

> share all the characteristics of the flakier specimens on offer: product performance that is at worst wildly erratic and at best sublime; constantly changing iconography (as the money men cash in on this season's strip); and an emotional appeal that transcends all reason. Was Dr Johnson thinking of football fans when he mused on 'a triumph of hope over experience'?

> Because it is hope that drives the game. Hope wrapped up in hero worship, fierce regional and national loyalties, endless tolerance of the antics of the sport's more pampered performers; '30 years of hurt' and a thousand other indignities. Greed too – and egos the size of a house. But we love it – and we invented it. We may no longer be very good at it, but for ninety minutes a week, around the country, football remains the ultimate fantasy brand. (Beverland, 2010)

Of course, Beverland's quote refers to the context of English football, and some of the cultural artefacts within it. Football is also marked out by being a game with a global appeal, and its roots can be traced back to 3BC when a predecessor of the game was documented in China, and other variants were played at or around the same time in the places that are now Japan, Argentina and the United Kingdom. One characteristic of football brands is that the game has global appeal, although major global brands, such as Manchester United, are global brands within a relatively small organization with between 200 and 500 employees.

This section now focuses on a number of the distinctive characteristics of the football brand and studies them to see why football might be viewed as 'the ultimate fantasy brand' (Beverland, 2010) and in what ways we might enhance our understanding of branding more broadly, in studying these brands whose 'product' varies so greatly in its level of performance and whose 'customers' are so passionately and tribally fierce in their loyalty (Maffesoli, 1996).

Sports marketing theory argues strongly that football and other sports clubs should be considered as brands (Tapp, 2004; Mahony, Madrigal and Howard, 2000; Wann and Branscombe, 1993). These arguments focus on a number of attributes of sports clubs, which make this appropriate.

First, there are high levels of *awareness* of football clubs and their players. Global broadcasting of football matches and the sheer appetite of fans to know detail about their favourites mean that a massive amount of football content is created and consumed. Football and Sports News has its own 24/7 channel and a fan, should they wish, could watch almost continual live football from somewhere in the world via satellite TV stations such as Sky TV, Al Jazeera, BT Sport and ESPN.

Second, this intense media and fan interest in football brands and their players means that they are increasingly conscious of their brand *identity and image.* The image of players, 'image rights' values and deals with players on transfer into clubs and the value of sponsorship deals which they are entering into reflect the dominance of image in football club thinking. As the behaviour of players and managers will be scrutinized by a global audience, with the power of multiple replays, it must be value-driven and consistent with the values of the club. Clubs increasingly focus on what their brand stands for, what are its distinctive values. For example, Norwich City emphasize the social and community role of the club in its area. Arsenal FC say that the brand is:

> synonymous with history, tradition and success. We believe that the Club exists to make our fans proud wherever they are in the world and however they choose to follow us. Everyone that works for the Club understands that we will fulfill our goal of making fans proud by being together, always moving forward and doing things 'The Arsenal Way'. This final element is a key ingredient of who we are. It's about thinking about others, getting the detail right and going above and beyond expectations. (BrandFinance Football 50, 2013)

Third, sports attract *loyal*, even fanatical, support. Within sports marketing literature there is a growing volume of work in the areas of 'fan identification' or the *relationships*, which fans have with clubs (Lascu *et al*, 1995; Sutton *et al*, 1997; Wann and Branscombe, 1993; Wann and Dolan, 2001) and their loyalty to particular teams or sports personalities (Tapp, 2004; Bridgewater, 2010).

Sports marketing research also addresses the different dimensions of these football brands to explore which aspects of a football brand fans want to engage with and to seek to understand what motivates this intense loyalty (Wann and Branscombe, 1993; Madrigal, 1995; Mahony, Madrigal and Howard 2000). Some of these are considered in the following section.

Brand value of football brands

When discussing the brand equity of football brands, many reports define their own methodology for measuring the value of the brand.

One such report, BrandFinance Football 50 (2013), for example, discusses the financial value of football brands using a 'Royalty Relief' method. Focusing on the brand as a trademark and the intellectual property which is associated with it, the method uses financial data to establish how much, if we assumed the organization did not own the brand itself, it would pay for the rights to use the brand. This is based on assessment of the strength of the brand, with reference to its heritage, record of success, honours, attendances and global reach and the 'Royalty Rate' based on comparable licensing agreements.

The focus on the financial indicators of brand value is echoed in some of the measures of brand equity adopted by football clubs. So, for example, Tottenham Hotspur refer to:

> tangible indicators of brand value, i.e. growth in commercial revenues, merchandising and licensing, fan base development, global TV audiences for our matches, estimated size of our fan base in key territories, volume of engaged fans across all our channels globally and the level of reach and increase in transacting supporters. (BrandFinance Football 50, 2013)

Brand equity, can, however, be measured in a number of different ways. If we adopt Aaker's (1996) dimensions of brand equity – Awareness, Image, Perceived Quality and Loyalty – we can see both similarities and differences between football brands and brands in general.

Awareness

In football, matchday attendance and revenue are very important to football clubs, but the extent to which clubs rely on fans attending in person, or on the televised rights to live matches and highlights packages, varies between leagues and countries. In general, the better the league, the more attractive it is to broadcasters. The broadcast rights package for the English Premier League was recently sold for £3 billion, but broadcast structure differs considerably even among the major leagues, with Bundesliga for example owning its own TV channel and selling its own content to broadcasters, and leagues differing in whether they sell rights individually by club as in La Liga, Spain, or collectively, English Premier League (Deloitte, 2013).

Global coverage of competitions such as the Europa Champions League has resulted in many European clubs having fans in all corners of the world. To build awareness and to encourage support of teams, football clubs, especially those in the leagues with larger global audiences such as the English Premier League or Spanish La Liga may undertake tours of different countries during their close season. Examples include Manchester United, in Asia Pacific and in South Africa. These tours may be the only time in which fans in those countries have the opportunity to see their heroes play and experience a live match, given constraints on stadium capacity. So, for example, Old Trafford, the stadium of Manchester United has a capacity of 80,000, although the club refers to a global fanbase of 650 million. While some clubs undertake a tour and play against local opposition, other clubs approach international tours differently. So, for example, in the summer of 2013, Italian Serie A clubs AC Milan and Inter Milan played in the Guinness International Champions Cup in the United States. Tottenham see their main focus outside of domestic football as being in the United States and Asia. Arsenal says that, as a club that already has a global fanbase, its main growth is currently in Africa and Asia.

Identity

Football brand logos

Football clubs usually use a traditional badge, often also displayed on the team shirt, as their logo. As with many other brand logos, such as McDonald's Golden Arches or the Nike Swoosh, the Real Madrid golden crown-topped circle or the Manchester United badge would be instantly recognizable, even if the name of the club were obscured.

Football club brands often contain a lot of symbolism. My own club, Sunderland AFC used to have a ship on its badge to reflect the shipbuilding heritage of the City. In 1997, after the demise of shipbuilding in Sunderland, and to coincide with the move into the new stadium, built on an old coal-mining site, the club unveiled a new club crest comprising images of local landmarks, such as Wearmouth Bridge and Penshaw Monument, with a colliery wheel to reflect the mining tradition. The club explains that the new crest is designed to pay tribute to the club's fans across the region and includes images from different parts of the area from which fans come.

Interbrand's work with Russian football club Rubin Kazan, was also to capture the brand's local identity:

> For the past decade, Rubin Kazan has been one of the fastest-growing European football clubs. Rubin Kazan's new identity was inspired by the club's desire to celebrate its success, prepare for future growth, and emphasize its role as an ambassador to the city of Kazan: a community where different cultures and religions have coexisted harmoniously for centuries.

The club's philosophy stems from the essence of the city it represents: constant change and harmony through diversity.

The new logo expresses this philosophy. The club name refers to the ruby, one of the hardest gemstones in the world. It evokes the club's constant commitment to achieving new goals. Keeping in line with the club's philosophy, the digitalization of the logo reflects its state of perpetual change. A westerly facing Zilant, a mythical creature and a symbol of the city, dominates the logotype and defines its shape (www.interbrand.com/Libraries/Press_Release/Rubin_Kazan_Press_Release_final.sflb.ashx).

Similarly, a number of other football clubs have changed their crest, or logo, over the years. Fulham FC explains a transition from the earliest badge which was a black and white representation of its ground, Craven Cottage, to the crest of the London Hammersmith Borough, used from 1947 to a 'retro' Fulham FC logo, a reversion to the London and Hammersmith Borough logo and finally, in 2001, based on research which showed that only 14 per cent of the club's fans recognized this logo (www.footballcrests.com/clubs/fulham-fc) to a simplified version of the club's initials. Given the growing commercial value of football brands, clubs increasingly employ teams of marketers and, as seen before, also high-profile branding professionals to help with repositioning and brand development.

Yet the intensity with which fans adhere to the traditions of their club, and maybe to a logo which they associate with a particular period in the club's history, can be seen in the campaigns which they have, on occasion, raised against changes to the club logo. Football brands are, often, heritage brands in which the geographic location of the club may be an essential component of the club. Accordingly, traditional elements or local references in a football club crest may have strong significance to fans. The challenge may be to refresh with a view to update and maybe simplify logos for digital communication, while preserving the heritage and unique identity for fans.

This was the case with Coventry City FC in England. In 2005, when Coventry City Football Club, then of the English Coca-Cola Championship (second league), proposed a new logo to mark the move from Highfield Road to the new Ricoh Arena, fans were not happy at the changes. Fans were happy to mark this development in the club's history, but were unhappy that the new logo did not feature the phoenix – supposed to represent Lady Godiva's husband Leofric – or else alternatively the postwar rebuilding of the city of Coventry. The castle on top of the elephant had also been removed, as had the football. The club responded to fans' concerns by dropping the proposed changes and sticking to the previous club logo.

As can be seen from the above, football clubs logos vary in their origins and style but tend to have some common features:

- Club logos tend to be based on historical club crests.
- Some of these have been redrawn – and often simplified – in relatively recent times.
- Many club logos incorporate the club's initials.
- Regional heraldic crests often feature.
- Colours are significant, with logos often heavily featuring the colour of the club's shirt colours often in conjunction with colours which have regional or other significance.
- Local buildings and landmarks also feature frequently on football club logos suggesting the importance of local and regional values.

The strength of fans' association with the club badge and other aspects of football brand might be explained by the intensity of the association between fans and clubs. In research conducted in 2001, Bridgewater identified 'History and Symbols' as one of the values of football brands. Fans prided themselves on their knowledge of the history, tradition, origins of crest and other facts about their chosen clubs.

Perceived quality

Deloitte and Touche (2013) shows a strong correlation between the quality of a club's squad (as measured by player wages) and the club's sporting performance. In academic literature, fans are found by economic studies to be more loyal to teams that are successful (Baade and Tiehen, 1990; Domazlicky and Kerr, 1990). This is measured both by high average attendances and lesser variability in attendances, although the latter is of course of limited use for successful football clubs, many of whom operate at capacity and have waiting lists for season tickets.

Yet perceived quality is not the only explanation for the level of engagement between football fans and the clubs that they support. Many clubs with little or no prospects of winning cups and leagues, still have strongly loyal fanbases. My own team, Sunderland have not won a cup since 1973 and are most often to be found flirting with relegation from the Premier League, but both they and their local rivals, Newcastle United, have strong fan attendance. The reasons why fans support teams with relatively low levels of perceived quality is explored in the section on loyalty to football brands, below.

Before moving on to loyalty, one or two other aspects of 'perceived quality' are worthy of mention, as these seem in many ways distinct from the issues facing brands in general.

First, that these brands vary in their quality between and even within seasons. A football team may have a very good season, or a good cup run, or a good match but at other times may have much poorer levels of performance and face the challenge of how to retain fans during these difficult periods. If other types of brands under-performed to the same extent, customers would surely switch (Aaker, Fournier and Brasel 2004).

Second, actual quality, as measured by points on a league table, or silverware, is often distorted in the minds of fans, who are so passionately attached to their clubs. Previous research (Bridgewater, 2010) shows Manchester United fans in the 1999–2000 season rating themselves as 'under-performing' despite winning the Premier League, but this is in comparison with the heights of the previous season 1998–1999, in which they had won the Treble of FA Cup, Premier League and Champions League. So the 'quality' of football brands is both relative and a perception of the fans.

Loyalty: The battle for the hearts and minds

Successful brands inspire loyalty, and this loyalty is often based on emotional as well as rational value placed on brands by their customers. Ries and Trout (2001) emphasize the need for positioning to be based on what happens in the customer's mind.

What is happening in the minds of football fans is intensely emotional. In many ways, football brands are close to Kevin Roberts' of Saatchi's concept of 'Lovemarks' described as a way of winning the consumer marketplace and later elaborated in both his follow-up book and the work of Sheehan (2013) *Loveworks* which discusses the need to make emotional connections to win the marketplace:

> Lovemarks reach your heart as well as your mind, creating an intimate, emotional connection that you just can't live without. Ever.

So in many ways, football brands sound as though they may be the ultimate 'Lovemark' and yet in others, football brands are most assuredly *not* similar to Lovemarks, the definition of which begins:

> Lovemarks are the future beyond brands. They deliver beyond your expectations of great performance.

These are intensely emotional brands, whose fans love them beyond reason *despite* what is often a poor or wildly fluctuating level of performance.

So how does loyalty work for football brands, and how do you manage this high level of interest and attachment when performance is not going well?

One insight into why loyalty to football brands is so intense comes from understanding why people support their chosen team.

In their Origins of Support research in 2009, Eon, then sponsors of the FA Cup identified reasons why fans began to support a particular club. Among these influences are family connections with a particular club; if either the person's father, mother, grandparent or other family member was a supporter of a particular club, they may have played a positive influence in the decision of which team to support.

Other reasons why fans decide to support a particular team include the influence of friends and social peers, or a particularly memorable match. I am one of a generation of Sunderland fans who were influenced not only by local and family ties to the club but also by Sunderland winning the FA Cup in 1973. Motivations might also include a star player or coach who captures the attention of the fan and triggers attachment to a particular club.

So, the emotional connection to a football brand may be to do with family loyalty, or local, geographic loyalty to a place of birth or family heritage. As these are often very important to individuals, so identification with a football brand may be about much more than just a sporting contest.

Furthermore, in their study of J-league football, Mahony, Madrigal and Howard (2002), building on Wann's (1995) broader sports fan motivation scale, identify seven needs that may be fulfilled by identification with a football brand. These are:

- *Drama*. Spectators who are more interested in the game of football than in a particular team want to see interesting and closely contested matches.

- *Vicarious achievement*. Fans often unthinkingly refer to themselves as playing a role in successful performances: 'We outclassed them'; 'We were the 12th man' while distancing themselves from poor performance: 'They were useless last night'; 'The manager got the team selection wrong'; 'The Board ought to put their hands in their pockets.' There is considerable evidence that fans feel the successes of their team to be their own successes and feel good about themselves when the team win. Cialdini *et al* (1976) refer to this as BIRGing or Basking in Reflected Glory. References to famous victories, legendary players and great sporting occasions may often be included both in match programmes, or websites and social media to increase fan connection with a football club.

- *Aesthetics*. That overhead bicycle kick, the way in which the leading striker chipped the goalkeeper or a heroic penalty save. Such moments are replayed and etch themselves on the consciousness of football fans. Many fans can recall in precise detail not only how these moments looked but also the television or radio commentary that went with media coverage of these incidents. The advent of club TV channels, and the ability to share clips on social media such as YouTube, Facebook and Twitter, mean that fans often generate their own content by capturing and sharing these moments.

- *Team attachment*. This is closest to the brand loyalty we might have to other types of organizations. The fan will develop an attachment to the club as an organization, to the squad of players and to the coaching and management staff. Football clubs have segmented their fanbase. At its simplest this might be by frequency of attendance, hard core 'bedrock' fans who attend every game and identify strongly with the club, more occasional support, new fans; but increasingly this might go further into benefit segmentation of the values which matter most to different types of fans. So some younger segments place more importance on the social elements of match attendance with friends, whereas the bedrock support is often characterized by stronger emotional attachment.

- *Player attachment*. Some fans are attracted to support a team because of a particular player who is playing for that team. This phenomenon can be seen clearly when a player of a particular nationality joins a club and interest in that club from both fans and media from that country increases, such as when Japanese player, Juanichi Inamoto, joined Arsenal, and

Ji-Sung Park of South Korea, Manchester United. Different clubs adopt different strategies with regards to building brands around specific players. So Juventus say of their players: 'There was a Juventus before them and there will be a Juventus after them, the club is more important than any one player' (BrandFinance Football 50, 2013) and the emphasis is placed on the club brand more than particular players, while other clubs may focus on Q&A sessions with particular players and build upon the image and identity of individual players within their clubs to enhance their football brand. Hence Arsenal say of their players: 'The players are undoubtedly the club's primaryasset and we work hard to ensure that they, like the rest of the club's staff, adhere to our vision and values both on and off the pitch. The growth in digital and social media means that many players now interact directly with supporters, and while this presents its challenges, we are able, through consistent engagement and comprehensive media training, to provide the players with clear parameters, whilst using their individual appeal and profile to enhance and support the club's own initiatives' (BrandFinance Football 50, 2013).

- *Sport attachment.* As a neutral supporter, fan of another club or fan of another sport, a fan may still enjoy watching a good, end to end football match. There is no particular affiliation to the club, but the experience of attending an interesting sporting event may still drive behavioural loyalty.

- *Community pride.* Many fans support a local team or a team associated with their family roots or a place where they have lived at some stage of their life. Tottenham Hotspur refer to the importance of community in their discussion of brand building (BrandFinance Football 50, 2013): 'What we do off the pitch is also important in determining our brand values and gaining new supporters, so on- and off-pitch activities are mutually supportive. By way of example, we are at the forefront of charitable efforts and CSR [Corporate Social Responsibility] through our Tottenham Hotspur Foundation, which is dedicated to utilizing the power of football to engage young people and create life changing opportunities. The Foundation runs a vast number of programmes which are fully supported by the players and coaching staff, who attend events on a weekly basis. This has earned the club a reputation for being responsible, caring and inspiring. Our global coaching programmes also take the "Tottenham style" of play to grass roots football at schools and colleges. Everything we do is guided by our core principles.'

How to keep fans loyal when times are tough

By their nature, football brands experience highs and lows. Without these, fan interest and attachment might not be so great. The possibility of a victory against the odds, is what keeps many fans gripped, even when on the pitch play is not wonderful. Cialdini *et al* (1976) referred to BIRGing, or Basking in Reflected Glory, but the flipside of the coin is the behaviour of fans in the face of poor performances.

While customers of other types of brands might switch in the face of poor performance, such is the intense and emotional loyalty of football fans to their clubs, that this is unthinkable. Poor performance hurts though, so fans often react by distancing themselves and avoiding rival fans who might glory in this hurt, and even steer away from media coverage and talking about the match. Cialdini *et al* (1976) refer to this as CORFing or Cutting Off Rejected Failure. So the level of activity and involvement of fans of a team which loses goes down, at least in the immediate aftermath of a poor result.

In research conducted across the Premier League in 2001, Bridgewater identified five key drivers of fan loyalty to football clubs. These were:

- Organizational values: the stability, financial health, governance and community involvement of the club.
- Team support: how successful the team is, how it is perceived by fans of other clubs.
- Social bonds: going to matches with a social group, maybe going for a drink or travelling to matches with friends.

- Self-esteem: how being loyal to the team makes the individual feel about themself.
- History and symbols: knowledge of the club, history, symbols, stories and heritage.

While all of these elements occurred to some extent in fans of all Premier League clubs, these varied in a number of ways.

First, different segments within the fanbase of individual clubs ranked higher on different elements, so younger fans placed more emphasis on social and self-esteem whereas History and Symbols and Team Attachment emerged more strongly for season ticket holders and older bedrock support.

Second, the weighting on these varied with the level of perceived success of clubs. Where teams *either* did better or worse than fans expected, greater emphasis was placed on the organization of the club. If the club exceeded expectations, fans were concerned at how it might push on to the next level, whereas if it under-performed they were similarly concerned to get better players and at how the club was run.

Finally, three distinct groups of clubs could be identified. While all placed value on all five of the above, the groups had different profiles with more or less weight on different values. In the 2000–01 season, analysis of 12 teams in the Premier League produced three groups:

- Group 1 (Sunderland, Aston Villa, Ipswich and Newcastle United) placed highest importance on emotional attachment to the club and to self-esteem. History and tradition were considered fairly important.
- Group 2 (Middlesbrough, Southampton and Manchester City) placed a mid level of emphasis on emotional attachment but were very active in their match attendance.
- Group 3 (Manchester United, Tottenham, Liverpool, Everton, Arsenal and Chelsea) placed high emphasis on match attendance as a social activity and considered success to be important. This may reflect their relatively higher levels of previous success than some of the other clubs.

The above groupings may suggest different strategies might appeal to different clubs, and to different segments within each club. The relative importance of emotional attachment and history and tradition, as well as the importance of the match day experience might suggest that building on these other elements might retain loyalty when results are less good. Moreover, the emphasis on organizational values in clubs which achieve below their expected level of success highlights the importance of good governance and strong links with the local communities and engagement with fans more broadly.

In summary, while winning would be nice, loyalty to football brands is often more based on them being value-driven and in doing the right things, even being open and accessible to fans who may wish to vent their frustration at performances or players or club governance.

Managing football brands is complex and often carried out in the full glare of fan and media attention. Strategies are needed for the bad times as well as good. And football has to guard against the tendency that success brings increased revenue so that the rich get richer and the poor poorer. While in many sectors it might be desirable even to drive competitors out of the market, in football, the future also depends on a – reasonably – level playing field and strong rivals.

The need to keep the football industry healthy

The continued success of football as whole, let alone of particular brands, depends on the game and the business handling a number of threats. Threats to revenue streams from piracy of broadcast content, from match-fixing and corruption which undermine football matches as fair sporting contests, threats that the proliferation of entertainment options and technologies might diminish support among future generations of fans and from the game becoming victim of its own success, as the costs of being a fan continue to rise. A number of football clubs have set up family enclosures, to encourage families to come to matches together. Children's football programmes in schools and out of school during holiday periods are used to encourage interest in and understanding of football. Discounted and free tickets to school children are offered by many clubs to get younger supporters to attend matches and develop loyalty to football brands.

The ultimate fantasy brand perhaps, and with a level of emotional attachment and engagement which marketers of other types of brands might only dream of, but this is no easy ride. The future health and well-being of football brands depend upon balancing the needs of football as a global business, without losing sight of football as a beautiful game.

Biography

Sue Bridgewater was international brand manager and new products manager with Nairn-Forbo and Unilever. She has a BA (Hons) in German from Durham University and an MBA and PhD (in emerging markets) from Warwick University. Sue joined Warwick Business School in 1991 as a teacher and researcher in marketing and international marketing. While there, she set up and ran successfully for 10 years, a course for the League Managers Association to train football managers and taught blue-chip clients including HSBC, Ford, Nestlé, Philips, Prudential, KPMG and in sport, the Football Association, League Managers' Association and the Professional Footballers' Association as well as a number of football clubs. Sue has written international journal articles and books including *Football Brands* (2010) and *Football Management* (2010).

In October 2013, Sue joined Liverpool University as Director of Sports Research. As well as teaching on the Football Industries MBA, Sue teaches Business of Football for clients including the Azeri Football Federation and the Josoor Institute in Qatar and is conducting a number of research studies in football and sport.

References

Aaker, D A (1996) *Building Strong Brands*, Free Press, New York
Aaker J, Fournier, S and Brasel, S A (2004) When good brands do bad, *Journal of Consumer Research*, 31(June), pp 1–17

Baade, R A and Tiehen, L J (1990) The impact of stadiums and professional sports on metropolitan area development, *Growth and Change*, 21, pp 1–14

Beverland, M (2010) review of Bridgewater, S (2010) *Football Brands*, Palgrave, Basingstoke, UK

BrandFinance Football 50 (2013), online report, 20 May, http://www.brandfinance.com/knowledge_centre/reports/brandfinance-football-50-2013

Bridgewater, S (2010) *Football Brands*, Palgrave, Basingstoke, UK

Bridgewater, S (2014) Football and Sponsorship, in (forthcoming) *Handbook on Economics of Professional Football*, eds P Sloane and J Goddard, Edward Elgar

Cialdini, R B, Borden, R J, Thorne, A, Wilker, M R, Freeman, S and Sloan, L R (1976) Basking in Reflected Glory: three (football) studies, *Journal of Personal and Social Psychology*, 34, pp 366–75

Deloitte (2012) *The Money League*

Deloitte (2013) *Football Finance Report*

Domazlicky, B R and Kerr, P M (1990) Baseball attendance and the designated hitter, *American Economist*, 34, pp 62–68

Eon (2009) *Origins of Support*, Research Findings

Gantz, W (1981) An Exploration of viewing motives and behaviours associated with television sports, *Journal of Broadcasting*, 25(3), pp 263–75

Gantz, W and Wenner, L A (1995) Fanship and the television sports viewing experience, *Sociology of Sport Journal*, 12, pp 56–74

www.theguardian.com/sport/2013/nov/09/bt-sport-champions-league-exclusive-tv-rights (accessed 9 November 2013)

Holt, R (1989) *Sport and the British: A modern history*, Oxford University Press, Oxford

Keller, K (2001) Building Customer-based Brand Equity, *Marketing Management*, Jul/Aug, pp 15–19

Kuper, S and Szymanski, S (2012) *Soccernomics*, revised and expanded edition, Nation Books, New York

Lascu, D-N, Giee, T D, Toolan, M S M, Guehring, B and Mercer, J (1995) Sport Involvement: a relevant individual difference factor in spectator sports, *Sport Marketing Quarterly*, 4(4), pp 41–7

Madrigal, R (1995) Cognitive and Affective determinants of fan satisfaction with sporting event attendance, *Journal of Leisure Research*, 27(3), pp 205–27

Maffesoli, M (1996) *The Time of Tribes: The decline of individualism in mass society*. Sage, London

Mahony, D F, Madrigal, R and Howard, D (2000) Using the Psychological Commitment to Team (PCT) scale to segment sports consumers based on loyalty, *Sport Marketing Quarterly*, 9(1), 15–25

Mahony, D F, Nakazawa, M, Funk, D, James, J D and Gladden, J M (2002) Motivational Factors influencing the behavior of J. League Spectators, *Sport Management Review*, 5, pp 1–24

Ohmae, K (1985) *The Borderless World*, Collins, London

Reichheld, F (1997) The bottom-line on customer loyalty, *Management Review*, 86(3), Mar, 16.

Ries, A and Trout, J (2001) *Positioning: The Battle for your mind*, McGraw-Hill

Roberts, K (2004) *Lovemarks, The Future beyond Brands*, Saatchi and Saatchi Co

Sheehan, B (2013) *Loveworks*, Saatchi and Saatchi Co

Sloan, L R (1989) 'The motives of sports fans' in J D Goldstein (ed) *Sports, Games and Play: Social and Psychosocial viewpoints*, 2nd Edition, Lawrence Erlbaum, Hillsdown, NJ, pp 175–240

Smith, G J (1988) The noble sports fan, *The Journal of Sport and Social Issues*, 12, pp 54–65

Sutton, W A, McDonald, M A, Milne, G R and Cimperman, J (1997) Creating and Fostering fan identification in professional sports, *Sport Marketing Quarterly*, 6(1), pp 15–22

Tapp, A (2004) The loyalty of Football Fans – we'll support you ever more, *Database Marketing and Customer Strategy Management*, 11(3), pp 203–15

Tapp, A and Clowes, J (2002) From 'carefree casuals' to professional wanderers: segmentation possibilities for football supporters, *European Journal of Marketing*, 36 (11/12), pp 1248–69

Wann, D L (1995) Preliminary validation of the Sport Fan Identification Scale, *Journal of Sport and Social Issues*, 19, pp 377–96

Wann, D and Branscombe, N R (1993) Sports Fans: measuring degree of identification with their team, *International Journal of Sport Psychology*, 24, pp 1–17

Wann, D and Dolan, T J (2001) Attributions of highly identified sports spectators, *Journal of Social Psychology*, 134 (6), pp 783–92

INDEX

The index is arranged in alphabetical, word-by-word order. The prefix 'Mc' and numbers in headings are filed as spelt out in full. Organization names spelt as acronyms (eg BMW) are filed as written. Headings in *italics* denote a document, programme or campaign title. Locators in *italics* denote material within a figure or photograph.

CPSIA information can be obtained at www.ICGtesting.com
Printed in the USA
BVOW02s1931041114

373661BV00002B/2/P